New Perspectives on Legislation

Lex et Res Publica
Polish Legal and Political Studies
Edited by Anna Jaroń

Volume 14

Zur Qualitätssicherung und Peer Review der vorliegenden Publikation

Die Qualität der in dieser Reihe erscheinenden Arbeiten wird vor der Publikation durch die Herausgeberin der Reihe geprüft.

Notes on the quality assurance and peer review of this publication

Prior to publication, the quality of the work published in this series is reviewed by the editor of the series.

Paweł Chmielnicki / Adam Sulikowski (eds.)

New Perspectives on Legislation

A Comparative Approach

PETER LANG

Bibliographic Information published by the Deutsche Nationalbibliothek
The Deutsche Nationalbibliothek lists this publication in the Deutsche Nationalbibliografie; detailed bibliographic data is available online at http://dnb.d-nb.de.

Library of Congress Cataloging-in-Publication Data
A CIP catalog record for this book has been applied for at the Library of Congress.

This publication was financially supported by Lazarski University, Warsaw.

Reviewed by Prof. Przemysław Kaczmarek

Printed by CPI books GmbH, Leck

ISSN 2191-3250
ISBN 978-3-631-79362-6 (Print)
E-ISBN 978-3-631-80038-6 (E-Book)
E-ISBN 978-3-631-80039-3 (EPUB)
E-ISBN 978-3-631-80040-9 (MOBI)
DOI 10.3726/b16071

Peter Lang – Berlin · Bern · Bruxelles · New York · Oxford · Warszawa · Wien

This publication has been peer reviewed

www.peterlang.com

Contents

Introduction

The issue of lawmaking is an important subject of interest in broadly understood legal sciences. Although many books have been written on this subject, new problems are still emerging. Especially, recent events in Poland make us think about new tendencies in creating law. The Polish parliament, dominated by the "Law and Justice" party, voted on various laws very quickly, without any serious discussion, by organizing votes of ten at night. The President signed the acts presented to him often on the day of their receipt from the parliamentary office. The so-called bottom-up mode (draft laws are reported by a group of deputies), allowing the legislative procedure to be carried out without the necessary public consultation was abused – the fact that the projects did not come from groups of deputies, but from the government, was widely known. The composition of expert bodies guaranteeing the appropriate formal and substantive level of bills in the parliament has been fundamentally changed in the personal aspect. The laws were voted even in the case of objections from experts (even those newly elected and essentially loyal to the new parliamentary majority). The changes were accompanied by a new legal discourse, combining revolutionary elements with a certain vision of conservatism.

Changes in Poland with all their specificity are not isolated. In many countries of the world and even in the hegemonic United States, current political and legal theories are becoming less and less adequate to the description of reality. The famous thesis about the end of history turns out to be false. However, it should be emphasized that what may concern the ideologues of liberal democracy and the rule of law, should be inspiring for researchers. The new issues expect new theoretical approaches, new concepts and new solutions.

The texts contained in this volume are the result of discussions of various researchers from different parts of the world. The conference organized by the Association of Research on Sources and Functions of the Law "Fontes" and the Lazarski University in September 2018 was an opportunity for these discussions. The importance of the subject matter and the substantive level of the lectures inducedus to work on the creation of a monograph that would allow the authors to reach the wider audience. Certainly, this book is not a typical monograph. It is more like an English garden. Everyone who has been in such a garden knows that it is seemingly chaotic, but it has its own deep, specific order.

Our volume includes chapters inspired by theory and legal philosophy, as well as texts written by dogmatists (researchers of particular branches of law) and practitioners. The multiplicity of points of view and the diversity of assumptions adopted by the authors, allows to create a multi-faceted image of law-making processes. Certainly, only such an approach allows to show the studied phenomenon in all its complexity.

The first chapter deals with the political nature of legislation. The author – Rafał Mańko, a well-known critical theoretician, attempts to build the theoretical basis of critical legisprudence.

The subject of the second chapter is the ideological nature of technology and its impact on the creation of law. The author is Dominik Góra, an experienced researcher of the processes of applying new technologies in legal practice.

The third chapter, written by Martin Škop, a Czech critical philosopher and sociologist of law, deals with very interesting issues inthe sociological context of legislation.

The next chapter is written by Paweł Chmielnicki, founder and first president of the Fontes Association for Research on Sources and Functions of the Law. The author, inspired by the theories of institutional economics, took up the subject of the impact of "micro" and "macro" factors on the creation of law.

The fifth chapter is more dogmatic (in the specifically legal sense of the word). The author, Alex Evans, an Australian legal researcher, examines the problem of creating Australian Income Tax Law.

The subject of the sixth chapter presents practical problems that have emerged in connection with implementation into the Polish law the Council Directive 85/374/EEC of 25 July 1985 on the approximation of the laws, regulations and administrative provisions of the Member States concerning liability for defective products. The author, a civil law specialist, is the head of the legal clinic at the Faculty of Law, Administration and Economics of the University of Wrocław.

The next, seventh chapter written by Professor Sanita Osipova, the judge of the Latvian constitutional court, deals with the problems of restrictions on the freedom of legislation.

The eighth chapter treats about role of the constitutional court in the process of legislation. The author of the chapter is Dobrochna Minich, a theoretician of law, an assistant professor at the Lazarski University.

The subject of the final chapter written by Rafał Chybiński, a doctoral student at the Department of Theory and Philosophy of Law at the University of Wrocław, is Carl Schmitt's views on the role of lawyers in lawmaking and the political struggle.

We are happy to give our volume to print, hoping that it will meet with a vivid reaction and the problems raised in it will encourage discussion about theoretical and practical issues of law making.

Part One Legislation and the Political

Rafał Mańko

1 Legislation and the Political: Towards Critical Legisprudence*

Abstract: Legislation – the social practice of creating abstract legal rules in (usually) a parliamentary process – inherently belongs to the sphere of the political. This is because, as Pashukanis observed, all law is born out of conflict of interests. Legislative rules are aimed at striking a certain balance between such conflicting interests, rendering winners (beneficiaries) and losers (maleficiaries). The actual social effects of legislation are difficult to judge in the abstract, and therefore empirical research is necessary. The methodology proposed in the Polish context by Professor Paweł Chmielnicki is an interesting step in this direction. Unmasking the dimension of the political, i.e. the social antagonisms, in legislation calls for the development of a new branch of critical legal theory – critical legisprudence. In contrast to non-critical legisprudence inaugurated by Luc Wintgens in the 1990s, critical legisprudence rests on the solid pillars of a hermeneutic of suspicion and emancipatory goal which are common to all strands of critical legal theory. In this perspective, any single legislative rule is treated as only the momentary outcome of ongoing social struggles. There is no perfect compromise, and a 'harmonious' society, at least within capitalism, is impossible. The practical task of critical legisprudence is, therefore, to become the 'lobbyist of the people', and on the basis of solid empirical research – for instance, along the lines of analytical realism proposed by Professor Chmielnicki – propose legislative solutions which will reduce oppression and promote emancipation.

Keywords: legislation, critical legal theory, critical legisprudence, analytical legal realism

* The present chapter has been prepared as part of the National Science Centre (Poland) project no. 2016/21/B/HS5/00164. All views presented in this chapter are exclusively those of the author and do not represent the position of any institution. I would like to thank Jakub Łakomy for reading an earlier version of this chapter and sharing his comments with me.

1 Introduction

Out of the four principal practices of legal culture[1] – legislation, adjudication, scholarship and education[2] – legislation stands out as the one which is most openly political. Especially in our times, when legislative texts are enacted by democratically elected parliaments, and where political pluralism (still) comes to voice in periodical elections. For this reason, formalistically oriented jurisprudence even refused to analyse legislation as a process, focusing exclusively on its outcome – binding legal texts.[3] Whereas the political aspect of legal education[4] or scholarship[5] or

1 By 'practices of legal culture' I understand 'repetitive, socially and culturally predefined actions performed by the agents of legal culture (lawyers) within the intersubjective systems of meanings constituting the interpretive community of lawyers' (Rafał Mańko, 'The Unification of Private Law in Europe from the Perspective of Polish Legal Culture' (2007–2008) 11 Yearbook of Polish Legal Studies 109, 112–113). See also: Brian Z Tamanaha, *Realistic Socio-Legal Theory. Pragmatism and a Social Theory of Law* (Oxford: OUP, 1997) 168 ff, Kaarlo Tuori, 'Legal Culture and the General Societal Culture' in Thomas Wilhelmsson (ed.), *Private Law and the Many Cultures of Europe* (The Hague: Kluwer, 2007) 32.

2 cf Mańko (n 1) 113. See also Martijn W. Hesselink, *The New European Private Law: Essays on the Future of Private Law in Europe* (The Hague-London-Boston: Kluwer, 2002) 11; Rafał Mańko, 'The Culture of Private Law in Central Europe After Enlargement: A Polish Perspective' (2005) 11(5) European Law Journal 527, 528.

3 Даце Шулмане and Полина Шевчук [Dace Šulmane and Polina Shevchuk], 'Легиспруденция – новый подход к вопросу о законотворчестве»' [Legisprudence – a New Approach to the Question of Law-Making] (2013) 97(6) Сравнительное Конституционное Обозрение 14, 16. This was, of course, a consequence of the 'modern logos of adjudication', whereby the judiciary is neatly separated from politics, and legal interpretation is seen as a rational and principled process, aimed at uncoding 'the law' already present in the texts. Cf. Adam Sulikowski, 'Trzy filary nowoczesnego logosu sądzenia i ich postmodernistyczna krytyka' [The Three Pillars of the Modern Logos of Adjudication and their Postmodernist Critique] in Michał Błachut (ed.), *Z zagadnień teorii i filozofii prawa. Ponowoczesność* (Wrocław: Kolonia Limited, 2007) 215 ff.

4 For an unmasking of the political nature of legal education see e.g. Duncan Kennedy, 'Legal Education and the Reproduction of Hierarchy' (1982) 32(4) Journal of Legal Education 591.

5 For an unmasking of the political nature of legal scholarship see e.g. Adam Sulikowski, 'Apolityczność w prawoznawstwie. Kryzys idei a zjawisko populizmu' [Apoliticality in Jurisprudence: Crisis of an Idea and the Phenomenon of Populism], (2018)18(3) Archiwum Filozofii Prawa i Filozofii Społecznej 74; Rafał Mańko, 'Nauki prawne wobec problemu polityczności: zagadnienia wybrane z perspektywy jurysprudencji

adjudication[6] is somewhat latent and needs to be unmasked through the operation of a hermeneutic of suspicion, the political character of legislation stands out patently before our eyes.[7] Despite that, and the fact that political parties and lobbyists[8] often have very concrete ideas on what legislation on given aspects should look like, I still think that a certain aspect is missing from our picture of this practice of legal culture, and this chapter aims at shedding more light on it. This aspect is *the political* – in contrast to (party) politics and (public) polices. The adjective 'political' refers to both 'the political' and to 'politics', but in this chapter I have in mind, the *concept of the political* (as a noun), drawing especially on the political theory of Chantal Mouffe.[9] Hence, I will argue that whereas it is broadly acknowledged that the practice of legislation – or parliamentary law-making – is 'political' in the sense of belonging to or being dominated by party politics and its ensuing phenomena (most notably, lobbying), the question of *the political*, in the sense of actual antagonisms being affected by the outcome of legislation, remains undertheorised and underestimated within legal discourse. I will also highlight that the recently created branch of legal theory focusing on legislation – legisprudence – due to its formalistic approach also fails to take stock of the dimension of the political in parliamentary law-making. Instead, critical and realistic approaches should be pursued, which could lead to the emergence of a 'critical legisprudence' – a critical analysis of legislation rooted in critical legal theory, but also conscious of the need for a thoroughly empirical approach, for instance along the lines of analytical legal realism developed in the Polish context by Professor Paweł Chmielnicki.[10]

---

krytycznej' [Legal Sciences Towards the Problem of the Political: Selected Issues from the Perspective of Critical Jurisprudence] (2018)18(3) Archiwum Filozofii Prawa i Filozofii Społecznej 38; Michał Stambulski, 'Polityczność w polskiej analitycznej teorii prawa. Zarys problematyki' [The Political in Polish Analytical Legal Theory: Outline of the Issue] (2018)18(3) Archiwum Filozofii Prawa i Filozofii Społecznej 64.

6 For an unmasking of the political nature of adjudication see above all Duncan Kennedy, *A Critique of Adjudication {fin de siècle}* (Cambridge MA: Harvard University Press, 1997).

7 Luc J Wintgens, 'Legisprudence as a New Theory of Legislation' (2006) 19(1) Ratio Juris 1, 1. As Wintgens notes, this has led to treating legislation as an object of political science, rather than legal theory.

8 cf Paweł Chmielnicki, 'Prawne i praktyczne uwarunkowania lobbingu' [Legal and Practical Conditions of Lobbying] (2014) 9 Przegląd Prawa Publicznego 34.

9 Chantal Mouffe, *On the Political* (London-New York: Routledge, 2005).

10 See section 4.1 for more details on Professor Chmielnicki's research method.

The chapter will be structured as follows. In section 2, I will introduce the concept of the political and its relation to the two adjacent concepts – those of politics and policies. This section will play a preparatory function for the rest of my argument. In section 3, I will briefly explain how I will understand the notion of legislation. In section 4, I will roll out a detailed theory on the way in which legislation belongs to the political, arguing that a realistic approach to social antagonisms is necessary, and that every rule made by the legislator gives benefits to some, but inflicts violence and harm on others. This aspect calls for a thoroughly ethical approach to legislation. In section 5, I will briefly analyse whether the new jurisprudential field of 'legisprudence', inaugurated at the end of the 20th century, is capable of addressing the question of the political (my claim is in the negative). Section 6 will conclude.

From a methodological perspective, this chapter is conceived as an intervention in legal theory, locating itself within the well-defined current of critical jurisprudence.[11] This entails a number of methodological assumptions and ontological presuppositions which are the building blocks of critical legal theory. These include, but are not limited to, the assumption that the social world is essentially political, i.e. ridden with conflict, and that the law does not represent a universal axiological foundation, but rather serves the interests of certain social groups or classes, or even individuals.[12] Critical jurisprudence boasts its hermeneutic of suspicion as a methodological approach, which boils down to the assumption that nothing in the world of legal culture should be taken at face value, but rather hidden meanings and hidden interests should be unmasked through a careful critique and deconstruction.[13] Finally, critical jurisprudence is characterised by its emancipatory approach,[14] meaning that it aims at removing

---

11 For an exposition of the methodological approach of critical jurisprudence see Rafał Mańko and Jakub Łakomy 'In search for the ontological presuppositions of critical jurisprudence' (2018) 10(2) Critique of Law 469; Rafał Mańko, 'Critique of the "Juridical": Some Metatheoretical Remarks' (2018) 11 Journal of the University of Latvia. Law 24.

12 cf Mańko and Łakomy (n 11) 475–476.

13 cf Brian Leiter, 'The Hermeneutics of Suspicion: Recovering Marx, Nietsche and Freud' (2005) 72 University of Texas School of Law Public Law and Legal Theory Working Paper, available at http://ssrn.com/abstract=691002 (accessed 21 March 2019).

14 Paweł Skuczyński, 'Typy myśli krytycznej w prawoznawstwie. Od krytyki poznania do walki o uznanie' [Types of Critical Thought in Jurisprudence: From the Critique of Cognition to Struggle for Recognition] in Tomasz Bekrycht et al (eds), 1 *Integracja zewnętrzna i wewnętrzna nauk prawnych* (Łódź: Wydawnictwo Uniwersytetu Łódzkiego, 2014).

violence and oppression, in line with the assumption that theory should not only interpret the world, but also change it for the better. It is with these considerations in mind that this chapter aims to analyse the phenomenon of legislation from the perspective of the concept of the political.

2 The Concept of the Political, as Opposed to Politics and Policies

2.1 The Political, or the Antagonistic Dimension of Social Life

There are three closely interconnected, yet distinct notions, which are useful for describing the relationship between the spheres of the juridical and of the political. These are: (1) the notion of the political; (2) the notion of politics; (3) the notion of policies.[15] *The political* denotes the dimension of antagonism present in society in which the interests of social classes and groups are in mutual conflict.[16] Without entering into a discussion on the pre-class formation of the original community, it can be safely said that all hitherto existing societies, including contemporary neoliberal capitalism, have been characterised by antagonisms. The same, sadly, applies to the systems of actually existing socialism where a strong antagonism between the *nomenklatura* and the rest of society replaced the antagonism between the bourgeoisie and the proletariat. On top of economic antagonisms, which can be said to be prototypical, one can also speak of cultural antagonisms (as between liberals and conservatists), ethnic antagonisms (as between different ethnic groups) and religious antagonisms. An antagonism, i.e. the dimension of the political, is based on a group identification (we vs. they) and has a collective character. Individual antagonisms can be individual instantiations of collective antagonisms, but may also have a purely individual character, without any reference to a collective conflict. As Damjan Kukovec points out: 'Struggle, conflict, and contradiction are central to our daily existence. There is a cost, a downside to everything in life.'[17]

---

15 Rafał Mańko, Adam Sulikowski and Jakub Łakomy, 'Polityczność prawa i ogólnej refleksji nad prawem: wprowadzenie' [The Political Character of Law and General Jurisprudence: An Introduction] (2018) 3 Archiwum Filozofii Prawa i Filozofii Społecznej 5, 5–6.

16 Mouffe (n 9) *passim*; *cf* Michał Paździora and Michał Stambulski, 'Co może dać nauce prawa polityczność? Przyczynek do przyszłych badań' [What Can Legal Scholarship Gain from the Political? Notes Towards Further Research] (2014) 1 Archiwum Filozofii Prawa i Filozofii Społecznej 55.

17 Damjan Kukovec, 'Hierarchies as Law' (2014) 21 Columbia Journal of European Law 131, 136.

2.2 Politics, or a Parliamentary-Democratic Way of Living Out the Political

The political, understood as the dimension of antagonism, must be clearly differentiated from *politics*, understood as a social practice of struggle for power over the community, which – in contemporary European societies – takes the form of struggle in democratic elections and in parliamentary struggles between opposing political parties.[18] Hence, we can speak about party politics (*Parteipolitik*) in order to differentiate it more clearly from the political. The links of legal scholarship to party politics are, perhaps, an interesting topic for historical or sociological research, but from the point of view of legal theory the issue seems rather trivial and will not be pursued any further.

2.3 Policies, or the Outcomes of Political Struggles

The third dimension, which I want to analyse, are policies (or *public policies*), understood as subject-matter areas of a given political community's activities.[19] Examples include foreign policy, security policy, economic policy, monetary policy, cultural policy, social policy, education policy, consumer policy and so forth. Whilst politics is about struggling for power, policies are about what is done with that power in precisely defined thematic remits. Clearly, the three dimensions – the political, politics and policies – remain closely interconnected. Specifically, outcomes of political struggles determine policies, and policies may favour one or the other side of the social conflict.

Most policies are juridified, i.e. expressed in legal terms or legally entrenched. The level of juridification of policies varies and the role of jurists in the co-creation of policies – in their *legal*, not political (e.g. as member of parliament) capacity, will be much greater in the case of deeply juridified policies, which enter into their proper realm of work. For instance, interpreting the rules on the Civil Code concerning unfair terms, or rules of the Criminal Code concerning the propagation of totalitarianism – both expressing certain public policies pursued by those in power – belong to the proper fabric of juridical work. For, as Sawa Frydman wrote already in 1936, 'dogmaticians, resorting to the force of persuasion and argumentation impose their views on other dogmaticians and upon practioners,

18 cf Kazimierz Opałek, *Zagadnienia teorii prawa i teorii polityki* [Issues of Legal Theory and Political Theory] (Warszawa: PWN, 1986) 238–239.

19 cf Mauro Zamboni, *Law and Politics: A Dilemma for Contemporary Legal Theory* (Berlin: Springer, 2008) 7–8, 71.

thereby *participating in political life*.'[20] Typical juridical tools of interpretation can therefore be deployed in order to strengthen or weaken a given policy (e.g. by resorting to a narrow or broad interpretation of vague concepts that denote the scope of application of a given rule).

From the perspective of both legislation and adjudication, it is also important to note that policies are not necessarily stand-alone phenomena. An individual case before a court or a proposed legal rule before parliament can fall into the scope of two or more policies, and the preference given to one or another policy is an object of struggle, and therefore belongs to the scope of the political. This is because, as critical jurisprudence claims, 'policies (. . .) are not neutral. Policies also cause distributive effects, so deciding cases by balancing such policies cannot be neutral either.'[21] Most significantly, 'for each policy there is a counter-policy',[22] and the choice between them belongs, in the stage of legislation, to the legislator, and in the stage of adjudication – to the judge. Policies are, therefore, a sphere in which the political is played out in parallel to politics.

3 The Phenomenon of Legislation

Legislation will be understood in this chapter as the phenomenon of creating, by parliamentary or other bodies, of texts containing general and abstract legal rules, i.e. rules directed to a broad class of addressees and covering repetitive situations or events.[23] The 'legislator' will be understood as 'any subject, especially a state organ, whose defined action (decision) is considered to be a law-making act according to an accepted conception of the sources of law'.[24] More specifically, however, the concept of legislation will be understood here as the creation of statutes (*leges*, *lois*, *Gesetze*), with the exclusion of sub-statutory regulatory activity, performed by ministries or specialised agencies.

---

20 Sawa Frydman, *Dogmatyka prawa w świetle socjologii. Studium pierwsze: o wykładni ustaw* [Legal Dogmatics in the Light of Sociology. A First Study on the Interpretation of Statutes] (Wilno: Księgarnia Kazimierza Rutskiego, 1936) 104. Emphasis added.

21 Siniša Rodin and Tamara Perišin, 'Transformation or Reconstitution of Europe: The European Critical Legal Studies Perspective' in Siniša Rodin and Tamara Perišin, *The Transformation or Reconstitution of Europe: The Critical Legal Studies Perspective on the Role of the Courts in the European Union* (Portland, OR: Hart Publishing, 2018) 7.

22 ibid 6.

23 cf Wiesław Lang, Jerzy Wróblewski and Sylwester Zawawdzki, *Teoria państwa i prawa* [Theory of State and Law] (Warszawa: Państwowe Wydawnictwo Naukowe, 1980) 374.

24 Jerzy Kowalski, Wojciech Lamentowicz and Piotr Winczorek, *Teoria państwa i prawa* [Theory of State and Law] (Warszawa: Państwowe Wydawnictwo Naukowe, 1981) 117.

Legislators do not function in a vacuum, but are confronted with various factors, especially of a socio-economic nature, including class forces, hegemonic ideology, political life etc.[25] With regard to this *status quo*, legislation can take three approaches: 'adaptation, regulation or innovation'.[26] Legislation thus enters into a dialectical relationship with the socio-economic and political reality it seeks to codify or change.[27]

As I will argue in the next section, this social reality is conflict-ridden, and legislative choices *nolens volens* have to take sides in the conflicts they seek to juridify, even if innovation is not sought after explicitly by the legislator. Due to the political nature of legislative bodies in today's democracies, political parties have to present a position on each and every piece of legislation (although sometimes there is no 'party discipline' and individual members of parliament may decide as they wish). Concerning the relationship between legislation and policies, it is clear that legislation is an instrument allowing to *juridify* policies in the sense discussed above.

4 All Legislation is Political

4.1 Legislation and Social Antagonisms

As Evgeny B. Pashukanis rightly claimed:

> A basic prerequisite for legal regulation is . . . the conflict of private interests. This is both the logical premise of the legal form and the actual origin of the development of the legal superstructure. Human conduct can be regulated by the most complex regulations, but the juridical factor in this regulation arises at the point when differentiation and opposition of interests begin.[28]

Therefore, any piece of legislation and any single rule in a piece of legislation can and indeed should be analysed from the point of view of the concept of the

---

25 Kowalski, Lamentowicz and Winczorek (n 23) 118–119.

26 ibid 119.

27 For a case-study of the dialectical relations between legislation and the socio-economic and political reality in times of transformation, see e.g. Rafał Mańko, 'Law, Politics and the Economy in Poland's Post-Socialist Transformation: Preliminary Notes Towards an Investigation' in Balazs Fekete and Fruzsina Gárdos-Orosz (eds), *25 Years After Transition in Central and Eastern Europe: Understanding the Transition from an Internal Perspective* (Frankfurt am Main: Peter Lang, 2017) 105–119.

28 Evgeny B. Pashukanis, *Law and Marxism: A General Theory. Toward a Critique of the Fundamental Juridical Concepts* [1924] (trans. by Barbara Einhorn, London: Pluto Press, 1983) 81.

political, which denotes the antagonistic dimension in society (in Pashukanis's words – 'the conflict ... of interests' or the 'differentiation and opposition of interests'). Indeed, legal rules usually decide upon social antagonisms belonging to the dimension of the political, as defined in section 2 above: they decide in which situation which side should prevail – the consumer or the trader; the worker or the employer; an ethnic majority or an ethnic minority (with regard to nationality, language rights, etc.); whether abortion or euthanasia should be legal and state-funded or should it be criminalised; whether same-sex couples should be allowed to marry and adopt children or not; whether progressive heroes of the past may be patrons of streets and have monuments or not, and so forth. The legislator is not fully free to pursue any kind of agenda, as he is constrained by various factors, including political, economic, social, ideological and cultural ones. As Rodin and Perišin point out, 'each legal norm is the product of a particular political conflict where one side won. Thus, legal norms are a snapshot of the distribution of power in political battles that created those norms.'[29]

However, the very nature of the legal form results in these choice being made in the abstract. People and their organisations, as well as legally relevant situations are classified, e.g. as a 'consumer' or 'parent' or 'contract' or 'tort', and the legal consequences are provided for, in principle, for all the people or situations falling under those abstractly framed categories. That is the nature of legislation (and the legal form).[30] Indeed, it can be said that the formalism of rules – making their outcomes dependent on purely formal, abstractly defined situations – is, in itself, political.[31] Even rules designed to protect consumers will operate independently of the real economic power and social position of the parties to a 'consumer contract'. A bourgeois consumer will benefit from consumer rights *vis-à-vis* a poor entrepreneur, selling hand-made objects to earn a minimum subsistence living for his large family. The formalism of law demands the judge to be blind to the entirety of the social context and to focus on what is 'legally relevant' for the situation at hand. In the case of consumer protection, the only legally relevant factor is whether a transaction is within or outside the scope of

---

29 Rodin and Perišin (n 21) 7.

30 Hugh Collins, *Marxism and Law* (Oxford: OUP, 1982) 132; Isaac D Balbus, 'Commodity Form and Legal Form: An Essay on the "Relative Autonomy" of the Law' (1977) 11 Law and Society 571, 576; Mańko, (n 5) 42–44.

31 Mańko (n 27) 43.

one's economic activity. If it is within – one has to bear the duties of being an entrepreneur and will be treated with all the harshness of the law, even if one is a poor craftsman struggling to earn a living by selling some hand-made objects on the internet. If the transaction is outside the scope – one will benefit from all the privileges of consumer law (such as the *pactum displicentiae* for online contracts) even if one is very rich, and the exercise of that right will cause detriment to the poor 'professional' side of the contract.

4.2 Identifying Beneficiaries and Maleficiaries

If we agree to the argument made above that all legislation belongs to the sphere of the political, not only by virtue of its content, but also by virtue of its form, one should definitely address the question of the actual beneficiaries (those who benefit from a rule) and maleficiaries (those who are harmed by the rule). Owing to the nature of legislation, i.e. its abstract form, the discussion necessarily has to have two dimensions – an abstract one and a practical one.

On an abstract note, one can attempt to identify the potential beneficiaries and maleficiaries of the rule. One can also try, as Kennedy suggests, to place each rule on a scale from individualism to altruism, and to show what kind of ideological project lies behind it.[32] However, the outcomes of such an abstractly framed, armchair analysis of legislation have limited applicability. What is necessary is to see beyond the text – into the context – and answer the question of who are the *actual* beneficiaries and maleficiaries of a given piece of legislation (or even a given rule within that legislation), as well as who were the expected beneficiaries and maleficiaries. These two aspects need not coincide. The effects of legislation are not necessarily symmetrical with their planned purpose. As Dace Šulmane points out, the effects of legislation can be expected or unexpected, desired or undesired, as well as direct and indirect.[33] According to the Latvian sociologist of law:

> The problems of efficiency of a legal provision are directly related to the achievement of desirable goals with the help of a law as the employed means. It is necessary to analyse whether the found consequences and impact is desirable and whether it existed in the legislator's intent, when creating the text as it is, which generated the consequences

32 Duncan Kennedy, 'The Political Stakes in "Merely Technical" Issues of Contract Law' (2001) 1 European Review of Private Law 7, 13–17.

33 Dace Šulmane, 'Versatility of Effects of Legal Provisions' in Jānis Rozenfelds and Jānis Pleps (eds), *The Quality of Legal Acts and its Importance in Contemporary Legal Space* (Riga: University of Latvia Press, 2012) 438–439.

> as they are ... The study of desirable and undesirable effects from the stance of sociology of law emphasizes political analysis, thus employing theories of political sciences. Nowadays, the law effectiveness studies serve as a policy instrument, because it helps the legislator choose and find their way, as well as plan the adoption of laws so that the majority of the society perceived it as the right direction.[34]

This kind of analysis, therefore, belongs to the domain of the sociology of law which has the necessary tools for this purpose. Since the present chapter situates itself within the discourse of the philosophy of law, it will limit itself to discussing the *conditions of possibility* of a political analysis of legislation, nonetheless one should mention in this context the socio-legal research– which could be dubbed 'analytical legal realism'[35] – as undertaken in the Polish context by Paweł Chmielnicki and his school, grouped around the Fontes Association for the Study of the Sources and Effects of the Law.[36] They have taken a closer look at some examples of recent Polish legislation showing interesting discrepancies between the declared beneficiaries and the actual beneficiaries of legislation. For instance, the well-known law on housing development, which was ushered in under the slogans of consumer protection, actually only provided benefits to banks.[37] Therefore, it can be said that banks were the *actual* beneficiaries of the legislation, in contrast to the consumers, who were only *declared* beneficiaries. Indeed, this kind of research must be done on a case-by-case and

34 ibid 439.

35 The proposed name for Professor Chmielnicki's research method stems from the combination of two elements: firstly, the legal realist element (as opposed to formalism), which is represented by the desire to go beyond the black-letter rules and explore the forces behind law-making and legal interpretation; secondly, the analytical element, represented by the rather formalised protocol of research proposed and applied by Professor Chmielnicki. Such a formalisation, in principle, is to be welcomed as it allows to make research repetitive and comparable, in contrast to unstructured approaches. However, the analytical element in Professor Chmielnicki's method does not make it formalist – it has, at its very heart, the objective of going *beyond* the textual layer of the law which is, as will become evident in section 5, inherent in the legisprudence proposed by Professor Witgens.

36 See especially: Paweł Chmielnicki, 'The Research Method of Association for the Research on Sources and Functions of Law' (2015) 3 Przegląd Prawa Publicznego 95. See also Paweł Chmielnicki, Michał Stachura and Anna Dybała, *Activity Rules of Economic Man in Society as the Source of Legal Norms* (Warszawa: LexisNexis, 2010).

37 Paweł Chmielnicki (ed.), *Nabycie lokalu lub domu od dewelopera. Wykładnia przepisów i efekty ich stosowania* [Purchase of a House from a Developer: Interpretation of the Legal Rules and the Effects of their Application] (Warszawa: Difin, 2014).

jurisdiction-by-jurisdiction basis. The variables include local interpretations, actual court practice and actual socio-economic effects of that interpretation and practice. They may even vary from region to region in one country, not to say – with regard to directives and regulations – across the Union.

What is important from a philosophical perspective is that legislation can and should be subjected to this kind of scrutiny, as it belongs to the sphere of the political. However, the tools for such an analysis cannot be purely textual, and as Chmielnicki's research clearly reveals, it requires access to extra-textual data concerning actual legal practice. Referring to the terminology used by Polish legal theorists, one needs a *post-analytical* approach,[38] whereby the entire socio-economic and political context of legal rules is given full weight.[39] In the case of the law on housing development, mentioned above, the necessary knowledge included *inter alia* data about the functioning of the banking sector.

4.3 What Is 'Better' Legislation?

There is a broadly disseminated slogan of 'better legislation', 'better law-making', 'better regulation'[40] or 'quality of legislation',[41] suggesting the legislation can be 'worse' or 'better'. As any slogan, it conceals more than reveals, and attempts to draw automatic conclusions closing the space for any meaningful discussion (after all, who would demand 'worse legislation'?). Critical jurisprudence, thanks to its hermeneutic of suspicion, approaches such slogans with distrust and immediately poses the fundamental question – better *for whom?* In other words, legislation is not just 'worse' or 'better' in the abstract, but rather is a better or worse *instrument* to serve the interests of a given social class, group or even some individuals.

---

38 See especially Andrzej Bator and Zbigniew Pulka (eds), *A Post-Analytical Approach to Philosophy and Theory of Law* (Berlin: Peter Lang, 2019).

39 I have referred to this method of research as 'non-analytical', rather than 'post-analytical', as it is based on a completely different way of thinking about the law when compared to the analytical tradition. See Rafał Mańko, 'Relikty w kulturze prawnej – uwagi metodologiczne na tle pozostałości epoki socjalizmu realnego w polskim prawie prywatnym' [Survivals in Legal Culture: Methodological Remarks Against the Background of Remnants of the Period of Actually Existing Socialism in Polish Private Law] (2015) 102 Przegląd Prawa i Administracji 201, 196, 204, 206.

40 See e.g. Olga Łachacz, 'Drafting the Legislation Within European Union Institutions – Towards Common Legal Acts Standards' in Rozenfelds and Pleps (n 33) 9 ff.

41 See e.g. Wim Voermans, 'Concern About the Quality of EU Legislation: What Kind of Problem, by What Kind of Means?' (2009) 2(1) Erasmus Law Review 59.

The critical approach advocated here presupposes that legislation (or even law as such) is not an aim in itself (a self-serving *telos*), but rather an instrument for protecting and furthering the interests of a certain group, and at the same time oppressing the interests of another group. Of course, legislation can be better or worse in its style, formulation, linguistic quality, transparency and the like, but we should not accept at face value that this would benefit all. Even if we agree with Olga Łachacz that '[i]f law is created in conformity with standards of good quality, it is also foreseeable and citizens enjoy legal certainty',[42] we should still keep in mind that the maleficiaries of legislation might prefer a specific legal act – which inflicts harm on them – to be vague in order to be able to protect, at least partly, their interests which have become vulnerable due to its enactment. Furthermore, vague, opaque and contradictory legislation serves the interests of lawyers as a social group (who can earn more on litigation), but also judges (whose power is enhanced, as they can fill in the lacunae in the written laws). Indeed, if we evaluate the legislator's purposes negatively (case of a 'wicked legislator'), a 'bad quality' piece of legislation, which can then be mitigated in its adverse effects by the courts, can paradoxically be the 'lesser evil'. Therefore, the 'quality' of legislation, its 'good' or 'bad' character cannot be discussed in the abstract but only in relation to a specific group of beneficiaries, even if limited or difficult to identify, and with regard to a specific legislator who need not always have good intentions.

4.4 Technical vs. Political Rules?

Another equally popular myth is the one according to which legislation, or specific rules (units of text in legislation) can be divided into 'technical' and 'political' ones, only the latter belonging to the sphere of the political. Thus, whereas rules on freedom of speech, political parties or redistribution of national income are readily classified as 'political', rules of private law, food safety law or detailed rules of tax law are treated as 'technical' (which implies that they are irrelevant for the political forces and boring to the non-expert, but should be left to 'technocrats'[43]). However, if we adopt the differentiation between *politics*, *policies*

---

42 Łachacz (n 40) 14.

43 Technocracy – the approach whereby 'technical' issues should be left to experts – effectively serves to mask the political dimension of society, resulting in a situation in which social and economic issues which would otherwise be politically contestable become the object of uncontested technocratic assumptions allegedly following from a body of commonly accepted knowledge. See Marija Bartl, 'Internal Market Rationality, Private Law and the Direction of the Union: Resuscitating the Market as the Object of the

and *the political*, as put forward in section 2, it will become evident that using the adjective 'political' as opposed to 'technical' can be misleading due to the fact that 'political' can refer to all three concepts (politics, policies, the political).

Duncan Kennedy writing about 'merely technical' issues in private law provides the following definition:

> By a 'merely technical' issue I mean things like how to treat the mistaken offeror in a simple contract situation, or the contract promisee who interrupts his own performance in retaliation for breach by his partner. I don't think the resolution of questions like these (. . .) has any importance at all for the shape of the economy. Nor indeed that choice about such rules have effects on any aspect of public or private, political, cultural or economic existence that are significant enough so that people can be expected to care about the choice in the normal matter of political concern.[44]

Indeed, these so-called merely technical rules do not figure high on political agendas in the sense that they are not the object of *politics*. To my knowledge, there has not been a political party which would demand changing the rules on declarations of will in the Civil Code or proposing to extend the grounds for launching a cassatory appeal in the Code of Civil Procedure. However, does this mean that these apparently technical rules are entirely apolitical in the sense of not belonging to the sphere of *the political*? Some light on this question could potentially be shed by introducing into the equation such notions as axiology (values) and ideology. Indeed, Rodolfo Sacco claimed that some legal institutions or rules are capable of surviving socio-economic transformation precisely because of their ideological neutrality.[45] The technical vs. ideological character of institutions and rules could change over time, as exemplified by certain socialist legal survivals which initially had a strongly ideological character (like the principles of social life), but later on became merely 'technical' tools.[46] But are these technical rules, even if outside the scope of interest of politics and ideology, true strangers to social antagonisms?

If we revert to the two examples given by Kennedy – mistaken offerors and contract promisees refusing to perform following the other party's breach – we

---

Political' (2015) 21(5) European Law Journal 572, 574. See also Rafał Mańko, 'Symbolic Violence in Technocratic Law and Attempts at Its Overcoming: Politicisation Through Humanization?' (2017) 11 Studia Erasmiana Wratislaviensia 31.

44 Kennedy (n 32) 7.

45 Rodolfo Sacco, 'Legal Formants: A Dynamic Approach to Comparative Law (Instalment II of II)' (1991) 39(2) American Journal of Comparative Law 343, 393–394.

46 Rafał Mańko, 'Transformacja ustrojowa a ciągłość instytucji prawnych – uwagi teoretyczne' (2016) 16(2) Zeszyty Prawnicze 6, 29–30.

can immediately identify the beneficiaries and counter-beneficiaries of the possible alternative rule formulations.[47] In ideological terms, the opposing rules can be arranged along a continuum from altruism to individualism.[48] This already reveals that social antagonisms are at stake. However, as Kennedy himself admits, the formality of rules means that the rules:

> . . .at least as formally stated, are not responsible either to the degree of vulnerability of the mistaken or breaching party, or, on the other hand, to the relative exposure of the other party. They ignore the quantitative dimension of the situation: it does not matter whether expectation damages will amount to a large windfall (. . .) or whether large losses to the breaching plaintiff could have been avoided by a virtually risk free extension of performance of the other party.[49]

This only reinforced the argument made above (in sub-section 4.2) that the actual effects of legislation can only to a limited extent be analysed in the abstract. They need to be referred to actual cases, with actual litigants and actual (class) interests behind them.

4.5 Legislation, Adjudication and Violence

In light of the above, it can be safely argued that most rules which could seem *prima facie* technical and ideologically neutral, may still have significant social consequences. A capitalist society is founded on the conflict of opposing interests, and legal rules are in place to 'strike balances' and 'solve conflicts'. However, each and every solution, no matter how much 'compromise' it has in itself, will benefit some people and harm others. As Damjan Kukovec rightly underlines:

> We injure and recognize others in every moment and make countless decisions for ourselves and others while doing so. It is in the structure of these decisions that the reproduction of hierarchies takes place. . .. Hierarchical struggle is daily, existential, inevitable, and not necessarily conscious or calculated. It is constant, never-ending, and ubiquitous.[50]

No rule can therefore, be dismissed as being outside the sphere of the political due to its allegedly technical character. Once a rule is applied to a real-life dispute, there will always be a winner and loser, a beneficiary and a harmed party. Violence will be inflicted. The question that critical jurisprudence needs

47 Kennedy (n 32) 9–12.
48 ibid 13–17.
49 ibid 13.
50 Kukovec (n 17) 156.

to address in its empirical dimension – that of critical legisprudence – is how to identify those beneficiaries and maleficiaries, how to find out who is going to be the victim of violence inflicted by the state legal apparatus.This is the empirical and analytical part of critical work that needs to be done, and the analytical legal realist approach, discussed above, is certainly a step in this direction.

However, the work of critical jurisprudence cannot stop here. In its ethical dimension, legal critique aims at rebuilding both legislation (including both parliamentary and judicial law-making) and adjudication in a way that will ensure that the legal process produces the most fair outcomes, with as much benefits and as little harm conferred to those who are oppressed in social and economic terms. It was Robert Cover who articulated this aspect in a poetic and very persuasive way, when he wrote that:

> Legal interpretation takes place in a field of pain and death. . .. Legal interpretive acts signal and occasion the imposition of violence upon others: A judge articulates her understanding of a text, and as a result, somebody loses his freedom, his property, his children, even his life. Interpretations in law also constitute justifications for violence which has already occurred or which is about to occur. When interpreters have finished their work, they frequently leave behind victims whose lives have been torn apart by these organized, social practices of violence. Neither legal interpretation nor the violence it occasions may be properly understood apart from one another.[51]

Legislation – the creation of rules that will be then interpreted – sets the scene for the violence later inflicted in adjudication, which Cover so persuasively depicted. Especially in civil-law jurisdictions, and in particular in the formalist ones, where judges worship legal rules and see their role as those who 'apply them', the significance of legislator-made rules for the generation and proliferation of violence cannot be overestimated. Paweł Skuczyński, a leading Polish specialist on legal ethics, told me once story of a judge who was faced with the cold rigour of a rule on funeral allowances, but decided the case against that rule, in order to do justice.[52] The decision was then upheld by the appellate court, which

51 Rober Cover, 'Violence and the Word' (1986) 95 Yale Law Journal 1601, 1601.

52 The facts of the case, as presented to me by Paweł Skuczyński, were as follows: a married couple of farmers had two children, both of whom died. The father asked the Farmers' Social Security Institution (KRUS) for a funeral allowance which he received. Four years leater, the KRUS found that the father was not entitled to the allowance because at the material time he was working outside agriculture, and filed a case against him demanding repayment. This caused emotional distress to the parents who had to go again through their grievance. After losing the case, the mother of the children – who was insured at KRUS at the material time – applied for the allowance. KRUS refused arguing that she missed the deadline of one year from the death. The legal rules were

called it 'courageous, yet fair'. As far as legislation is concerned, it should be framed in such a way to give judges the greatest opportunities not only to 'apply the law', but to do justice – social justice – to the litigants.[53] This, of course, opens up further significant questions which cannot be possibly addressed in this brief contribution, namely the role of general clauses and legal education of judges.

5 Legisprudence: A Right Step in the Wrong Direction

Until now, I have been trying to argue for a 'critical' or 'political' legisprudence as a new field of applied critical legal theory. However, these proposals should be placed in the broader jurisprudential context and I see the need of delimiting the critical stance from that of (non-critical) legisprudence, a branch of legal theory created in 1997 by Luc Wintgens.[54] Of course, jurists addressed the problem of legislation earlier,[55] nonetheless Wintgens promised to provide a new quality. According to him:

> A legisprudential theory of law in contradistinction to the widespread jurisprudential approach no longer takes for granted the central position of the judge as the main legal agent. It aims instead to enlarge the spectrum of legal theory as the meta-theory of legal science by including the legislator as a legal agent thus downplaying his mainly political role in lawmaking.[56]

In that theory, the legislator is treated in a similar way as the judge, and his choices in implementing the constitution through legislation are to be subject to four leading principles: the principle of alternativity, the principle of normative density, the principle of temporality, and the principle of coherence.[57] Let

---

very clear: if the cold form of law were to be applied, KRUS was right on both counts. The judge, however, decided the case not applying the cold law, but resorting to empathy – the mother of justice. He ruled in favour of the mother (but against the legal text) and she received the funeral allowance despite the expiry of the one-year deadline.

53 cf the remark of Dace Šulmane who points out that: 'It is important to distinguish between the undesirable effects of legal provisions, which can be prevented only by political decisions, and such undesirable effects, which can and should be improved by the court for the sake of justice' (Šulmane (n 28) 439).

54 Шулмане and Шевчук (n 3) 16.

55 Šulmane and Shevchuk point to such researchers as Jeremy Bentham or Friedrich Carl von Savigny (Шулмане and Шевчук (n 3) 14–16).

56 Luc J Wintgens, 'The Rational Legislator Revisited. Bounded Rationality and Legisprudence The Rational Legislator' in Luc J Wintgens and A Daniel Oliver-Lalana (eds.), *The Rationality and Justification of Legislation* (Heidelberg: Springer, 2013) 2.

57 Wintgens (n 7) 10.

me briefly recall the content of these four principles, as expounded by Professor Wintgens:[58]

1) the principle of alternativity 'requires that an external limitation of freedom be justified as an alternative for failing social interaction';[59]
2) the principle of normative density implies that 'sanctions need justification because they include a double restriction of freedom. First, external limitations are conceptions about freedom, and exclude action on a conception of freedom. (. . .) Secondly, if they are accompanied by a sanction, the purpose, goal, or end of the rule can only be realised in the way that is prescribed';[60]
3) the principle of temporality 'constrains normative propositions subject to justification on the [principle of alternativity] and the [principle of normative density] from the perspective of time. An external limitation can be justified on both these principles at a certain point in time';[61]
4) the principle of coherence means that 'the legislator (. . .) has to justify both the status quo and the change of external limitations'[62] and that new rules should 'fit the system as a whole when seen from inside the system.'[63]

The undoubtedly complex principles of legisprudence have one element in common: they are patently formalist in the sense of focusing on purely formal aspects of rule-making by the legislator, and deliberately abstracting from the *substance* of legislation which, as is well known, affects ongoing class struggles, group interests, ideological conflicts and so forth. In other words, Wintgens's theory of legisprudence can be characterised as highly formalist.

The perspective of non-critical legisprudence, as proposed by Wintgens, takes the perspective of the 'freedom' of the subject which is arguably, a bourgeois subject,[64] enjoying the privileges of class, such as property and exploitation of labour.

---

58 The following is a simplified account of the rather complex system put forward by Professor Wintgens, especially with regard to the multi-level principle of coherence. However, I hope to have indicated its most characteristic features which are patently *formalist*.

59 Wintgens (n 7) 10.

60 ibid 11–12.

61 ibid 14.

62 ibid 18.

63 ibid 20.

64 cf Pashukanis (n 26) 40: 'the principle of legal subjectivity (which we take to mean the formal principle of freedom and equality, the autonomy of the personality, and so forth) is not only an instrument of deceit and a product of the hypocrisy of the bourgeoisie, insofar as it is used to counter the proletarian struggle to abolish classses, but is at the

The position of that subject is taken for granted; any 'limitations' of this subject's freedom require justification (principle of alternativity), especially if they include legal sanctions (principle of normative density) and should be lifted as soon as possible (principle of temporality). These three principles are, in effect, a reformulation of the principle of proportionality, permeating contemporary legal systems as a 'paradigmatic' mode of legal reasoning.[65] Proportionality as such is a formal device for balancing:[66] what counts are the preferences for interests of concrete classes and groups, as well as ideological choices, both cloaked under the idealistic form of 'values' or 'axiology'. Just like proportionality, embodied in principles 1–3, the final (4th) principle of coherence is *par excellence* formalist. Commenting on legisprudence's declared ambition to address the issues of law and politics,[67] one cannot but quote here Pashukanis's critique of the extreme formalism of Kelsen – which fits very well to legisprudence – claiming that it 'spends itself in sterile methodological and formal-logical humbug and parades its own complete dissociation from actual reality'.[68]

Therefore, it can be said that Wintgens made the right step but in the wrong direction. His step was right in the sense of recuperating legislation as a proper object for the general reflexion upon law (jurisprudence). His step was taken, however, in the wrong direction, because he refused to acknowledge the element of the political and constructed his system in a highly abstract and formalist manner. What we need, therefore, is a properly *political legisprudence*, understood as a critical inquiry into the theory of legislation. It could be referred to, as I have already hinted to above, as 'critical legisprudence'.

6 Conclusions

Legislation, due to its connection to the political process, is broadly regarded as being 'political', as opposed to the allegedly 'technical' phenomenon of adjudication or academic interpretation. However, this acknowledgement confuses

---

same time a concretely effective principle which is embodied in bourgeois society from the moment it emerges and and destroys feudal-patriarchal society.'

65 Kukovec (n 17) 136. See also Duncan Kennedy, 'A Transnational Genealogy of Proportionality in Private Law' in Roger Brownsword (ed.), *The Foundations of European Private Law* (Portland OR: Hart 2011) 185 ff; Duncan Kennedy, 'The Hermeneutic of Suspicion in Contemporary American Legal Thought' (2014) 25(2) Law and Critique 91.

66 Kukovec (n 17) 136.

67 Witgens (n 7) 1.

68 Pashukanis (n 26) 70.

two notions – that of 'politics' and 'the political'. All legislation belongs to the latter sphere, even if – from the point of view of politics – it passes off as 'technical' because it is not an object of a direct political conflict, voiced by parties or lobbyists. However, due to the essential features of legislation – the fact that it affects the rights and duties of actually existing groups of people – legislation is inherently political, as it impacts more or less directly upon the interests of social classes and other groups. Taking into account that legislation affects actual social antagonisms, its political analysis must be based on the impact that it has upon such antagonisms. In section 2, I mentioned a number of such antagonisms, such as the consumer vs. trader, employer vs. employee or liberal vs. conservative. The list is by no means exhaustive and the relationships can overlap or have a more complex, multi-pronged nature. For instance, the example mentioned in section 4 concerning the Polish law on housing development involved three groups in conflict – consumers (purchasers of a house), development companies and bankers. All three groups have conflicting interests vis-à-vis the two other groups. The declaratory aim of the legislation was to help consumers in their antagonism with developers, but in fact, it helped banks in their conflict with developers and consumers. This example poignantly shows that antagonistic relationships tend to be more complex than one could have *prima facie* considered (a triangular, rather than bipolar) and that the actual beneficiaries can be concealed from the original picture (parliament justified its stance mentioning only developers and consumers, but concealed the bankers).

The political analysis of legislation – critical legisprudence – must therefore combine two elements: on the one hand, a solid theoretical foundation allowing to properly identify social classes and groups, as well as their conflicts, and on the other hand, an extensive sociological research, linking the operation of a given piece of legislation and the interests of such classes or groups. The added value of such research cannot be underestimated, potentially leading to a more conscious and transparent political debate (as advocated by Martijn Hesselink with regard to the European Civil Code[69] and later, to contract law in general[70]), and at the very least seriously increasing the scientific understanding

69 Martijn W Hesselink, 'The Politics of European Contract Law: Who Has an Interest in What Kind of Contract Law for Europe?' in Stefan Grundmann and Jules Stuyck (eds), *An Academic Green Paper on European Contract Law* (Hague: Kluwer, 2002) 181–191; Martijn W Hesselink, 'Five Political Ideas of European Contract Law' (2011) 7(2) European Review of Contract Law 295.

70 Martijn W Hesselink, 'Democratic contract law' (2015) 11(2) European Review of Contract Law 81.

of legislation in its broader, socio-economic, and not only purely juristic, context. This does not necessarily mean that an open debate will lead to a compromise: contrary to Habermas,[71] I definitely subscribe to Mouffe's agonistic vision of the political (and *eo ipso* legal) order,[72] whereby conflicts cannot be eradicated in a society based on class antagonisms. I am sceptical of the possibility of reaching a compromise 'reflecting the joint interests of the society – a social compromise of different interests, a nation's history, traditions and culture',[73] as Darijus Beinoravičius argues for.

The social struggle is characterised by its ongoingness and pervasiveness, and it is played out *inter alia* in the field of legislation. Therefore, any single legislative solution should be treated as reflecting the state of social forces at the time of its enactment. Law is not written in stone, but is the effect of struggles in which some interests are preferred over others. Law arises from violence.[74] Indeed, each and every legal rule has its beneficiaries who impose their interests upon the maleficiaries, and the role of critical jurisprudence – and specifically the proposed approach of *critical legisprudence* – is to actively take part in the legislative debates (as 'lobbyist of the people') to ensure that new rules lead to the emancipation of human beings from opression and violence in its economic, social, cultural and symbolic facets, and old rules, imposing such violence or limiting the emancipation – are repealed.

This ever ongoing struggle (moving from 'compromise' to 'compromise') encompasses each and every legal rule, even those 'merely technical' ones on revoking offers or withholding performance that Kennedy mentioned. Even the most minute, technical legal rule is capable of being applied (that is, ultimately, the reason of its enactment), thereby enhancing the situation of one litigant (the beneficiary) and deteriorating that of another (the maleficiary). There are no 'win-win' solutions in litigation, but those whose just interests are sacrificed may be trained to accept the oppressive results and even avoid trying to defend them

---

71 For an application of Habermas's political theory to law-making in the field of contract law, see Hesselink (n 70) 109–111.

72 Chantal Mouffe, *Agonistics: Thinking the World Politically* (London: Verso, 2013).

73 Darijus Beinoravičius, 'Role of Legislative Sociology in Drafting Just Laws' in Jānis Rozenfelds et al (ed), *Tiesību efektivitāte postmodernā sabiedrībā* (Rīga: LU Akadēmiskais apgāds, 2015) 15.

74 Walter Benjamin, 'Critique of Violence' in Walter Benjamin, 1 *Selected Writings* (ed Marcus Bullock, Cambridge MA: Harvard University Press, 2004) 236 ff. Cf Saul Newman, 'Terror, Sovereignty and Law: On the Politics of Violence'(2004) 5(5) German Law Journal 569.

which can sometimes conceal the antagonistic dimension and contribute to diffusing an illusion of a 'harmonious' society.

Obviously, as it has become apparent in section 4, an *in abstracto* analysis of the effects of legislation, without empirical material, has only a limited role to play in the proposed project of critical legisprudence. However, the stakes are too high to limit critical research on legislation merely to its armchair dimension. A thoroughly pluridisciplinary approach needs to be taken, and the analytical legal realism proposed in the Polish context by Professor Paweł Chmielnicki is certainly a step in the right direction.

References

Balbus, I.D. 'Commodity Form and Legal Form: An Essay on the "Relative Autonomy" of the Law' (1977) 11 Law and Society 571.

Bartl, M.'Internal Market Rationality, Private Law and the Direction of the Union: Resuscitating the Market as the Object of the Political' (2015) 21(5) European Law Journal 572.

Bator, A., Pulka, Z. (eds.), *A Post-Analytical Approach to Philosophy and Theory of Law* (Berlin: Peter Lang, 2019).

Beinoravičius, D. 'Role of Legislative Sociology in Drafting Just Laws' in Jānis Rozenfelds et al. (eds), *Tiesību efektivitāte postmodernā sabiedrībā* (Rīga: LU Akadēmiskais apgāds, 2015).

Benjamin, W. 'Critique of Violence' in Walter Benjamin, 1 *Selected Writings* (Cambridge MA: Harvard University Press, 2004).

Chmielnicki, P. (ed.), *Nabycie lokalu lub domu od dewelopera. Wykładnia przepisów i efekty ich stosowania* [Purchase of a House from a Developer: Interpretation of the Legal Rules and the Effects of their Application] (Warszawa: Difin, 2014).

Chmielnicki, P. 'Prawne i praktyczne uwarunkowania lobbingu' [Legal and Practical Conditions of Lobbying] (2014) 9 Przegląd Prawa Publicznego 34.

Chmielnicki, P. 'The Research Method of Association for the Research on Sources and Functions of Law' (2015) 3 Przegląd Prawa Publicznego 95.

Chmielnicki, P. et al. *Activity Rules of Economic Man in Society as the Source of Legal Norms* (Warszawa: LexisNexis, 2010).

Collins, H. *Marxism and Law* (Oxford: OUP, 1982).

Cover, R. 'Violence and the Word' (1986) 95 Yale Law Journal 1601.

Frydman, S. *Dogmatyka prawa w świetle socjologii. Studium pierwsze: o wykładni ustaw* [Legal Dogmatics in the Light of Sociology. A First

Study on the Interpretation of Statutes] (Wilno: Księgarnia Kazimierza Rutskiego, 1936).

Hesselink, M.W. 'Democratic contract law' (2015) 11(2) European Review of Contract Law 81.

Hesselink, M.W. 'Five Political Ideas of European Contract Law' (2011) 7(2) European Review of Contract Law 295.

Hesselink, M.W. 'The Politics of European Contract Law: Who Has an Interest in What Kind of Contract Law for Europe?' in Stefan Grundmann and Jules Stuyck (eds.), *An Academic Green Paper on European Contract Law* (Hague: Kluwer, 2002).

Hesselink, M.W. *The New European Private Law: Essays on the Future of Private Law in Europe* (Kluwer, 2002).

Kennedy, D. 'A Transnational Genealogy of Proportionality in Private Law' in Roger Brownsword (ed.), *The Foundations of European Private Law* (Portland OR: Hart, 2011).

Kennedy, D. 'The Hermeneutic of Suspicion in Contemporary American Legal Thought' (2014) 25(2) Law and Critique 91.

Kennedy, D. 'The Political Stakes in "Merely Technical" Issues of Contract Law' (2001) 1 European Review of Private Law 7.

Kennedy, D. 'Legal Education and the Reproduction of Hierarchy' (1982) 32(4) Journal of Legal Education 591.

Kennedy, D. *Critique of Adjudication {fin de siècle}* (Cambridge MA: Harvard University Press, 1997).

Kowalski, J., Lamentowicz, W., Winczorek, P. *Teoria państwa i prawa* (Warszawa: Państwowe Wydawnictwo Naukowe, 1981).

Kukovec, D. 'Hierarchies as Law' (2014) 21 Columbia Journal of European Law 131.

Łachacz, O. 'Drafting the Legislation Within European Union Institutions – Towards Common Legal Acts Standards' in Jānis Rozenfelds and Jānis Pleps (eds.), *The Quality of Legal Acts and its Importance in Contemporary Legal Space* (Riga: University of Latvia Press, 2012), 9–15.

Lang, W.,Wróblewski, J., Zawawdzki, S. *Teoria państwa i prawa* [Theory of State and Law] (Warszawa: Państwowe Wydawnictwo Naukowe, 1980).

Leiter, B. 'The Hermeneutics of Suspicion: Recovering Marx, Nietsche and Freud' (2005) of Texas School of Law Public Law and Legal Theory Working Paper, available at http://ssrn.com/abstract=691002 (accessed 21 March 2019).

Mańko, R., Łakomy, J. 'In search for the ontological presuppositions of critical jurisprudence' (2018) 10(2) Critique of Law 469.

Mańko, R. 'Critique of the "Juridical": Some Metatheoretical Remarks' (2018) 11 Journal of the University of Latvia. Law 24.

Mańko, R. 'Law, Politics and the Economy in Poland's Post-Socialist Transformation: Preliminary Notes Towards an Investigation' in Balazs Fekete and Fruzsina Gárdos-Orosz (eds.), *25 Years After Transition in Central and Eastern Europe: Understanding the Transition from an Internal Perspective* (Frankfurt am Main: Peter Lang, 2017) 105–119.

Mańko, R. 'Nauki prawne wobec problemu polityczności: zagadnienia wybrane z perspektywy jurysprudencji krytycznej' [Legal Sciences Towards the Problem of the Political: Selected Issues from the Perspective of Critical Jurisprudence] (2018) 18(3) Archiwum Filozofii Prawa i Filozofii Społecznej 38.

Mańko, R. 'Relikty w kulturze prawnej – uwagi metodologiczne na tle pozostałości epoki socjalizmu realnego w polskim prawie prywatnym' [Survivals in Legal Culture: Methodological Remarks Against the Background of Remnants of the Period of Actually Existing Socialism in Polish Private Law] (2015) 102 Przegląd Prawa i Administracji 201.

Mańko, R. 'Symbolic Violence in Technocratic Law and Attempts at Its Overcoming: Politicisation Through Humanization?' (2017) 11 Studia Erasmiana Vratislaviensia 31.

Mańko, R. 'The Culture of Private Law in Central Europe After Enlargement: A Polish Perspective' (2005) 11(5) European Law Journal 527.

Mańko, R. 'The Unification of Private Law in Europe from the Perspective of Polish Legal Culture' (2007–2008) 11 Yearbook of Polish Legal Studies 109.

Mańko, R. 'Transformacja ustrojowa a ciągłość instytucji prawnych – uwagi teoretyczne' [Systemic Transformation and the Continuity of Legal Institutions – Theoretical Remarks] (2016) 16(2) Zeszyty Prawnicze 6.

Mańko, R., Sulikowski, A., Łakomy, J. 'Polityczność prawa i ogólnej refleksji nad prawem: wprowadzenie' [The Political Character of Law and General Jurisprudence: An Introduction] (2018) 3 Archiwum Filozofii Prawa i Filozofii Społecznej 5.

Mouffe, C. *Agonistics: Thinking the World Politically* (London: Verso, 2013).

Mouffe, C. *On the Political* (London-New York: Routledge, 2005).

Newman, N. 'Terror, Sovereignty and Law: On the Politics of Violence' (2004) 5(5) German Law Journal 569.

Opałek, K. *Zagadnienia teorii prawa i teorii polityki* [Issues of Legal Theory and Political Theory] (Warszawa: PWN, 1986).

Pashukanis, E.B. *Law and Marxism: A General Theory. Toward a Critique of the Fundamental Juridical Concepts* [1924] (trans. by Barbara Einhorn, London: Pluto Press, 1983).

Paździora M., Stambulski, M. 'Co może dać nauce prawa polityczność? Przyczynek do przyszłych badań' [What Can Legal Science Learn from the Political? Notes Towards Further Research] (2014) 1 Archiwum Filozofii Prawa i Filozofii Społecznej 55.

Sacco, R. 'Legal Formants: A Dynamic Approach to Comparative Law (Instalment II of II)' (1991) 39(2) American Journal of Comparative Law 343.

Skuczyński, P. 'Typy myśli krytycznej w prawoznawstwie. Od krytyki poznania do walki o uznanie' [Types of Critical Thought in Jurisprudence: From the Critique of Cognition to Struggle for Recognition] in Tomasz Bekrychtet al. (eds.), 1 *Integracja zewnętrzna i wewnętrzna nauk prawnych* (Łódź: Wydawnictwo Uniwersytetu Łódzkiego, 2014).

Stambulski, M. 'Polityczność w polskiej analitycznej teorii prawa. Zarys problematyki' [The Political in Polish Analytical Legal Theory: Outline of the Issue] (2018) 18(3) Archiwum Filozofii Prawa i Filozofii Społecznej 64.

Sulikowski, A. 'Apolityczność w prawoznawstwie. Kryzys idei a zjawisko populizmu' [Apoliticality in Jurisprudence: Crisis of an Idea and the Phenomenon of Populism], (2018) 18(3) Archiwum Filozofii Prawa i Filozofii Społecznej 74.

Sulikowski, A. 'Trzy filary nowoczesnego logosu sądzenia i ich postmodernistyczna krytyka' [The Three Pillars of the Modern Logos of Adjudication and their Postmodernist Critique] in Michał Błachut (ed.), *Z zagadnień teorii i filozofii prawa. Ponowoczesność* (Wrocław: Kolonia Limited, 2007).

Šulmane, D. 'Versatility of Effects of Legal Provisions' in Jānis Rozenfelds and Jānis Pleps (eds.), *The Quality of Legal Acts and its Importance in Contemporary Legal Space* (Riga: University of Latvia Press, 2012).

Šulmane, D., Ševčuk, P. [Шулмане, Д. Шевчук П.]. 'Легиспруденция – новый подход к вопросу о законотворчестве' (2013) 97(6) Сравнительное Конституционное Обозрение 14.

Tamanaha, B.Z. *Realistic Socio-Legal Theory: Pragmatism and a Social Theory of Law* (Oxford: OUP, 1997).

Tuori, K. 'Legal Culture and the General Societal Culture' in Thomas Wilhelmsson (ed.), *Private Law and the Many Cultures of Europe* (The Hague: Kluwer, 2007).

Voermans, W. 'Concern About the Quality of EU Legislation: What Kind of Problem, by What Kind of Means?' (2009) 2(1) Erasmus Law Review 59.

Wintgens, L.J. 'Legisprudence as a New Theory of Legislation' (2006) 19(1) Ratio Juris 1.

Wintgens, L.J. 'The Rational Legislator Revisited. Bounded Rationality and Legisprudence The Rational Legislator' in Luc J Wintgens and A Daniel Oliver-Lalana (eds.), *The Rationality and Justification of Legislation* (Heidelberg: Springer, 2013), 1–31.

Zamboni, M. *Law and Politics: A Dilemma for Contemporary Legal Theory* (Berlin: Springer, 2008).

Rafał Chybiński

2 The Role of Lawyers in Law-making and the Political Struggle from the Perspective of Carl Schmitt

Abstract: Carl Schmitt, alongside Hans Kelsen and Leon Petrażycki, is currently considered one of the most famous philosophers of law. His views are strongly controversial, but increasingly they seem to be very pertinent today. One can observe a great influence of his thought/philosophy on modern Europe, especially on such countries as Hungary or Poland.This article focuses, above all, on Carl Schmitt's decisionism in the context of the politics of Nazi Germany. Subsequently, it shows the pertinence of Nazis' behaviour and the attempts to transpose that behaviour onto the current political reality. On the whole, the article aims at revealing how modern jurisprudence is entangled in politics. It is, without a doubt, a huge problem which under the current circumstances should be considered impossible to solve.

Keywords: Lawyers, Carl Schmitt, Decisionism, Constitution

Introduction. The Concept of the Political According to Schmitt

When starting any considerations on the political nature of jurisprudence, it would be worthwhile to briefly explain the significance of this "Political" in the context discussed. Contrary to the often-encountered understanding of the term of the Political, it is difficult to speak of explaining it as an activity centered around any political party. One should look at the political nature of jurisprudence more in the spirit of Schmitt's rivalry of friends and enemies, in which the public authority points to the new enemy, whose task is to serve as the scapegoat for the manipulation of the current governors, with its finger. The aim of the present work will therefore be to check the compatibility of Carl Schmitt's theory with the current political situation.

It is no secret that we have been witnessing the creation of ever newer public enemies for almost two years. For the purposes of the present publication, those enemies, who are to allow the governors to maintain their power by evoking universal fear or hatred at the mere thought of an "imaginary" adversary, may be omitted. The most interesting category of enemies will be those who in reality are on the side of the authority, but their role is a mystifying one – they are supposed to be the bad cop, while the governors are the good one, the one who offers the society a relaxation of the restrictions announced by the former. Such practices resemble the actions of stores preparing for great discounts – products in their offers are sold at a price much higher than the previous one, while containing an information about a fictional discount.

In order tounderstand the topic discussed in the present work better, one should briefly present how the concept of the Political is understood in the spirit of Carl Schmitt, crown jurist of the Third Reich, a professor at the University of Berlin. It was precisely Schmitt's doctrine that helped Nazis justify their policies in a scientific manner. He argued that not all countries are equal in the face of law, denied legal universalityand also predicted the division of the globe into appropriate regions managed by an entity whose task was to prevent any interventions from the outside[1]. In his opinion, a peculiar feature of the Political was the friend-enemy relationship, about which we will talk in situations when different groups enter into a conflict of some kind. An entity participating in this friend-enemy relationship will therefore be referred to as a political one[2]. According to previous declarations, I will try to present the political nature of jurisprudence from a different point of view than before. I will not try to look for public enemies created by those currently in power in the form of politicians representing "total opposition." Lawyers will be the "enemies" who are more important to me. Undoubtedly, those determined to support the drafts of amendments proposed by the current authorities have been drawn into a political game whose consequences they were not able to foresee. Carl Schmitt himself was in a similar situation in 1933. He gave his support to Nazis and was therefore subsequently treated with contempt until the end of his days in the Federal Republic.

1 Stanisław Musiał, „Historyczne i ideologiczno-polityczne źródła Nazistowskiego projektu „Neue Europa" i jego realizacja w Europie środkowo-wschodniej, [eng. Historical and ideological-political sources of the Nazi project „Neue Europa" and its implementation in Central and Eastern Europe]", (2012) <http://bazhum.muzhp.pl/media//files/Colloquium/Colloquium-r2012-t-n3/Colloquium-r2012-t-n3-s27-48/Colloquium-r2012-t-n3-s27-48.pdf> accessed 27 March 2018.

2 Paul Hirst, „Decisionism of Carl Schmitt" in Chantal Moufee (eds), *The Challenge of Carl Schmitt* (OUP 1999).

1 Takeover of Legal Structures on the Example of Actions of the Third Reich

The content presented below is intended to show the horrible things that may be achieved while simultaneously acting "in accordance with the law". The fact that legislation was created by lawyers acting on orders of the Nazis is not without significance.

Precisely on 14 July 1933, a law was passed, in accordance with which, NSDAP was the only party recognized as operating legally on the territory of Germany. It was undoubtedly the most important change thus far, one that allowed Nazis to seize power completely. The Third Reich was slowly becoming a centralist country, and any manifestations of state federalism were meticulously eliminated. Another important attack on the freedom of public life was a legal act which made it possible to oblige state officials and judges to swear their allegiance to Adolf Hitler. The slow takeover of all state institutions took place at the expense of lawyers who created the new, "tailor-made" legislation of the Third Reich[3]. A huge violation of the principles *lex retro non agit* and *nulla poena sine lege* was the imposition of the death penalty in relation to people suspected of setting fire to the Reichstag. All these activities of jurists cooperating with the Nazis were dictated by thinking in terms of the alternative "Hitler or chaos". They were convinced that only thanks to such actions they would be able to protect Germany from the internal enemy in the form of Jews and communists, and also to save their own lives.

In 1935, by virtue of the Act, citizenship, as well as the right to marry German people, was withdrawn from all those who were not "people of German blood." In this way, it was easy to "legally" deprive of citizenship those enemies of the regime who refused to support the national revolution. It is worth noting here that the entry into force of the Nuremberg Laws did not take place at Adolf Hitler's initiative, but upon request of the extremely anti-Semitic officials from the Ministry of Internal Affairs. They considered it necessary to clarify any issues related to German citizenship. When the draft was presented to the Führer, he crossed off the last sentence of the legal act: "This law applies only to full Jews," which caused interpretation problems. It was only after a supplement to the Act

---

3 Łukasz Bolesta, Prawo Karne III Rzeszy instrumentem polityki państwa totalitarnego, [eng. Criminal Law of the Third Reich as an Instrument of Policy of a Totalitarian State], (2013) <https://www.journals.umcs.pl/szn/article/viewFile/1413/1125> accessed 27 March 2018.

was issued, that it was clearly stated: "Jews mean German Orthodox Jews who have Jewish grandparents or those who married a person of Jewish origin"[4].

However, it should be pointed out that all these activities were in accordance with the letter of the law. This situation could only take place under the most influential trend in legal thought, which is undoubtedly legal positivism. As Adam Sulikowski indicates: "the sense of positivist legal practice determines its inseparable connection with a war and striving to defeat opponents, to take a better position in an imaginary community." Phrases such as "to defeat the opponent,""to win the case", which often appear in professional practice, may be a testimony of perceiving the trend in this way. All this indicates the aggressive nature of legal positivism, which had a significant impact on allowing the activities discussed above. I would not like to present here a full description of this way of understanding the law, which is why I will confine myself to expressing a statement which is the most important for the purposes of this work and says that legal positivism assumes the separation of the law and non-legal normative systems[5]. This is important because of the way in which non-compliance of the law with moral principles will influence the validity of legal norms. The Third Reich could afford to take over all legal institutions precisely because the previous perception of law assumed the independence of the law and in its validity from morality[6]. In literature, however, it is possible to find voices of opposition to the allegations made against legal positivism. Maria Zmierczak was of the view that, in fact, the attitude of Nazis to positivism was critical. Lawyers of the Third Reich were constantly trying to explain that the spirit of *Gesetzespositivismus*[7]is not *compatible with the* Nazi understanding of the law. Arnold Wagemann, in the magazine "Volkischer Beobachter," published an article whose title clearly revealed the attitude of "lawyers of the Reich" to the Act and formalism – "Under the yoke of the Act. The slogan of the struggle against the enemy nation and formalism that destroys the law"[8]. Another German lawyer – Roland Freisler, not concealing his dislike towards positivism, wrote – "National Socialist law, while

4 Richard Overy, *The Rhird Reich: A Chronicle,* (Quercus Publishing 2011).

5 Adam Sulikowski, Opresywność pozytywizmu prawnego i jej postmodernistyczna krytyka, [eng. Oppressiveness of legal positivism and its postmodern criticism], (2010) <http://bibliotekacyfrowa.pl/Content/35300/0003.pdf> accessed 28 March 2018.

6 Lech Morawski, *Wstęp do prawoznawstwa,* [eng. Introduction to jurisprudence], (first published 1996, Toruń 2012) p. 44.

7 German translation: statutory positivism.

8 Manfred Krohn, *Die deutsche Justiz im Urteil der Nationalsozialisten 1920–1933,* (Peter Lang 1991) p. 317–322.

it has found a means of expression in the Act, aims to include remedies against the fossilization of statutory law in the Act itself. [. . .] Preambles to National Socialist acts and their program assumptions were mocked. [. . .] It is indeed these introductions that give the acts a direction; they guarantee that their political intention will be faithfully observed in their implementation and execution. Obviously, an act itself cannot achieve this"[9]. In this way, he clearly emphasized that law is not defined in acts at all, but in the spirit of national socialism. Helmut Nicolai was of a similar opinion, pointing to the strength of legal conviction present in the German nation – "only a national state can create just law that is always and everywhere biologically and morally dependent, and it must be like this to ensure the life and existence of the nation." It is also worth mentioning the new theory of sources of law, about which wrote Curt Rothenberger. The Act, although it was situated at the top of the pyramid, could no longer be understood in the spirit of positivism but only as the plan and will of the leader. It is clear that lawyers obeying the Nazi rhetoric did not want to recognize law as an entity separated from morality. They pointed to the obligatory relationship of regulation with the commandments of decency, but a decency that was understood in an unquestionably distorted manner. There is no other source of law than the conscience of the nation – Walther Merk points out[10].

It is difficult to have any doubts that the Nazis used elements of positivism perfectly to legitimize their actions. With the help of jurists, they shaped only the understanding of regulations in the spirit of national socialism, which was to be done using introductions and preambles to acts. This did not change the very essence of the positivist understanding of the law completely. It was only after the end of World War II that German philosopher Gustav Radbruch included three theses, now known as the Radbruch formula, in his work "Statutory Lawlessness and Supra-Statutory Law." The reason why he created them was to prevent instances of "hiding" behind the provisions of law in such a blatant manner in the future, even if these provisions are in clear opposition to the principle of justice and, by doing so, he simultaneously strengthened the assumption he initially put forward. The first thesis states that in some situations of an internal conflict of law, we may not take into account the provisions and instead focus on

9 Maria Zmierczak, *Pozytywizm prawniczy a prawnicy i prawo w Trzeciej Rzeszy - powojenna dyskusja niemieckich historyków i teoretyków prawa o przyczynach upadku prawa w czasach nazizmu,* [eng. Legal positivism and lawyers and law in the Third Reich – post-war discussion of German historians and law theorists on the causes of the collapse of law in the Nazi era], [2001], p. 11.

10 *Ibidem.*

the implementation of justice. The second one concerns the fact that extremely pervasive acts should be deprived of the privilege of calling them laws. The third one, meanwhile, places the full burden of responsibility for all the horrors of Nazi crimes, which, nota bene, were committed in accordance with the law, precisely on legal positivism, which created a habit of absolute obedience towards the law in the society from those years[11].

One may ask themselves the question, what is the purpose of recalling the Radbruch formula today anyway?However, in this chapter, I will not include it along with its historical context, which would justify the doubt as to the reasonable nature of this procedure, but instead, I will treat it in an instrumental manner, while attempting to transfer its message onto our domestic events. In the subsequent part of the work, I will try to recall the actions of those currently governing, evidently attempting to take over consecutive legal institutions in our country, as well as the behavior of previously respected lawyers, which could easily be compared to the actions of Carl Schmitt.

2 The Enemy within the Fourth Polish Republic

As I noted at the beginning of this chapter, I will not focus in my considerations on the enemies created by the present authorities in the form of "total opposition," judges or politicians of the European Union. My main goal will be to present the hidden manipulations of the governors, who try to create, by means of their lawyers, controversial regulations or opinions arousing hostility in the society only to then reject them altogether, a fact which is so characteristic of Carl Schmitt's philosophy of politics. Such an action serves to create the conviction in people that the current authorities do not agree to the use of such radical legal measures, which lawyers have previously deemed "lawful." This builds up an increasing anger towards this professional group, at the same time strengthening the peculiar relationship of the society with the "ruling friend."

The first situation confirming the assumptions made by me will concern the veto exercised by President Andrzej Duda in relation to the acts on the Supreme Court and the National Council of the Judiciary. The president noted that he had talked about the above-mentioned acts with many specialists in law, philosophy, sociology or politics. However, it was Zofia Romaszewska's opinion that had the greatest influence on his final decision: "Poland needs a reform of the justice

11 Jerzy Zajadło, *Polska pod pręgierzem formuły Radbrucha,* [end. Poland under the pillory of the Radbruch formula] (2018) <http://konstytucyjny.pl/polska-pod-pregierzem-formuly-radbrucha/> accessed 29 March 2018.

system and I am a supporter of this reform. But Poland needs a wise reform that will ensure the efficient functioning of the justice system, one which will increase the sense of justice. I feel deeply that the reform will not increase security and justice in this form."[12] One might consider this behavior of the President to be an expression of his autonomy, that is, independence of the president of the ruling party. However, in reality, the situation may be completely different. It is no secret that Andrzej Duda's position has been weakening with each passing month, and opposition parties have even called him a "puppet." To strengthen the President's political status, the current authorities had to reach for radical measures. Thanks to the maneuvre of introducing controversial laws into the legal order, which the Head of State will then reject, he will regain support and will begin to appear to the public as a real defender of the Constitution.

Another example of using drafts and opinions to transfer the responsibility for controversial regulations onto lawyers and thus "whitewash" the politicians of the ruling party may be the Report of the Team of Experts on the Issues of the Constitutional Tribunal (hereinafter referred to as the Report), which was coordinated by Professor Jan Majchrowski[13]. It was created as a result of the Venice Commission issuing an opinion on the problem surrounding the Constitutional Tribunal. It was Witold Waszczykowski – the then Minister of Foreign Affairs who had asked the Commission for such an opinion. In the Report, the authors emphasized that such an established position of the Constitutional Tribunal may completely distort the image of the country which has been shaped thus far. We will no longer be dealing with the so-called political nation exercising the utmost power in the state, but only with a state in which the "Proponents (. . .) in turn recognize the legal order as a field, which is not only superior to a political community and binds it, as well as all bodies of public authority but also as one that legitimizes the functioning of this community and public institutions."[14]Such a perspective leads the authors to the conclusion that the second solution transfers the attribute of sovereignty onto law, which they consider a significant disadvantage. This creates an impression as if the creators of the Report forgot the main

12 President Andrzej Duda signed the bill about common courts, <http://wyborcza.pl/7,75398,22145773,jednak-dwa-weta-prezydent-andrzej-duda-podpisal-ustawe-o-sadach.html> accessed 30 March 2018.

13 Report of the Experts' Group on the Issues of the Constitutional Tribunal of 15 July 2016, <http://www.sejm.gov.pl/media8.nsf/files/ASEA-ADRKBW/%24File/Raport%20Zespołu%20Ekspertów%20do%20spraw%20Problematyki%20Trybunału%20Konstytucyjnego.pdf> accessed 31 March 2018.

14 *Ibidem* p. 3.

goal of creating the Constitution as a peculiar social contract. It is thanks to the Basic Law that we have an increased sense of security in situations of controversial regulations being created by the government. The story of Odysseus returning from the Trojan War is a parable which illustrates this well. When Odysseus passed by the island of sirens, ordered his subordinates to tie themselves to the mast, so as not to be seduced by their beautiful singing. He ordered his helpers to plug their ears. In this parable, the mast is to symbolize the Constitution, which will protect Odysseus (the people in power at a given moment) from seemingly attractive but, in reality, destructive decisions (the sirens)[15]. Taking into account the message of the quoted narrative, one may assume that the authors of the Report are attempting to justify, by virtue of the strength of their authority, the fact of the position of the Constitutional Tribunal being habitually weakened by the current government. By doing so, they are building the conviction in the society that citizens are owed real power over the law, a power, access to which is blocked by the Constitution, or rather its provisions. "With this assumption, neither the "sovereign" nor the body that represents him, are "above" such a court anymore; instead – like him – they are bound by law and treated as its "organs."""[16] It is clear from the wording of the content of the Report that a properly functioning Constitutional Tribunal, according to the Experts, treats the sovereign (i.e., all citizens) as a body which is subordinate to it. However, the Report's authors completely forgot that (first of all) democracy is not equivalent to the rule of the majority and (secondly) that the Constitutional Tribunal most often acts as the defender of minorities. Such a defence is perfectly illustrated by a situation when a party which, most often as a consequence of differences in the view of the world, does not represent a certain social group starts to rule in the Parliament. This group, which is in the minority at that time, may, in the event of a violation of their rights and freedoms use the help of the Constitutional Tribunal, which is obliged to protect this community from attempts to remove it from power made by the currently ruling party. It is difficult to say unequivocally whether the authors of the Report are aware that all their current activities can only lead to creating the image of a lawyer as an enemy of the society which, simultaneously, will also begin to have a negative impact on them.

---

15 Marcin Matczak, *Lesson about Constitution*, <https://www.youtube.com/watch?v=YHodsdPKS4M> accessed 31 March 2018.

16 Report of the Experts' Group on the Issues of the Constitutional Tribunal of 15 July 2016, <http://www.sejm.gov.pl/media8.nsf/files/ASEA-ADRKBW/%24File/Raport%20Zespołu%20Ekspertów%20do%20spraw%20Problematyki%20Trybunału%20Konstytucyjnego.pdf> accessed 31 March 2018.

The increasingly frequent dispersion of elements from American realism into the legal discourse is also worthy of mention. After all, the rotation of judges is indicated as the antidote to solving current problems. This builds the conviction that the justice system is not based on provisions that form the basis for rendering judgements, but on the internal feelings and views of judges. According to the government, removing the current judges, which, at present, is happening before our eyes will be the ideal remedy for systemic diseases in the form of the excessive length of proceedings or penalties which are not always commensurate with the committed acts. New judges will render their rulings much faster, while investigating the facts of a case much more thoroughly. An excellent demonstration of the "people's justice system" were the sessions of the Verification Commission under the leadership of Minister Patryk Jaki. Often, one could hear the chairman's words referring to the legal loopholes that "bad lawyers" are trying to use against "ordinary citizens." All these maneuvres may resemble the ones taking place in Germany before 1939. It is obvious that we are no longer dealing with such cruel physical violence. However, the "enemy" is still "alive." People who agree to cooperate with the governors for their own benefit will also stay "alive."

In March 2017, a report was prepared containing information on the number of opinions commissioned by the Sejm. Over the course of the year, nearly 250 analyses have been commissioned, the authors of which were lawyers verifying, among others, the situation surrounding the Constitutional Tribunal. Over PLN 250 000 was allocated for their work[17]. The opinions written by the late Professor Bogusław Banaszak and Professor Paweł Sobczyk are particularily noteworthy. The former stated that continuing the 33th session of the Sejm of December 16, 2016 in the Column Hall was in accordance with the Constitution and the Regulations of the Sejm. The latter of the professors confirmed the compliance of the decision made by the Speaker of the Sejm, who called a vote by show of hands and had the secretaries count all the votes cast, with the Regulations of the Sejm. The intentions of the authorities are therefore very clear and still filled with the spirit of American realism[18]. By taking full control over the right people, it is possible to gain complete control of the law. One question arises in and of itself.

17 Mateusz Ratajczak, *Analysis of the Sejm*, <https://www.money.pl/gospodarka/wiadomosci/artykul/ekspertyzy-sejmu-lista-ekspertow-sejmu,153,0,2290329.html> accessed 31 March 2018.

18 Marcin Matczak, *A debate on amending the Act – Law on the common court system,* <https://www.youtube.com/watch?v=aEi7bzqyQA0&t=2066s> accessed 31 March 2018.

How much farther are those lawyers, who are able to deny everything they have been taught thus far for their own benefit, willing to go?

Conclusions

All the previous considerations made in this chapter prompt one to draw the conclusion that the party currently in power has created a new "enemy" who is protecting the ancient regime. The "enemies" are, above all, the lawyers who refuse to blatantly violate the provisions of the Constitution. Those who have agreed to create opinions that are supposed to "legitimize" the actions of the authorities now benefit from the situation by strengthening their positions. It is not out of the question that in a few years' time they might repeat the fate of Carl Schmitt as infamous lawyers. However, these are currently merely speculations.

At this point, assessing the usefulness of Carl Schmitt's theory itself for contemporary political or social reality would also be worthwhile. Despite the many similarities between the actions of those currently in power and the politicians of the Third Reich, it is not entirely possible to assume full compatibility of the views of the "crown jurist" with the system functioning at present. As I have already mentioned, in spite of the clear power of politics over law and the instrumental use of its provisions to pursue political goals, such behavior will not bring benefits in the immediate future, as is clearly indicated by Schmitt and the other lawyers referred to above. This is for two reasons. First of all – the society is neither ready nor willing to accept such an aggressive policy – like a legislative hammer striking into the previous order. This is evident even in the actions of the authorities themselves. It tries to suit the "taste" of its electorate, treating it every now and then to a "legislative candy," rather than forcefully changing the image of the social life against its will. Secondly – nowadays, Carl Schmitt's Theory is ideally suited primarily for criticism, but it is difficult to build anything on its foundations, as the only fruit born by it will be the creation of a totalitarian state.

So, what position should one take at present? Jerzy Zajadło points out that the ruling party is increasingly more frequently approaching a certain boundary, beyond which it will be possible to consider any legislative action as statutory lawlessness. This applies to both factual and legislative activities[19]. Unfortunately, one cannot outright refuse to abide by the rules, even if these rules are issued in violation of the provisions of the Basic Law. This is because they benefit from

19 Jerzy Zajadło, *Polska pod pręgierzem formuły Radbrucha,* [end. Poland under the pillory of the Radbruch formula] (2018) <http://konstytucyjny.pl/polska-pod-pregierzem-formuly-radbrucha/> accessed 29 March 2018.

the presumption of constitutionality. But what happens in a situation where the Radbruch formula is applied, as suggested by the previously mentioned Jerzy Zajadło? In his opinion, the violations of the Constitution are clear and far-reaching enough that relying on the above-mentioned principle is perfectly justified. It seems, however, that such a radical action would only serve to reaffirm the current governors in their conviction about actual power lying with lawyers and not the law. That is why it is worth to wait out this whole legal mess, hoping for a "better change."

References

1. ŁukaszBolesta, Prawo Karne III Rzeszy instrumentem polityki państwa totalitarnego, [eng. Criminal Law of the Third Reich as an Instrument of Policy of a Totalitarian State], (Lublin 2013) <https://www.journals.umcs.pl/szn/article/viewFile/1413/1125> accessed 27 March 2018.
2. PaulHirst, "Decisionism of Carl Schmitt" in ChantalMoufee (ed), *The Challenge of Carl Schmitt*,(London, OUP 1999).
3. ManfredKrohn, *Die deutsche Justiz im Urteil der Nationalsozialisten 1920–1933*, (Frankfurt/M., Bern, New York, Paris, Peter Lang, OUP 1991).
4. MarcinMatczak, *A debate on amending the Act – Law on the common court system*, <https://www.youtube.com/watch?v=aEi7bzqyQA0&t=2066s> accessed 31 March 2018.
5. MarcinMatczak, *Lesson about Constitution*, <https://www.youtube.com/watch?v=YHodsdPKS4M> accessed 31 March 2018.
6. LechMorawski, *Wstęp do prawoznawstwa*, [eng. Introduction to jurisprudence], (first published 1996, Toruń, Dom Organizatora 2012).
7. StanisławMusiał, „Historyczne i ideologiczno-polityczne źródła Nazistowskiego projektu „Neue Europa" i jego realizacja w Europie środkowo-wschodniej, [eng. Historical and ideological-political sources of the Nazi project „Neue Europa" and its implementation in Central and Eastern Europe]", (Gdynia 2012) <http://cejsh.icm.edu.pl/cejsh/element/bwmeta1.element.cejsh-fc3aa56b-12ce-49cb-a99b-5a3594e4b065/c/Stanislaw_Musial.pdf> accessed 27 March 2018.
8. RichardOvery, *The Rhird Reich: A Chronicle*, (London, Quercus Publishing 2011).
9. President Andrzej Duda signed the bill about common courts, <http://wyborcza.pl/7,75398,22145773,jednak-dwa-weta-prezydent-andrzej-duda-podpisal-ustawe-o-sadach.html> accessed 30 March 2018.

10. MateuszRatajczak, *Analysis of the Sejm*, <https://www.money.pl/gospodarka/wiadomosci/artykul/ekspertyzy-sejmu-lista-ekspertow-sejmu,153,0,2290329.html> accessed 31 March 2018.
11. 'Report of the Experts' Group on the Issues of the Constitutional Tribunal of 15 July 2016, <http://www.sejm.gov.pl/media8.nsf/files/ASEA-ADRKBW/%24File/Raport%20Zespołu%20Ekspertów%20do%20spraw%20Problematyki%20Trybunału%20Konstytucyjnego.pdf> accessed 31 March 2018.
12. AdamSulikowski, Opresywność pozytywizmu prawnego i jej postmodernistyczna krytyka, [eng. Oppressiveness of legal positivism and its postmodern criticism], (Wrocław 2010) <http://bibliotekacyfrowa.pl/Content/35300/0003.pdf> accessed 28 March 2018.
13. JerzyZajadło, *Polska pod pręgierzem formuły Radbrucha,* [end. Poland under the pillory of the Radbruch formula] (2018) <http://konstytucyjny.pl/polska-pod-pregierzem-formuly-radbrucha/> accessed 29 March 2018.
14. MariaZmierczak, *Pozytywizm prawniczy a prawnicy i prawo w Trzeciej Rzeszy - powojenna dyskusja niemieckich historyków i teoretyków prawa o przyczynach upadku prawa w czasach nazizmu, [eng. Legal positivism and lawyers and law in the Third Reich - post-war discussion of German historians and law theorists on the causes of the collapse of law in the Nazi era*], (Acta Universitatis Wratislaviensis No 2214, Wrocław 2001).

Dominik Góra

3 Politicalness of Law and Technological Ideology

Abstract: This paper tries to combine two very modern and interesting fields of our society: politicalness and new technology. The author believes that new technologies will certainly impact (or have already done it) politics so powerfully that it will give rise to self-technocracy.

Keywords: new technologies, technocracy, law, politics, politicalness

The problem[1] of the political[2] nature of the law was raised for the first time in the 1930s by the German philosopher C. Schmitt, who is considered a co-creator of the so-called political theology. In his time, the concept of politics was associated with considerations regarding the recognition of a particular subject as a sovereign, and the same politicalness was a prism through which he saw a "certain social order" which he had established and that he considered as close to the ideal. Following H. Kelsen, who claimed that law might be the sovereign itself, it can be undoubtedly concluded that a certain transition of politics to the discourse of law was made, which in its essence was politically neutral, what was mentioned in a work "What can politics give to science?" A contribution to future research" by M. Paździora and M. Stambulski[3]. For this reason, the political system, affecting the legal system, is woven more and more into new areas. Politicalness, which is characterized by C. Mouffe in her works, claims that it is a kind of antagonism that is the center and at the same time, a condition for the possibilities of society, while politics itself considers the background formed on elements of social practice and legal institutions themselves, which

---

1 This paper was created as a part of the NCN OPUS research project no. 2016/21/B/HS5/00164.

2 M. A. Cichocki, '*Teologia polityczna i inne pisma*'[Political theology and other writings] [selection], (Cracow, Znak, 2000).

3 M. Paździora, M. Stambulski '*Co może dać nauce prawa polityczność? Przyczynek do przyszłych badań*' [What can the law of politics give to science? A contribution to future research]in2014 1 *ARCHIWUM FILOZOFII PRAWA I FILOZOFII SPOŁECZNEJ*, 56.

as if they enable existence in this society[4]. There is an immanent connection of politics with other areas of social existence, among which there is undoubtedly also the law. Hailing from the Cracow region, M. Król notes that "every view of political philosophy presents a concept of politicalness[5]". For this reason, it should be considered whether the legal discourse related to the implementation of new technologies into the law is not an element of political activity that takes place before our eyes, that is, the eyes of entities whose political decisions affect directly. For the purposes of this work, the starting point may also be the concept of M. Weber, who assumed that politics is a specific and targeted action of politicians and politically active citizens at the decision-making levels affecting the fate of both the state and citizens. He believed, creating one of the more well-known philosophical thought, the state is an organization that can shape the law and enforce it with the help of even physical strength, which he presented in his famous lecture entitled "Politics as a Vocation[6]." D. Bell noted that technological development will have an impact on political and economic decisions that will cause further social change. The production of knowledge is to a lesser extent an individual matter, and increasingly to the social activity of communities that apply and acquire knowledge[7]. It is difficult to disagree with this thesis.

Contemporary technological development, and hence social, is different from the previous stages of civilization development and at the same time much faster than it was possible to be observed in the past[8]. This otherness, which has been distinguished in the document, consists in the fact that the current technological revolution is based on the change of information into knowledge, and not, as it has been before, on the creation of new machines and technologies. Nowadays, it is not enough to create new technologies, which also takes place at present, but also their skilful use. The consequences of the dynamic technological development are widely noticeable changes taking place in society and the economy, which will allow to explain the impact of new technologies on society and law,

---

4 C. Mouffe, for instancje in'Polityczność. Przewodnik Krytyki Politycznej'[On the political. Guide to Political Critics] (Warsaw, Krytyka Polityczna, 2008).

5 M. Król, '*Filozofia polityczna*' [Political philosophy], (Cracow, Znak, 2008) 129 and next.

6 M. Weber,*'Polityka jako zawód i powołanie' [Politics as a vocation]* in M.'*Racjonalność, władza, odczarowanie'[Rationality, power, disenchantment)*, Wydawnictwo Poznańskie, Poznań: 2011.

7 J. van Dijk, „*Społeczne aspekty nowych mediów*", op.cit., p. 104.

8 "*Living and Working in Information Society: People First*", Green Paper of Commission of the European Communities, (24.07. 1996).

both in terms of its creation and application. Most often, these are technologies related to the transmission of information and communication, but it is not a closed catalog.

Going further above the set course of thinking, nowadays it may be noticed that a widely understood "technologization" of law, which is visible above all in implementation of new technologies into law systems, and even situations where new technologies become law itself. Considerations about the political nature of the law towards technological ideologies can be started from the analysis of the work of J. Habermas, titled "Science and technology as an ideology", which in a specific way began a discussion on the impact of technology on modern societies, including the legal system. As the German philosopher writes, "Rationalization means, above all, extending the scope in which social life is subject to measures of rational resolution. The counterpart of this process is the industrialization of social work, as a result of which instrumental criteria also penetrate other areas of life (urbanization of lifestyle, "technization" of relations and interpersonal communication[9].As rightly claims Wojciech Bober –"(. . .) technology development is the result of non-technical determinism, but the purpose for which it arises[10](. . .)." This quote shows that the development of science, and hence also of new technologies, is determined by human needs and emerging opportunities that this development brings. The evolution of modern times is based on knowledge, which in the form of new inventions and technological solutions, has made significant changes in the functioning of societies. J. Habermas adds: "(. . .) it is about imposing a pattern of purposeful-rational action, which refers here to the organization of resources, there to choose between alternative solutions (. . .). Fasting rationalization of society is associated with the institutionalization of scientific and technical progress. To the extent that science and technology penetrate the institutionalized fields of social life, and thus transform institutions, old validations become invalid[11]. "

Undoubtedly, the new politics is peculiar technocratic politics, while the technology itself is nothing but the substrate of a new ideology that directly affects politics (*sensu stricte*) and forces politics to perform technical tasks, including

---

9 J. Habermas, '*Nauka i technika jako ideologia*'[*Science and technology*] [*w*] '*Czy kryzys socjologii*? [Is tere a crysis of philosophy?)', (Ed.) J. Szacki. (Warsaw, Czytelnik, 1977) 342.

10 W. Bober, 'Powinność w świecie cyfrowym. Etyka komputerowa w świetle współczesnej polityki moralnej' [Duty in the digital world. Computer ethics in the light of contemporary moral politics, (Wydania Akademickie i Profesjonalne, Warszawa 2008)32.

11 J. Habermas, „*Nauka* 342.

the implementation of new technologies as a reliable and effective tool of power. It could be tempting to make a statement, referring to the ideas propagated by J. Habermas, that the rhetorical and rational activity presented by him is nothing different than exercising control or willingness to strive for this control. In other words, technocratic politics has become a certain ideology that leads to the achievement of previously set goals, one of which is control. Ideology, as a certain community of worldviews, in its essence strives to carry out, as a rule, a specific interest either of the indicated group, or of the social class or, more broadly, of the nation. K. Marx in "The German Ideology" even identified ideology with philosophy, indicating that all human thought is nothing but a reflection of material conditions[12]. In this approach, human consciousness becomes the realization (reflection) of the material conditions in the society. It would seem that ideology functions in an unreal, spiritual or illusory world. As S. Żiżek accurately points out, ideology is not an illusory illusion that we build to escape the unbearable reality; in its basic dimension, it is a fantasy that serves as a support for our "reality": "Illusion" which builds our effective, real social relations and masks some unrealistic, real, unreal core (conceptualized by E. Laclau and C Mouffe as "antagonism": a traumatic social division that cannot be symbolized). The function of ideology is not to offer us a starting point from our reality but to offer us social reality in itself as an escape from a traumatic, real kernel[13]. It is therefore necessary to consider the situation when the political nature of the law becomes (directly or indirectly) ideology. The law, as a tool that ruling politicians have from centuries, is often used to achieve political goals, addressing the issue of politicalness of law in connection with its instrumental function. As J. Jankowski rightly says, we are faced with great state interventionism through electronic control of law and by law[14]. Therefore, the technological determinism of ITC tools in the law makes some of the behaviors of entities are regulated or even modelled in an intended manner. The impact of infrastructure is modelled: "creating the so-called infrastructural systems of human behavior control,

12 K. Marks, F. Engels '*Ideologia niemiecka: I. Feuerbach*' [The German Ideology: I. Feuerbach] (Warsaw, Książka i Wiedza, 1975).

13 S. Żiżek, '*Wzniosły obiekt ideologii*' [A lofty object of ideology] (Warsaw, Verso, 1989) 45, [after] R. Mańko *"Reality is for those who cannot sustain the dream: Fantasies of selfhood in legal texts"*, [in] 2015, 5, *Wroclaw Review of Law, Administration and Economics*, 26–27.

14 . Jankowski 'Cyberkultura prawa. Współczesne problemy filozofii i informatyki prawa' [Cyberculture law. Contemporary problems of philosophy and computer science law], (Warsaw, Difin 2012) 219–239.

which are directly influenced by codes and architectures of ICT systems and not by standards[15]."Considering at this point the issue of technological determinism of ICT tools that affects the instrumental function of the law, attention should be paid to the instrumental properties of these ICT technologies. S. Kaźmierczyk recalled that "The instrumental understanding of law is essentially the same as the instrumental understanding of any other tool, about which – in reference to empirical knowledge – it can be expressed that the used leads to the achievement of a specific goal[16]." Therefore, it seems correct to state that communication and information technologies have instrumental properties because they are undoubtedly used as tools for a specific purpose. The functioning of e-democracy is a natural effect of the functioning of the information society and, undoubtedly, the architecture of the network, which determines the creation of such and no different law. When new opportunities arise, and in this case they are related to the development of information and communication technologies, then the society, and consequently also the legislator, try to maximally use their potential in order to improve the functioning of the state and other objectives appropriate for them. It can be said that the functioning of e-democracy is based on controlled action, fully dependent on the will and preferences of a human being. It should be agreed following the thesis of H. Marcuse that "Dominion is perpetuating today and expanding not only through technology but as technology; it provides the perfect validation of expansive political power encompassing all areas of culture. In this universe, technology also perfectly rationalizes slavery, lack of autonomy, and the inability to decide about one's own life. This bondage does not reveal its irrational or political character, but it shows as a subordination to a technical apparatus that increases the comfort of life and increases work efficiency. In this way, technological rationality does not abolish the legitimacy of domination, but on the contrary – it protects it[17](. . .)". It follows from the above that technocratic ideology can perfectly support politics, through the conscious shaping of the functioning of society. Assuming a

15 Ibid. P. 273.

16 S. Kaźmierczyk, '*Założenia metodologiczne rozważań o relacjach między prawem w znaczeniu instrumentalnym a prawem w znaczeniu pozainstrumentalnym*' [Methodological assumptions of considerations about the relationship between the law in the instrumental sense and the law in the non-instrumental sense] in 'Z zagadnień instrumentalizacji prawa' [From the issues of law instrumentalization] (ed.). A. Kozak, (Wroclaw, Kolonia Limited, 2000) 11.

17 J. Habermas, *Nauka* 346 [after] H. Markuse „Der eindimensionale Mensch", (Neuwied, 1967) 172 and following.

large dose of skepticism, it may be tempted to say that technology is the material goal of reigning and taking power, which also makes it as belonging to the form of technical reason. New technology is used to increasingly better and effectively manipulate and govern people who depend on the ruling spheres. According to J. Habermas: "(. . .) the development of the social system seems subordinated to the logic of scientific and technical progress. The internal regularity of this process seems to generate objective necessities that must be obeyed by politically obedient functional needs[18]."

It is not uncommon that this ideology is invisible to society, in other words a set of entities that it directly concerns. It can have both positive and negative overtones. The negative appears especially in relation to subjects of law, which the technocratic ideology imposes on certain rights and obligations. There are a lot of examples of this state of affairs. One of them, referring to the Polish universally binding law, is the possibility of using electronic writ-of-payment proceedings, colloquially and briefly known as the EPU. In general, the purpose of implementing this highlytechnologized tool was to facilitate the conduct of simple civil lawsuits, relieve district courts, speed up proceedings or widen access to the judiciary. These objectives were met, however, in an indirect way they also generated the negative effects of their existence. One of them was the possibility of making fraud by entering a false PESEL number in the electronic form, as well as a certain social stratification. Some people, for example, older people, have touched the so-called electronic exclusion, a situation in which they cannot use "electronic legal activities", so that their rights have been minimized in relation to younger people who have a computer, access to the Internet and the ability to navigate in the virtual world. People excluded in general only minimally engage in the use of new technologies on a daily basis, which is also reflected by the lack of use of new technologies in law. All legal activities are carried out in a "conventional" manner, which does not require the use of a computer or the Internet. Due to this, the above social stratification leads to interesting statements and conclusions, among which the most important is that it is not always a man who decides whether or not he is a participant in a life in an information society that is based on new technologies. Wanting or not wanting, it becomes an element of the functioning of this community and often has to categorically apply to the standards prevailing in its area. Otherwise, there may be a lack of acceptance of such an entity directly or indirectly by other participants in the environment in which it exists, and at the same time may have limited rights, which is the effect

18 J. Habermas, *Nauka* 372.

of not so much the will of the lawmakers, but the dislike of the person excluded to comply with this law. It may seem that in the described case, new technologies functioning in the information society give individuals some possibilities and it is up to them whether they want or do not want to use them. These electronic exemptions are often a consequence of deliberate human decisions based on which they decide to be turned off. This results from the lack of will to submit to new legal solutions, the lack of willingness to learn what is new and the lack of proper education in the necessary scope. Because of this, we notice an ideology that we do not actually see, and the lawmaker forces us to behave in a certain way and submit to his will, which we adapt to, however, in consequence. The legislator tries to convince us, through the implementation of useful tools, to be right in his own case, creating in us the ideological manner of "what is new and modern is good". In many aspects of the modern (some would say post-modern) reality it is difficult not to agree with such a thesis, nevertheless it is easy to cite arguments against such a way of understanding these reasons. It is impossible to mention here M. Foucault, who in his reflections also dealt with the ideologies of invisible supervision over individuals. One should then think about the vision of using new technologies in law that will allow for perfection to supervise the life of the individual, introducing the theory of panopticism created by M. Foucault. The power and supervision of the state over man will be invisible to people, but they will allow full surveillance by the authorities, where Orwell's vision of the world will be fulfilled[19]. "M. Foucault wrote that"(...) Power is to be like a look without a face, which transforms the whole of the social body into the field of perception: thousands of eye locations everywhere, busy and ready-made observation points, extensive hierarchical grid[20]. Thanks to this, the law can be more effective and legal awareness in people should be deepened, but such a vision of law carries with it a dose of anxiety, excessive intervention or even over-instrumentalization of law.

The technocratic ideology, in which the post-modern politics, based and connected with new technologies and their dynamic development, has also changed, has also caused that the existing patterns and behaviors of individuals in society have been reduced to the technological conditioning of the ability of usage of the new technologies. This issue can be considered in several key areas.

---

19 This vision, G. Orwell, in his work entitled "1984", portrayed the society as a creation completely subordinated to surveillance by the state apparatus that interfered with the behavior of even the thoughts of its citizens.

20 M. Focault, '*Nadzorować i karać*' [Discipline and punish], (Warsaw, Aletheia, 2009) 208.

First, the dependence on technology is noticeable, and secondly, when looking through the prism of technological posthumanism, the machine is interwoven with man, which in turn leads to the taking over of the logic of the equipment as the only proper one. According to A. Sulikowski "After all, as you can imagine, the machine *sensu stricto* is a product of intelligent human culture, the effect and tool of control over nature, hence making it a philosophical key can also lead to the strengthening of human domination[21]." In this aspect of politics, it can be concluded that the strengthening of technocratic politics will strive for this.

In summary it can be concluded that technologization begins to usurp the role of the acquisition and interpretation of the world becomes hidden ideology, which is also mentioned by P. Markuse, who claimed that technology and science today also take over the function of the validation rule. Moreover, the political rights wades so far technocracy that often practical interest policy is covered by the gain or further development of technocratic. Above it may also seem that the political rights as an ideology will evolve in the direction of maximum impose its authority over the units, the ability to manipulate and create subordinate units of power, even indirectly, subconscious and hidden. H. Marcuse says: "In the industrially developed capitalist societies reign disposes of such features as afflictions exploitation Praz seeks to "rationalize", which, however, does not lead to anything but to the disappearance of political domination: dominion is subject only to maintain the interest and ability of the camera as a whole[22]". Therefore, many technological tools, which is used as an expression of the new technocratic ideology are introduced slowly, often they are not initially clear overtones as to their functions, which become apparent only at a particular time or circumstances. Mentioned J. Habermas notes that "Modern science produces knowledge, therefore, that in terms of form (and not the subjective intention) is technically useful knowledge but the possibility of its application reveal generally only later[23]." A great summary of considerations of this work will also be a reference to A. Gehlen about which he writes in the quoted work of J. Habermas: "If, according to A. Gehlen, the internal logic of technical development consists in the fact that the circle of purposeful-rational action gradually breaks away from the substrate of the human body and transferred to the plane of machines,

21 A. Sulikowski, '*Posthumanizm a prawoznawstwo*'[Posthumanism and jurisprudence] (2013) *492 Studia i monografie Uniwersytetu Opolskiego* (Opole, Uniwersytetu Opolskiego, 2013) 123.

22 J. Habermas, *Nauka* 344 as cited in H. Markuse „*Treiblehre Und Freiheit*" [in] „Freud In der Gegnwart", vol. XI, Frankfurt, 1957.

23 J. Habermas, *Nauka* 364.

technocracy could pass as the last phase of this process. Human being, as *homo Faber*, may for the first time completely objectify and stand against achievements independent of his own creations. Moreover, if we manage to reconstruct the structure of purposeful-rational action on the level of social systems, man will also be able to become an integral part of his own technical devices as *homo fabricatus*[24]." "Depoliticization of the masses of the population validated by technocratic consciousness is at the same time the self-objectification of people both in the category of adaptive behavior: the deliberate scientific models penetrate into the field of socio-cultural life and gain objective power over the process of self-understanding[25]". In the view of Marx's theory, technocratic politics, as ideology, will be able to serve both the power that creates it, but also – perhaps – itself, when it takes the form of a self-regulatory social process. The future is also doomed to a significantly increased demand for modern law, which has ceased to regulate only real reality, but has also begun to regulate virtual reality. Computerization of the law may ultimately aim at the complete automation of its application. Can the same be said about politics? Will new technologies really become a factor that completely determines its development and evolution, and at the same time, it will become an ideology that will only be appropriate in post-modern times? At this time, it is difficult to find an unambiguous and only right answer. Surely, further technological development, as well as human thought progress, will indicate whether the answer to the above-mentioned questions will be positive.

References

1. J. Habermas, „*Nauka i technika jako ideologia" [in] „Czy kryzys socjologii?*", ed. J. Szacki, Czytelnik, Warszawa 1977.
2. J. Jankowski,„*Cyberkultura prawa. Współczesne problemy filozofii i informatyki prawa*", Difin,Warszawa 2012.
3. K. Marks, F. Engels,„*Ideologia niemiecka: I.Feuerbach*", Książka i Wiedza, Warszawa 1975 r.
4. S. Żiżek, „*Wzniosły obiekt ideologii*", Verso, Warszawa 1989 r.
5. S. Kaźmierczyk, „*Założenia metodologiczne rozważań o relacjach między prawem w znaczeniu instrumentalnym a prawem w znaczeniu*

24 Ibid. 373.

25 J. Habermas, „*Nauka i technika jako ideologia*" [in] „*Czy kryzys socjologii?*", ed. J. Szacki. Czytelnik, Warszawa 1977, p. 381.

pozainstrumentalnym". [w:] „Z zagadnień instrumentalizacji prawa", ed. A. Kozaka, Kolonia Limited,,Wrocław 2000.

6. W. Bober, „*Powinność w świecie cyfrowym. Etyka komputerowa w świetle współczesnej polityki moralnej*", Wydania Akademickie i Profesjonalne, Warszawa 2008.
7. R. Mańko, „*Reality is for those who cannot sustain the dream: Fantasies of selfhood in legal texts*", [in] Wroclaw Review of Law, Administration and Economics, vol. 5, 2015.
8. M. Weber,„*Polityka jako zawód i powołanie*" [in] *M.„Racjonalność, władza, odczarowanie*", Wydawnictwo Poznańskie, Poznań 2011.
9. M. A. Cichocki, „*Teologia polityczna i inne pisma*", Znak, Kraków 2000.
10. M. Paździora, M. Stambulski „*Co może dać nauce prawa polityczność? Przyczynek do przyszłych badań*", [in] Archiwum Filozofii PrawaiFilozofii Społecznej, no. 2014/1.
11. Por. C. Mouffe [in] „*Polityczność. Przewodnik Krytyki Politycznej*", Krytyka Polityczna, Warszawa 2008.
12. M. Król, „*Filozofia polityczna*", Znak, Kraków 2008.
13. „*Living and Working in Information Society: People First*", Green Paper of Commission of the European Communities, 24.07. 1996.
14. M. Focault, „*Nadzorować i karać*", Aletheia, Warszawa 2009.
15. A. Sulikowski „*Posthumanizm a prawoznawstwo*", Studia i monografie Uniwersytetu Opolskiego, nr 492, Uniwersytetu Opolskiego, Opole 2013.
16. J. Van Dijk, „*Społeczne aspekty nowych mediów*", PWN, Warszawa 2010.

Part Two In Search of New Approaches

Paweł Chmielnicki

4 "Macro" and "Micro" Approach to Research on Law as a Part of Socio-Economic System

Abstract: In legal science, too little empirical research is still conducted on the connections between the legal system and its socio-economic environment. Meanwhile, such research can be carried out successfully, both in relation to the entire legal system (on a "macro" scale) and in relation to individual legal acts or individual legal norms (on a "micro" scale). Research on a "macro" scale concerns the genesis of lawmaking (material sources of law) and reveals long-term trends occurring in the legislative process. These trends result from periodic changes in demand for regulating specific social, economic or political problems in a certain way. Research on the "micro" scale is based on the concept of a "normative set", which is made up of formal (including legal) and informal (for example, rules of economic activity) norms that serve the purpose of achieving some goals of human activity. Analysis based on a normative set allows the assessment of the importance of individual norms for human decision making.

Keywords: material sources of law, normative set, legislative process

Introduction

The chapter treats about two new research assumptions aiming at significant expansion of a typical, common paradigm of law sciences. The research assumptions on which the methods are based are completely original. Although they have some methodological connection with some earlier research proposals reported within the law sciences (especially with the so-called legal realism in its various versions), they are not their repetition or a simple expansion. They constitute an entirely new proposal of research on normative order of the contemporary society, having no direct prior precedent. This proposal is based on a holistic study of the nature of relations (connections) between all legal norms relating directly to the aim to act, the aim set by man for himself, as well as on the study of relations occurring between legal norms and other norms which make up the socio-economic order of the contemporary society (such as the informalized rules of commodity-money exchange). The research findings for this purpose relate to both the sources of origin of the law as well as to its socio-economic effectiveness.

1 The "Macro" Approach – Research Method[1]

It is about determining long-term trends in the law-making process. This scientific method is based on assumption that law is a product of civilization, just like any other; therefore, over the years, demand and supply are changing into legal regulations concerning specific issues. These changes are not accidental, but result from changes in socio-economic needs, are of an evolutionary nature and are arranged in legible long-term trends. By means of evaluation of individual, completed legislative projects, it is possible to determine the level of attention that the legislator devotes in a given year to the implementation of particular social, political and economic aims. The use of mathematical tools allows the analysis of test results from various points of view. The results of a research project based on this method are presented below. The project provided for carrying out comprehensive research on the entire legislative process in a country (Poland) in the long term, i.e., over more than twenty years.

The research results proved the main initial hypothesis, whereby it was assumed that the establishment of formalized institutions (law) followed long-term trends which resulted from the forces of supply and demand, similar to the provision of any other goods, whether tangible or intangible. The project was financed by the Polish National Science Center awarded based on the number of decision-DEC-2013/09 / B / HS5 / 04078. This project was titled 'Application of Statistical Methods to Determine the Nature of Long-term Trends Occurring inthe Legislative Process'.

At the outset of the project, detailed research problems were defined following the theoretical assumption on the presence of the main categories of economic and social factors which determined the matters addressed in legal regulations. Research into these problems led to the assessment whether or not, to what extent, and how frequently the same factors affected the course of the legislative process. The assessment of a factor's impact (evaluation) was carried out taking

---

1 Section 1 is based on the article Paweł Chmielnicki, Elżbieta Ingot-Brzęk, Igor Styn. "Reduction of entrepreneurial risk as the purpose of legislative initiatives: research results", Studia Prawa Publicznego, 1/2018, 9–25. The research project described in this article was financed by the polish National Science Center awarded based on the number of decision-DEC-2013/09 / B / HS5 / 04078. This project was titled 'Application of Statistcal Methods to Determine the Nature of Long-term Trends Occuring inthe Legislative Process'. The method and the theoretical assumptions underlying the research this presented were developed by Paweł Chmielnicki who was also the team leader of the research project, the authors of the final conclusions were also Elżbieta Inglot – Brzęk and Igor Styn.

into consideration the importance of such factor in the adoption of a legislative act. The research method was based on expert reviews: each legislative act was reviewed by three experts (a lawyer, an economist, and a sociologist) who independently provided their evaluation by way of answering the research question. Subsequently, an average value was calculated separately for each of the acts, based on all the expert assessments. Thus obtained data were aggregated into numerical sequences corresponding to periods of time (time sequences), where the time unit was one year, and then, the variations in numerical values were laid out in the graphic form as diagrams.

The assumption was made to study the effect of factors determining legislative proposals in relation to only one of the sources of law, namely, the legislation passed in Poland in the years 1990–2013 (twenty-four years). The justification underlying this assumption was substantial, as the laws of a lower rank in Poland are, by and large, solely implementing regulations, and their provisions solely elaborate on those of the respective legislative acts, thereby following the directions set out by the legislature. Therefore, the laws of a lower rank cannot produce a major change in the trend related to the social and economic requisites of the legislative process. The analysis covered a vast majority of legislative acts passed by the Sejm of the Republic of Poland (the Polish parliament) in the years 1990–2013 (3,087 acts of law). The only acts to be excluded from the analysis were those of a technically legal nature. Another very important aspect was the fact that a prevailing majority of the acts of law (at least 95 %) concerned a specific area of socio-economic relations (i.e., a law was meant to achieve a specific socio-economic purpose, to resolve a specific matter, which may be easily seen from the formal justification assessments accompanying the legislative acts).

The evaluation process consisted in each of the acts of law being assessed from the point of view of the detailed research questions on a seven-grade scale. The point was to highlight clear differences in the socio-economic importance of some of these regulations.

For each of the research questions, in relation to each of the 3,087 acts of law, one of the following values was to be determined:

-3 -2 -1 0 1 2 3

The values were assigned depending on the level of convergence between the effect of the regulation and the assumption underlying a given research question: from "3" (a strong, substantial positive correlation with the effect assumed in the research question), to "-3" (a strong, substantial negative correlation with the effect assumed in the research question), where the "0" value implied the absence of the effect assumed in the research question.

Mathematical methods were applied in order to transform the values assigned by experts to acts of law for each of the research questions, into time sequences. The sequences obtained this way were quantifiable variables (figures), for which levels could be calculated year to year. These variables were used, among others, to graphically illustrate (as diagrams) the changing trends in the values assigned for successive years.[2]

Overall, two main mathematical modelling approaches were used: the values and the changes thereof were aggregated, which was referred to as the aggregate figures approach, and average values and changes in the average values were calculated, which was referred to as the average figures approach. Without going into the details of the two mathematical approaches, it is enough to note for the purposes of this publication that the aggregate figures approach can basically applied to establish the actual values assessed for particular years and for specific detailed research questions, which roughly reflected the emphasis placed in the legislative process, while the average figures approach was more oriented towards measuring the socio-economic importance of the regulations adopted in a given year. In other words, the quantitative approach also alluded to the qualitative aspect of the process (whether or not the focus placed by law makers on a particular issue was translated, on the one hand, into the number of the adopted laws, and on the other, into their significance from the point of view of shaping the socio-economic relations in a particular year). An auxiliary method was also used to determine successive time sequences which were referred to as discrete sequences. The purpose to establishing these discrete sequences was to identify the sequences of solely positive or clearly positive values (or, alternately, solely negative or clearly negative values) in a given year, while, at the same time, disregarding all other values, i.e., zero and negative values, or (accordingly) zero and positive values. Therefore, as part of the discussed method, it is possible to graphically present results based solely on positive or negative evaluations ("cut by 1" or "cut by -1"). [3]

---

2 For a more elaborate discussion of the statistical methods used for the purposes of the project see Sobczyk Mieczysław, *Statystyka*, 1st edn, Państwowe Wydawnictwo Naukowe 1991 and Magiera Ryszard, *Modele i metody statystyki matematycznej*, 3rd edn, Oficyna Wydawnicza GiS 2002.

3 For a more detailed discussion of the mathematical modelling approach used to interpret the research results see Michał Stachura in Paweł Chmielnicki (edt) Anna Dybała, Michał Stachura, *Activity Rules of Economic Man in Society as the Source of Legal Norms*, 1st edn LexisNexis 2010, 174 – 184.

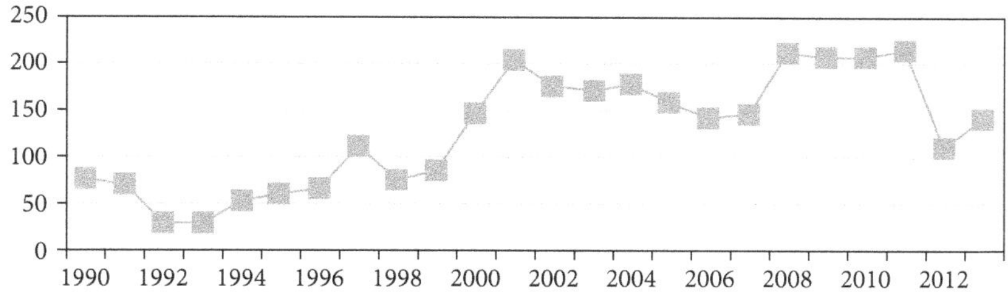

Fig. 1: The number of analyzed legislative initiatives for particular years (own materials). Source: own materials.

It is important to note the quantitative distribution of the total number of legislative initiatives in particular years, which were included within the scope of this research. The figures reflecting the numbers of legislative acts in specific years are presented in the diagram below.

The analysis of the diagram presenting the number of legislative acts for the respective years, that were included in the research, is important to the extent that it allows determining whether or not the diagram which illustrates the scope of this particular research project by and large reflected the overall numbers of adopted legislative acts. If this is the case, indeed, it would imply that, roughly speaking, law makers continued to focus in their work on specific matters, on which regulations were adopted, or in other words, that certain issues enjoyed a steady interest from the legislature, which was proportional to the overall volume of legislative work. A similar approach may be applied in order to interpret any diagram presenting average figures for a more or less stable trend, with no major growth or decline. A more rapid growth (or decline) in the values attributed to a particular area, as compared to the growth (or decline) in the total number of legislative acts adopted in a particular year, would indicate, respectively, either a reinforcement or weakening of the factors which determined the formalization of specific types of activity. The diagram shows that the number of adopted laws continued to grow quite rapidly during the first ten years following the collapse of communism, until 2001 (an increase from about 50–100 bills passed per year in the early 1990s, up to 250–300 acts in the early 2000s).This growth trend slowed down in the following years, and the number of adopted acts remained at a stable level until 2012–2013 when it rapidly declined to a little over 100 bills passed in one year.

2 Examples of Research Findings

2.1 Transaction Costs

The first and obvious issue to be tackled by scholars whose research interests focus on economic institutions, concerns transaction costs. "The defining of a transaction as the basic unit in research, turned out to be of crucial importance to the results of systematic study of real-life economic mechanisms and business organizations. Although the applicability of quantitative models was thereby reduced, at the same time, opportunities were created for developing the microeconomic basis of all economic strategies. This assumption resulted in the necessary departure from the concept of a business organization as an autonomous entity, capable of allocating its resources in a fully rational manner. Once it was recognized that technology and human needs were universal, this implied that the most important research problem did not concern the technology, but the institutions that constituted management structures, and organizational innovations that determined the costs of relationships, which were defined as transaction costs" [Michał G. Woźniak 'Niesprawności kapitalizmu globalnego w świetle podejścia ekonomii instytucjonalnej. Wnioski dla Polski' in *Dokonania współczesnej myśli ekonomicznej. Ekonomia instytucjonalna – teoria i praktyka*, Urszula Zagóra-Jonszta (edt), Wydawnictwo UE Katowice 2006, 251–252].

In economics, the notion of transaction costs is discussed in parallel with that of barriers to entry, being the obstacles encountered by the economic man seeking to enter into a transaction. These concepts reflect, in a sense, the same research problem which may be reduced to the assessment of obstacles and burdens arising in the course of economic activity.

In order to facilitate a better understanding of the research findings presented herein, it should be stressed that the matters discussed in this part of the chapter concern barriers to entry and costs, and not returns (gains and profits), whereby the allocation of additional funds does not automatically justify the assignment of a negative value in assessment (it is not the opposite of the earlier described situation when costs are generated and barriers established), save for some exceptional situations. On the other hand, the assignment of a negative value was justified in relation to a regulation which reduced costs and barriers (by lifting burdens, e.g., through a reduction in taxes).In other words, the regulations considered to correspond with the trend in question, were those which increased (in different ways) the entrepreneurs' costs, or which established barriers to entry. At the same time, the regulations treated as counteracting the trend suggested in the research question were those, which reduced costs and abolished or reduced barriers to entry.

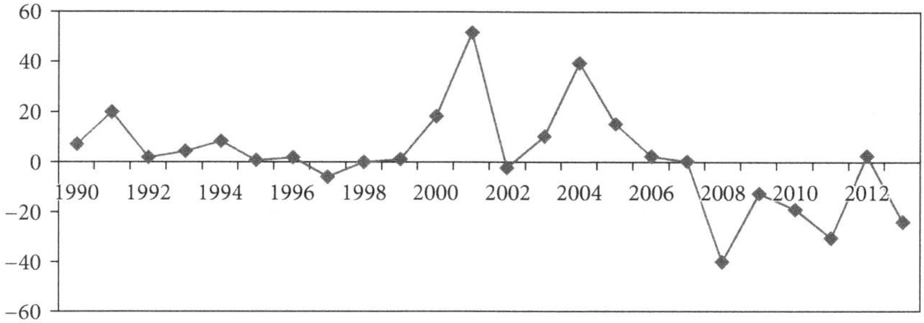

Fig. 2: Diagram based on aggregate figures for the years 1990–2013. Source: own materials.

The research results may be analyzed, first of all, as providing a general picture of the trend established on the basis of the net outcome of all the legislative acts, both those which were to increase business costs or create barriers to entry and those which were to reduce the costs and/or barriers. Another approach may be to look separately at the law makers' initiatives leading to an increase in costs and barriers, and separately at their attempts to reduce the same. Each of the different aspects of the research results contributes in a different way to a better understanding of the trends seen in the development of the institutional order in Poland, and each leads to conclusions concerning somewhat different angles of the process.

Let us begin by looking at the overall trend (the net outcome based on the positive and negative values assigned).

As shown in the diagram, over the entire twenty-four-year period, the long-term trend was for the volume of legislation to decrease with regard to the regulations creating costs and establishing barriers. There was only one clear correction in this long-term trend in the years 2000–2004. It should be noted that the same trend is even stronger in the diagram based on the average figures (Fig. 3), i.e., using the method which better reflects whether or not the law makers' efforts dedicated to specific matters translate not only into the number of adopted legislative acts, but also into their importance for the entire legislative process. The period from 1990 to 2013 included, among others, the years when the Polish law was harmonized with the laws of the European Union. Poland was entering into a new supersystem, which mostly involved increasing various requirements, costs of business operations in the broad sense of the term, etc. The studied period was also marked by global economic crises, which may

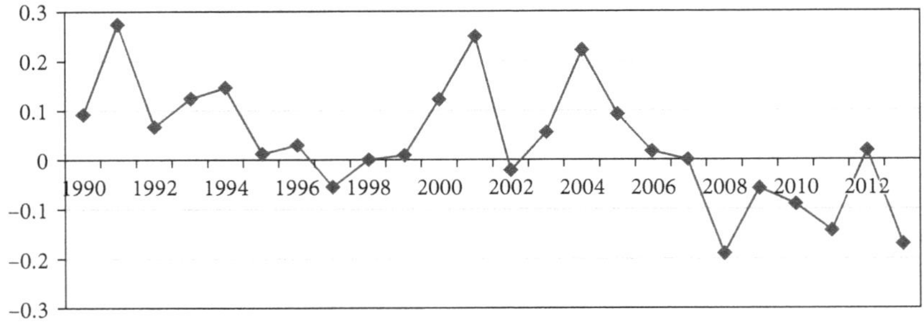

Fig. 3: Diagram based on average figures for the years 1990–2013. Source: own materials.

explain the saddle point on the diagram corresponding to the years 2001–2002 (the government was trying to stimulate the economy and not to suppress it with higher costs and stricter requirements). A very clear decline trend may be observed following the year 2004 (after Poland's accession to the EU), which notably resembles the situation after 1990. Back then, the dramatic change of the years 1989–1990, brought about by the change of the political and economic system was followed by many years of a decline trend when costs were rationalized. Then, there was another peak when the costs grew in connection with the preparations for the EU accession, following which, once Poland had entered the European Union, transaction costs were rationalized again. However, soon after that, another global economic crisis broke out in 2008, very strongly affecting the EU member states. This leads to a question whether the period after 2008 shouldbe seen as another breakthrough, bringing about dramatic changes in the institutional order, also in Poland. It is still too early to pass definite judgments, but the data shown in the diagram for the last years covered in the research presented herein, may seem to suggest that this may indeed be the case.

A brief description of the socio-economic circumstances which affected the course of the above described general trend should begin with a recollection of the parliamentary elections held in Poland on June 4, 1989. These elections resulted in the formation of the government dominated by the earlier anti-communist opposition (for the first time ever in a Soviet Bloc country), which originated from the Solidarity tree trade union movement. The most important undertaking of the cabinet headed by then Prime Minister Tadeusz Mazowiecki in relation to establishing a new institutional order was the commencement of work on the government package of bills on corporate finance management, taxes, and employment. On December 17, 1989, then deputy prime minister Leszek Balcerowicz presented the package of new regulations in the Sejm, and the parliament passed nine acts which became to be known as "the Balcerowicz Plan" [Karpiński Jakub, *Trzecia niepodległość. Najnowsza historia Polski*, 1st edn, Bertelsmann Media 2001, 70]. The Balcerowicz Plan was a program of thorough reforms of the national economy, and comprised three main policies: (1) a reform of state finances and balancing the government budget; (2) establishment of a market economy; and (3) reform of the ownership structure in the economy [Michalak Ryszard, Andrzej K. Piasecki, *Historia polityczna Polski 1952–2002*, „Akapit" 2003, 189].

The first term of the Sejm in a sovereign Poland (also referred to as the Third Republic; in the years1992–1993) was a period abounding in political developments, but, at the same time, it was largely a waste of time in the context of building an institutional order for the economy. The political elites were preoccupied with factional conflicts, and legislative initiatives often concerned strictly political issues, which were hardly or not at all related to establishing the basis for economic growth. These issues diverted attention away from work on a number of matters crucial to the economy. A slow-down in work on the establishment of the new institutional order may be very well seen, for instance, in the number of new laws passed in the years 1992–1993. At that time, the number of passed bills reached a record low (see Fig. 1), never to be repeated again. The slow-down occurred right at a time when swift legislative measures were particularly needed. Political parties which emerged from the former anti-communist opposition lost control of the creation of the institutional order for the economy within as little as three years after the celebrated collapse of the communist system in Poland. The successive parliamentary elections (for the 1994–1997 term) were won by two parties associated with the former system, namely, the Democratic Left Alliance (SLD), consisting mostly of the former PZPR communist party members, and the PSL peasant party.

In principle, both parties declared their will to continue the institutional reforms oriented towards the establishment of capitalism and a market economy, but the means they chose to do so were not always the same as those used by their predecessors.

A comparison of the above information with the data obtained from legislation assessment values shows a clear correlation. There is a visible decline in figures for the years 1994–1997 on the diagram reflecting the trend in the formalization of measures related to creating costs and establishing barriers to entry. The political situation changed during the next term of the Sejm, and the legislative outcome was also different.

The following parliamentary elections were won by the Solidarity Election Action (AWS) and the Freedom Union (UW), which formed a coalition. Leszek Balcerowicz (who was again appointed the deputy prime minister) returned to his earlier leading position in the process of developing formal institutions of the economy. The policies of successive SLD governments to stimulate investment, accompanied by the generally good economic situation in international markets, must have produced the desired effects, and maybe even too much so, since right after taking over the office, then deputy Prime Minister Balcerowicz declared a need to cool down the economy which, in his opinion, had been overheated under the previous government coalition. In fact, at the time when the government in Poland was taken over by the AWS–UW coalition, a decline started in global markets. In 1997, a crisis broke out in Asia. As a result, the demand for oil decreased, and consequently, a crisis broke out in Russia in the summer of 1998. A rapid decrease in demand on the Russian market strongly affected Polish exports. In 1998, the level of Polish trade deficit reached its record highest since the beginning of economic reforms, and amounted to over US$18 billion [Morawski Wojciech, *Dzieje gospodarcze Polski*, 2nd edn, Difin 2011, 309–310].

The end of term of the AWS government (years 2000–2001, after the UW had left the coalition), saw a fast growth in the number of regulations increasing costs and establishing barriers to entry. This was partly due to the continued difficult situation of public finances (resulting, among others, from the initiated large-scale reforms).However, another factor which contributed to the adoption of regulations generating costs and barriers was related to Poland's working to adjust its institutional system to EU requirements. The volume of these regulations started to grow dramatically from 2000, and the adopted laws often involved stricter requirements, higher costs to businesses, and thresholds to be achieved.

Based on the diagram showing the values corresponding solely to those regulations which reduced costs and barriers (i.e., negative values obtained in responses to the research question, Fig. 4), it is possible to note that the AWS–UW tried to fulfil the promises made in their political programs with regard to reducing the burdens. Nevertheless, these efforts did not prevail over the opposite trend in the existing circumstances.

The SLD-PSL coalition returned to power in the following term, in the years 2002–2005. Since then, the leading parties in the parliamentary elections in Poland from 2005 onward have been parties originating from the former anti-communist opposition: the Law and Justice (PiS) and the Civic Platform (PO), with similar outlook on the economy, provided that the PO has been clearly referring to neoliberal concepts of the state and the economy.

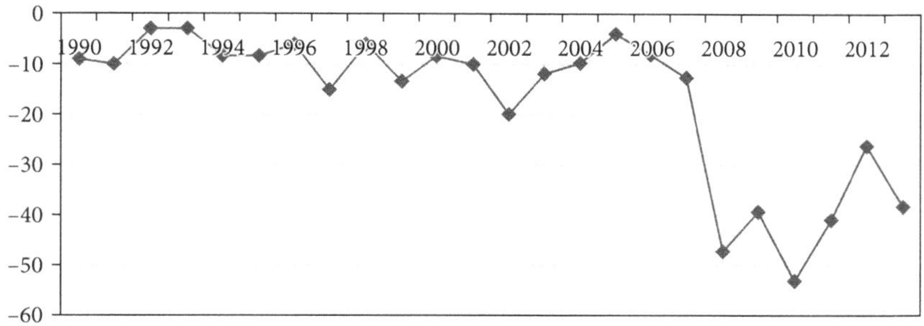

Fig. 4: Diagram based on aggregate figures with a "cut off at -1" for the years 1990–2013. Source: own materials.

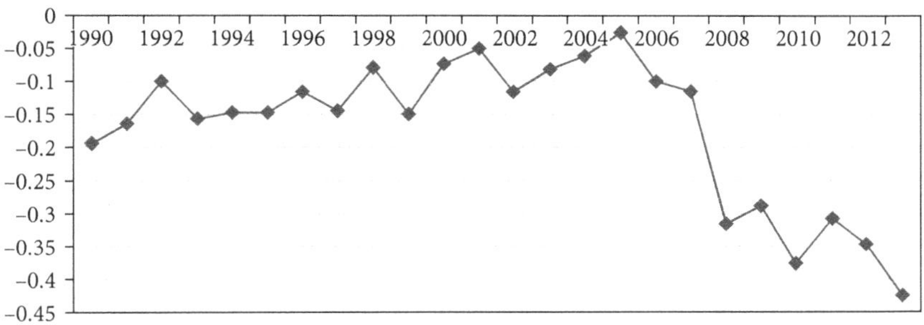

Fig. 5: Diagram based on average figures with a "cut off at -1" for the years 1990–2013. Source: own materials.

An accurate assessment of the policies under the governments run by the PiS and the PO may be made based on the results of legislation evaluation with regard to solely those regulations that reduced costs and abolished barriers to entry.

A striking decline trend may be noted on the diagram beginning exactly in 2005. There is no doubt that it was during the 2005–2007 and 2007–2011 terms of the Sejm that the largest number of legislative acts were passed with the aim of establishing an institutional order based on the concept of low transaction costs and reduced barriers to entry wherever possible.

The analysis of research results leads to the conclusion that legislative proposals aimed at reducing business operating costs, abolishing restrictions, removing administrative barriers, making the regulations more liberal, etc., are put forward regularly, in the program of each of the political parties, and are even actually acted on through numerous legislative initiatives. This is certainly the case, as proved by the findings discussed above.

A question may be asked then about the origin of the aforementioned phenomenon. It would be interesting to establish why there is a stable (typical) trend for law makers to reduce transaction costs and barriers to entry.

It would be interesting to establish whether or not the trend may be explained solely by efforts to be popular among voters, or it is also founded on some more profound premises inherent to the institutional system itself.

Clearly, based on the research data presented above, it is possible to establish that the volume of regulations increasing the costs incurred by the economic man and the level of formalization of economic activities occurs rapidly at discrete intervals. One may say that the research results discussed here are generally consistent with the economic theory of transaction costs, but it is not entirely so.

The transaction costs theory actually stipulates a continued increase in transaction costs, and does not provide for a possibility of extended periods of cost decline, whereas the research results prove that the reality (at least in Poland) is somewhat different.

As it happens, the increase in the number of legislative initiatives generating costs was of a short-term nature: it was observed only at times of breakthroughs which tipped the critical balance (such as the transition from a centrally planned economy to a market economy in 1990, and the EU accession in 2004). At the same time, each such situation was followed by a much longer adjustment period of streamlining and reduction in transaction costs and barriers to entry.

This leads to the conclusion that increases in transaction costs (and barriers to entry) occur rapidly in discrete intervals, in situations when the critical balance of socio-economic relations is tipped and there is a transition to a new set of institutional arrangements (when a new frame of reference is established as basis for obtaining goods).

The critical balance in socio-economic relations may be tipped due to factors which are external in relation to the institutional system (being the set of norms, rules, and institutions used by the economic man in society).These may be, for instance, changes in economic resources or geopolitical events (such as accession to an international community). There may also be internal factors, i.e., factors originating from within the system, which may tip the critical balance. These would involve factors leading to system evolution as a result of the very forces of competition for access to the most efficient ways of obtaining goods. Both categories of factors may also be closely connected with each other.

As it is frequently observed in economic sciences, in order for institutional change to occur, "(...) there must exist certain encouraging opportunities arising from the lack of institutional balance, i.e., there must be a reason for the existing institutional system to no longer be the most efficient of possible choices. Starting from the initial point of balance, there may be four sources of the lack of institutional balance: (1) changes in the institutional choice set; (2) technological changes; (3) long-term changes concerning relativity factors and product prices; and (4) changes in other institutional systems. At the same time, each of these fours sources of imbalance comprises several various factors" [Michał Turek, 'Ekonomiczne podstawy zmiany instytucjonalnej, zmiana mikroekonomiczna i makroekonomiczna' in *Dokonania współczesnej myśli ekonomicznej. Ekonomia instytucjonalna – teoria i praktyka*, Urszula Zagóra-Jonszta (edt), Wydawnictwo UE Katowice 2006, 48 ff.].

However, from the point of view of the business cycle theory, internal factors are of fundamental importance, being intra-systemic factors (construed as the reasons underlying system evolution as a result of the very forces of competition for access to the most efficient ways of obtaining goods) which are not included in the enumeration above.[4]

A change occurring in the institutional system due to internal reasons is caused by different rates of decline in the usefulness of a specific solutions (including legal norms) to its particular users. Some of the entities which need to abandon the use of a particular mechanism as a result of an overly large comparative advantage of other users begin to satisfy their needs in more difficult circumstances, and the new solutions employed by them are more complex and require incurring higher costs. The tipping of the critical balance is followed by a transition to a restructured economic and social system, and a process begins, whereby the adopted institutional solutions are optimized and the costs of their application are reduced. However, this process takes place in an environment involving generally higher costs of system functioning as compared to the previous arrangement. For example, in the case of Poland, there is no doubt that, generally speaking, the EU accession hasbrought about stricter requirements imposed on business operators compared to the times before the accession. One may say that the entire Polish economic system has jumped to a higher level of complexity in connection with the EU accession, which has involved an overall increase in the costs of functioning of socio-economic structures.

---

4 Further considerations concluding this subsection are based on: Paweł Chmielnicki 'Mechanism of growing complexity of the system of normative sets' in Paweł Chmielnicki (edt), Anna Dybała, Michał Stachura, *Activity Rules of Economic Man in Society as the Source of Legal Norms*, 1st edn LexisNexis 2010, 133 – 139.

A question may be asked then how these rapid and discrete changes in the level of transaction costs and barriers to entry come to produce a cycle effect.

First, a note should be taken of the fact that each system of socially approved activity patterns derives from the current conditions in which needs are satisfied at a given time. It reflects the level of available natural resources, the demographic situation, and the available technologies. At a time when an institutional solution (i.e., new legal norm) is introduced into social circulation, it (most often) has certain span and potential sufficient for the current circumstances. The potential of a solution may be reduced by external conditions, but, it is necessary to add, that the same may happen due to the attractiveness of the potential benefits to be obtained through a particular institution. The more attractive the potential benefits, the greater number of those wishing to apply a particular solution, even if this would involve incurring higher costs, and even if the institutions used to date are still available and continue to enable the satisfaction of needs (obviously, in some less attractive way). The more an economic activity set-up is likely to suffer as a result of the tragedy of the commons, the more likely and quickly will those of its users who have achieved the greatest comparative advantage seek to keep out potential newcomers, and the more likely they will be to establish barriers to entry. Therefore, those to whom such set-up no longer presents itself as useful will start to look for new ways to achieve their ends.

Solutions used at a given time are more or less adjusted to the current conditions, which is why the development of new patterns poses greater challenges. The use of already existing institutions is the simplest and the most effective at a particular time because these solutions rely to the greatest extent on the resources available at the time. Those who are discouraged from using the initial institutions must therefore create new ones based, for instance, on the use of less readily available resources, a greater competition, or simply operating under more difficult circumstances. Thus, a new institutional solution must take into account new, more difficult operating conditions which, as a rule, involve higher costs because the adjustment to new a new set-up requires more complex rules of activity to be put in place, as compared to the to-date solutions, and more efficient than the earlier ones which were adjusted to easier conditions for achieving particular purposes.

Taking this further, the greater the number of those who are kept out (due to transaction costs and barriers to entry) from the application of the most attractive business institutions (that offer the greatest benefits to individuals) and from using easy ways to achieve goals, the more solutions are being developed on the basis of more complicated and complex activity patterns (since the easier method is no longer productive because its use is being controlled by the strongest players, and it is necessary to apply a more difficult and costly method). Higher operating costs mean a greater risk of suffering a loss in the event of failure, and therefore it becomes necessary to arrange for the protection of the new activity set-up so as to minimize the risk and better secure the outcome of a more cost-intensive activity. The users of the new institution are more willing to incur additional costs by investing in mechanisms securing order and collective security, and thereby a greater protection of the outcome of their activity. There is a growing demand for determining the course of interactions between those who are protected and those who protect, and there are pressures for the most important elements of a particular set-up to be formalized, which leads to an increase in the number of formal rules.

At the same time, the establishment of new formal institutions limits the scope of freedom to act without complying with the new ready-made activity schemes that are promoted and protected by society. Consequently, it becomes increasingly difficult to put in place new institution because of a growing probability of their interference with the already existing ones. On the other hand, more complex activity patterns (including new legal institutions) factor in a greater range of possible scenarios (because although they continue to rely on the basic variant, they also include new elements which were absent in the original set-up). This makes it possible to maximize their utility function under more difficult circumstances. Therefore, new solutions start to become more advantageous compared to the traditional ones, which used to be optimal under simpler and easier conditions.

This leads to a very important point, namely, the relationship between the establishment of new solutions and a decline or increase in transaction costs. According to most institutional theories, a new institution eliminates earlier ones because it better enables to minimize costs. Cost minimization is to be a natural factor decisive for the evolutionary success of the new institution, and determining its greater ability to adjust. Indeed, if the term "institution" is construed to comprise such broad categories as agreement, money, or government [Tomasz Gaweł, Michał Klimczak, 'Pojęcie instytucji w prawie i ekonomii' in *Ład instytucjonalny w gospodarce*, Barbara Polszakiewcz, Jerzy Boehlke (eds), Toruń 2005, 73 ff.], this view could hardly be contested. Money or legal regulations applicable to making agreements certainly reduce transaction costs in general. It should be noted, however, that an increase in system complexity must be distinguished from improving its mechanisms, which are generally oriented towards removing interference between particular solutions, as well as to reduce functioning costs with regard to institutions, which have already been accepted by man.

The process of system improvement is often felt as an ability to act more swiftly, to simplify certain mechanisms, and to make their application cheaper. Nonetheless, this means simplifying and facilitating the operation of a system which, overall, is much more complex compared to the previous one. There is some reduction in costs, but it occurs in a situation of a generally greater complexity and cost intensity of the entire system. Purchase agreements are nowadays made much more swiftly and efficiently than before (with very little risk of interference), but the apparently simple rules of entering into purchase agreements are founded on complex mechanisms of guarantees, warranties, insurance, dispute resolution, and payment enforcement, which are available and may be used in case of infringement on the rules of exchange of money and goods. These mechanisms create, among others, a risk of high costs to be incurred in the event of breach of trust by a party to an agreement.

The costs of man's activity are being reduced cause the formal and informal institutions used by man, although the reduction is not a linear process. It begins after a rapid discrete transition of the system (or a part thereof) to a higher level of complexity, which involves higher overall operating costs of the entire system.

It should be added that growing advantages of new solutions (new activity patterns) cause some response within the original ones: either the old solution lose and are abandoned, or their operating parameters are enhanced and are able to better adjust to various conditions, including new and more difficult ones (e.g., higher standards required by trading partners) compared to the earlier set-up [see Rafał M.Jakubowski, 'Efektywność gospodarcza w ujęciu ekonomicznej teorii prawa własności – wybrane zagadnienia' in *Ład instytucjonalny w gospodarce*, Barbara Polszakiewcz, Jerzy Boehlke (eds), Toruń 2005, 68 and Friedrich August v.Hayek, 'The Results of Human Action But Not of Human Design' in *Studies in Philosophy, Politics and Economics*, 1st edn, Simon and Schuster 1967, 96–105]. Hence, also the old institutions (old activity patterns), if they continue to be used, begin to provide for a greater number of possible scenarios, a higher level of protection, and become more complex.

Therefore, there are a growing number of solutions (activity patterns) which are better adjusted to specific circumstances, alternative patterns emerge, and the to-date basic patterns start to break down into more narrow, purpose- or participant-specific paths enabling the achievement of goals.

This fosters the emergence of a growing number of functionally restricted solutions ("specialized" patterns of activity and allocation of resources), while a greater number of sets further complicates the system. As new solutions (new activity patterns) gradually gain superiority over the old ones by being more refined and better adjusted to the socio-economic conditions, they become

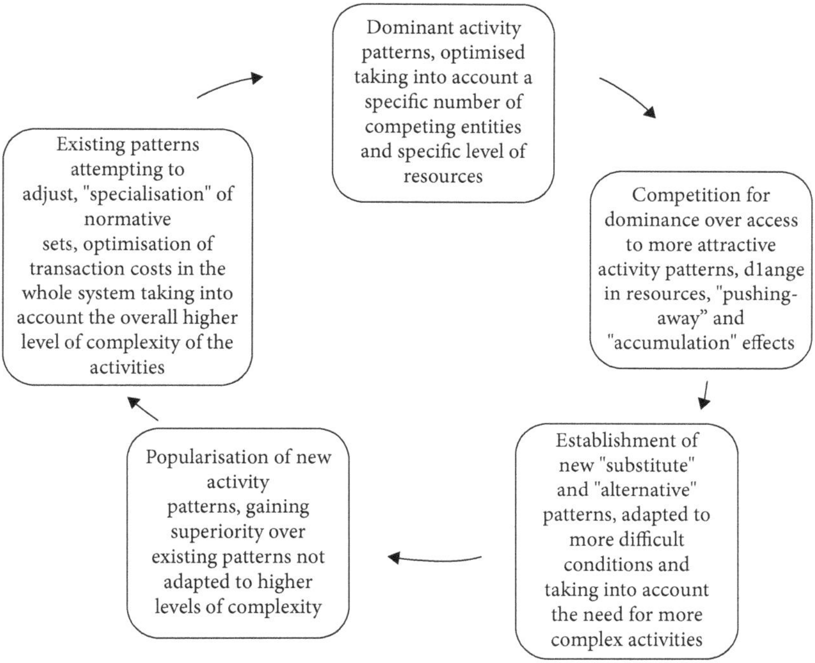

Fig. 6: Intrasystemic mechanisms of the system evolution cycle. Source: Paweł Chmielnicki (edt), Anna Dybała, Michał Stachura, *Activity Rules of Economic Man in Society as the Source of Legal Norms*, 1st edn LexisNexis 2010, 138.

even more attractive, and it turns out to be no longer reasonable to follow old solutions which were optimized for specific resources of the state and of the economy. Now, the new institutions achieve dominance and can fully optimize their mechanisms in line with the currently available resources.They begin to offer the highest returns and become the most popular. A balance between the institutional system and external factors (with regard to the system) moves to a different point at a higher level of complexity, and the cycle starts over again.

2.2 Competition and Comparative Advantage

The next research question was one of the central issues in economic sciences, namely, maintaining competition in the market.

A natural purpose of activities undertaken by the economic man is to achieve advantage over competitors. From the point of view of an entrepreneur, the best situation is to monopolize a particular sector of the economy. This obviously would not be advantageous to other actors involved in socio-economic relations, including consumers who are forced to bear the cost of a monopolist seeking to maximize its utility function. Therefore, they press for rules to be formalized in order to restrict opportunities for market consolidation. These pressures are further reinforced by other entrepreneurs whose interests are threatened by stronger competitors.

The law makers are always faced with the dilemma whether to build institutions that allow for the consolidation of a particular sector of the economy, which implies the growth of strong market players with a large potential. The opposite approach would be to prevent excessive market consolidation, and to counteract the natural trend for bigger marker players to drive companies with a smaller economic potential out of the market. A choice in favor of either of the two options has its advantages and disadvantages, and their assessment always depends on the adopted viewpoint on the purpose of legislation and the situation of entrepreneurs. If priority is given to the stability of the business environment, or the competitiveness of Polish companies on international markets, this would call for proposals aimed at reinforcing the potential of individual strong market operators and stimulating consolidation processes. Such approach in recent years may be illustrated by the laws regulating the banking sector or the energy sector. On the other hand, if the priority is to maintain the competition in a given sector of the economy, this would require quite opposite measures, such as reinforcing the powers of regulatory authorities, protecting the interests of small and medium-size companies, etc. Unfortunately, there is no approach which would make it possible to reach both of these aims at the same time. Measures intended to reinforce the potential of local companies in relation to their foreign competitors, at the same time lead to reducing the competition on the domestic market, especially in the context of the supplier-consumer relationship. On the other hand, measures taken to protect smaller business operators against the expansion of bigger market players, result in market fragmentation, discourage large investors, and may lead to the outflow of capital. Such considerations better than anything else illustrate the relativity of statements justifying any specific legal measure. They also point to the key importance of seeking a balance when establishing normative institutions of the economy, which stimulate various responses by the affected parties. An imbalance towards any of the radical options, although it may appear advantageous at a time, produces reactions and requires to be corrected in the longer term.

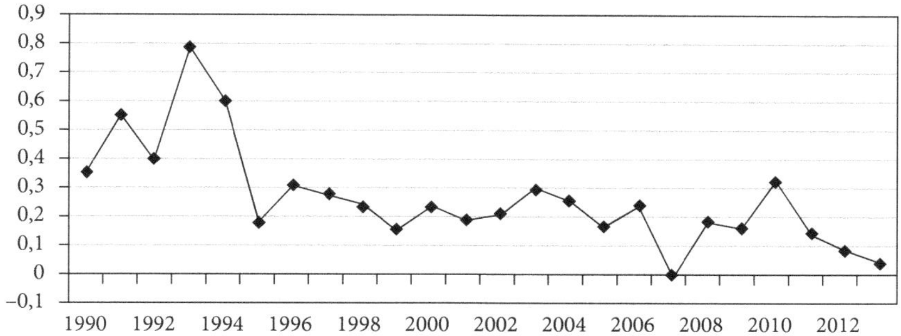

Fig. 7: Diagram based on the average figures for the years 1990–2013. Source: own materials.

Theoretically, due to consumer pressures alone, the evolution of the legal system should proceed towards a gradual formal reduction of comparative advantages enjoyed by large market players, which should be manifest not only through the development of legal remedies against the abuse of an advantageous position, but also through a decreasing share of regulations ensuring support for large market players in the economy as a whole. The results of research which is being presented here, concern an analysis of the law making process seeking to address the question whether or not a particular regulation fosters the interests of large market players, and in particular, those which enjoy or are close to achieving a dominant position in the respective sector of the national economy. The specific question asked was therefore whether or not the regulation supports a growing ability to surpass market competition, and whether or not it fosters the achievement of better economic results. It was analyzed whether or not the regulation protects the interests of large companies, including state-owned enterprises. A negative value of the evaluation result would then be appropriate in a situation where the regulation would hinder the activities of entrepreneurs seeking to monopolize a sector of the economy, or it would reinforce the position of smaller market players against the companies enjoying a dominant position in the market.

The diagram presenting the net effect of the two trends combined: the trend to curtail the advantageous position of companies dominating the markets, and the counter trend (Fig. 7), actually shows a long-term decline trend. It is interesting to note that the decline does not correspond with the trend in the overall number of adopted legislative acts, which indeed continued to grow for many years. It is

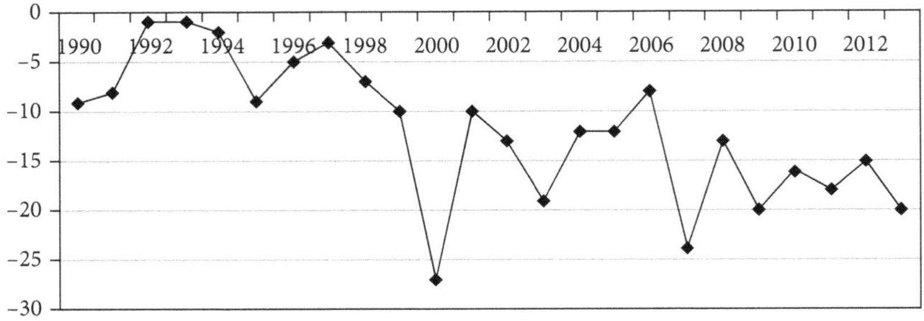

Fig. 8: Diagram based on aggregate figures for values "cut off at -1" for the years 1990–2013. Source: own materials.

also striking that the figures do not reflect at all the peak observed in numerous other research findings for the years 2000–2001.

Already during the 1992–1993 parliamentary term, the Sejm adopted regulations to adjust certain shortfalls of the market. The Act on Preventing and Fighting Unfair Competition of 16th April 1993 (published in the *Dziennik Ustaw* official journal No. 47, 1993, Item 211) regulated preventing and fighting unfair competition in business operations, which served the public interest, as well as the interests of entrepreneurs and their clients, and especially consumers. The law defined acts of unfair competition such as: providing misleading information as to the identity of a company, providing false or fraudulent designation of origin of products or services, using misleading designation of goods or services, breach of company privileged information, soliciting termination or non-performance of agreements, copying products, preventing market access, as well as deceitful or prohibited advertising and organization of avalanche sale. Nevertheless, as shown in the diagram based solely on data reflecting negative values assigned to legislative acts (Fig. 8), i.e., covering only the regulations which counteracted consolidation of economic potential by dominant players on the market, including monopolists, the figures clearly support the thesis that the most intensive efforts to establish an institutional order of the economy based on competition and de-monopolization were undertaken under the government formed by the AWS-UW coalition, specifically in the years 1998–2000. This conclusion is not surprising bearing in mind that the main initiator of these activities was Leszek Balcerowicz who had been the author of the package of bills which at the end of 1989 set Poland on the path of market reforms.

Increasing economic competitiveness remained to be one of the main directions of the legislative policy under the government formed by the AWS-UW coalition as long as it was in power. As then Deputy Prime Minister Balcerowicz claimed, the need for such legislative initiatives "(. . .) existed particularly in those sectors in which to date there had been temporary protection, sometimes extended in time. Such protection could no longer be extended. It was simply not possible to maintain it without jeopardising Poland's fundamental external interests in negotiations with the European Union. I am referring to: the steel industry, in a certain time perspective, also railroad transport – there should also be opening of the market there, and the energy sector" [the address to the Sejm made by Leszek Balcerowicz, then deputy prime minister and finance minister, during the first reading of the 2000 budget bill on October 14, 1999].

The most significant legislative project carried out by the AWS government with regard to creating the institutional order of the economy was probably the Act on the Protection of Competition and Consumers of 15th December 2000 (published in the *Dziennik Ustaw* official journal No. 122, 2000, Item 1319) which replaced the earlier anti-monopoly law. The Act provided for the President of the Office of Competition and Consumer Protection to be appointed as the national government authority responsible for effectively preventing interference with competition on the market. The law provided for broad inspection powers of anti-monopoly authority and unconditionally prohibited abuse of a dominant market position.

Concerning the analysis of research results with regard to regulations, which fostered the interests of companies with a large economic potential, one may notice two clearly distinct periods. The first one was the period until 1993 during which the largest companies' position on the market was consolidated, and the second period from 1994 until 2013 which saw a gradual decrease in the share of the respective regulations.

To sum up, based on the research on the legislative process in Poland, it transpires that the long-term trend among the law makers has nevertheless been to attempt to reduce the advantages of companies with a large economic potential, i.e., to protect competition. The trend has been to make it more difficult for monopolies and oligopolies to emerge. Here as well, just as it was the case with transaction costs and barriers to entry, the prevalence of the trend does not depend on the political orientation of legislators. Two peaks in building institutions which foster the interests of big market players occurred in the years when the power was held by parties with entirely different outlooks on the economy. In 2003, the left was in power (the Democratic Left Alliance (SLD), and in 2010, it was the liberal Civic Platform (PO) (crisis in the financial markets, and the need to stabilize the banking sector). On the other hand, the most determined actions to foster market competition were taken by the government formed by the Solidarity Election Action (AWS) and the Freedom Union (UW). However, the record of its successors from the SLD does not differ very much in this respect (the period of Poland's preparations for accession to the EU, regulations related to the free movement of goods and services). An analysis of the research data may therefore lead to the conclusion that the establishment of competition regulatory mechanisms increasingly depends on global factors, and to a lesser and lesser extent on the intentions of national legislators.

2.3 Costs of Maintaining the System

Another issue concerns costs related to maintaining the environment which fosters unobstructed trade in goods and cash flows, which comprises conditions for the satisfaction of basic life needs by ordinary members of the population.

The more developed the social system is, the greater the need for system safeguard measures to encourage cooperation, and not only to discourage unilateral abuse of the system to achieve one's own ends. Where the needs are satisfied to a greater extent through social, and not individual means, this necessitates the use of a greater number of instruments based on cooperation between individuals, thereby implying a greater complexity of the system, which makes the system more vulnerable to interference. Therefore, an unobstructed operation of the formal institutions depends much more on the prevalence of active cooperation attitudes, intentionally oriented towards minimizing the effects of interference. In order for individuals to be interested in adopting such attitudes, it is necessary for them to strongly deem the system as useful. They must believe that they will achieve personal gains by supporting the system. Or, when looking at the same situation from a different angle, they must be convinced that by breaching the rules of the system they will be deprived of specific gains.

The level of system maintenance complexity itself requires the leaders to offer more in exchange for social consent to follow the imposed rules. The leaders must react to relative deprivation sentiments [Piotr Sztompka, *Socjologia. Analiza społeczeństwa*, 1st edn, Znak 2002, 287–290], and conceal their advantages in order for subordinated individuals not to increase their expectations and demands addressed to the leaders, which would bring about a growth in the costs of leadership (whether political or economic). Therefore, the importance of the redistributive function of the public spending policy continues to grow, especially in the indirect sense (reduction of inequalities in living standards).

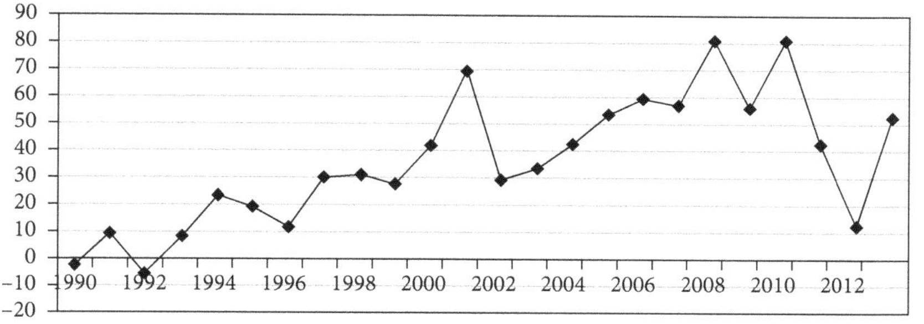

Fig. 9: Diagram based on the aggregate figures for the years 1990–2013. Source: own materials.

The purpose of research was therefore to establish whether the regulatory effect is to be redistribution (allocation) of some goods (whether tangible or intangible) solely based on the rule of membership in a particular group (national, ethnic, professional, gender, etc.), and not by way of compensation for work which has been or is being performed. In other words, the purpose was to determine whether a regulation made it possible for a gain to be obtained through the exercise of rights arising from membership in a group. Hence, positive values in the diagram reflected the regulations which provided for public welfare, introduced early retirement benefits for the unemployed, granted privileges to specific groups based on their occupation, increased the amounts of child support benefits disbursed from public funds in lieu of non-performing parents, etc., whereas negative values were recorded, for instance, when discounts were cut down on public transport rates, disability pension restrictions were introduced, public support was reduced for the creation of jobs for the unemployed, etc.

As may be seen in the diagram which shows both positive values (for regulations involving the provision of benefits) and negative values (for regulations involving the withdrawal of benefits), the figures for regulations under which gains could be obtained (needs satisfied) on the basis of membership in a group grew continuously over a very long period.

A growing importance of the redistributive function in the public spending policy and a high concentration of regulations under which goods could be obtained on the basis of membership in a group, were actually observed until 2010, save for the years 2001–2002 when the trend was reversed. In the years 2011–2012, a dramatic change of trend was observed, following which the growth trend was restored in 2013. The strong correction in the trend for the welfare

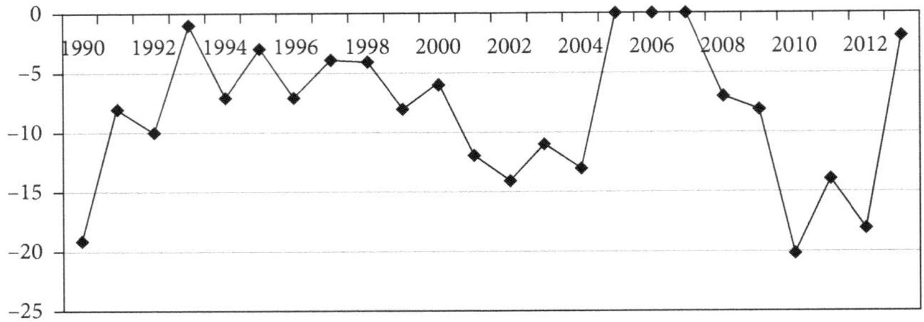

Fig. 10: Diagram based on aggregate figures with a "cut off at -1" for the years 1990–2013. Source: own materials.

state to expand, noted in 2001–2002, may be explained by a major correction in the projected government spending for the years 2000–2002, which was due to the overestimation of the government deficit projection for the years 2000–2001 by then Finance Minister Jacek Bauc. The correction in public spending in 2011–2012 may have resulted from a high government deficit during the period 2009–2011, while the surge in redistributive functions of the state in 2013 may be explained by a decline trend in the government deficit, with the lowest deficit figure recorded in 2012 (unfortunately, the deficit increased in 2013 up to 4.3 % of the GDP, but government deficit effect on legislative policies is delayed by approximately one year). It should be noted that Poland has not been the only country afflicted by the tendency to consolidate the welfare state functions since the beginning of its structural reforms (unless public spending levels were threatened by an overly large public deficit and limitations on incurring public debt). Similar trends of varied intensity were observed in practically all of the former so-called people's democracies in Europe, i.e., members of the Soviet Bloc.

Interesting findings were obtained by cutting off the regulation assessment values at -1 (Fig. 10). This method was applied in order to separate only those legislative initiatives which reduced or withdrew benefits.

Paradoxically, one of the periods of the most intensive legislative efforts in this respect was under the government of the Democratic Left Alliance (SLD; in the years 2001–2005), which is a party declaring its left-wing orientation, while the left wing is associated with state welfare, income redistribution, and the provision of benefits. On the other hand, under the government of the Law and Justice party (PiS) which designates itself as a right-wing party (2006–2007), the values reached zero levels. After all, it is usually the political right-wing that is expected to cut welfare spending. This example shows clearly how relative the use of "left-wing" and "right-wing" labels may be nowadays, at least with regard to the economic policy.

It is also interesting to note in the above diagram that the greatest prevalence of negative values was recorded for the most recent terms of parliament when the Civic Platform (PO) had a majority in the Sejm. Its election programs and neo-liberal language used during election campaigns announced a change of trend in structuring the institutional system, and the party indeed acted on its program.

A note should be made as well that, whereas the total number of legislative acts increased approximately by a twofold during the period concerned, the number of acts indirectly providing for redistributive functions grew as much as six times. It was not until 2008 that the long-term growth trend was turned. For the time being, it is difficult to determine to what extent this has been a correction, and to what extent it may mean a change of trend.

Summing up, should be noticed, that providing for the needs of those who do not participate in the production of goods constitutes one of the costs of safeguarding the entire socio-economic system. The necessary costs of safeguarding the institutional order include not only the costs of keeping the services whose function is to physically uphold law and order in domestic or external relations of a state. The costs of financing welfare benefits are transactions costs for those competing to maximize their profits on the market in which goods and services are supplied, and these transaction costs are just as necessary as those related to purchasing gear for police officers who protect shops against thieves. This is due to the fact that the principal task of a group leader, also an economic leader, is to ensure access to means through which needs may be satisfied. This function is assigned to the leader instinctively, based on the deepest felt mechanisms of social interaction and identification of social roles, which evolved in the course of social history of mankind. In some situations, this comes down to directly providing specific goods.

The more the social system is developed, the more the measures used to protect the system must rely on encouraging cooperation, and not just discouraging unilateral use of opportunities to satisfy an individual's needs. This is related to the fact that, if needs are satisfied to a greater extent through social and not only individual methods, this makes it necessary to apply a greater number of measures based on cooperation among individuals, thereby implying an overall higher degree of system complexity and, consequently, a higher system susceptibility to interference. This is reflected in the actions taken by law makers, as confirmed by the figures presented in the diagram (Fig. 9). Therefore, an uninterrupted use of the formal institutions of socio-economic order depends to a much greater extent on the prevalence of active cooperation attitudes intentionally oriented towards minimizing the consequences of interference. However, this implies that the perceived rewards from cooperation must be higher than yields from breach of solutions supported by the group. Enforcement of the rules through negative stimuli (penalties, aggravation) often need to be kept in the background due to structural limitations of the system of sanctions in a contemporary democratic system. After analyzing the diagram based on figures reflecting the general trend in development of the institutional order with regard to redistribution of goods on account of membership in a group, one may come to the conclusion that the evolution of the Polish institutional system follows the foregoing assumption.

2.4 Free Rider Effect: Reducing Unnecessary Costs of the System

The issue discussed above relates closely to another one, namely, how to secure the system against unjustified costs being incurred. Measures commonly applied within the socio-economic system factor in, among others, the problems of providing for the necessities of those who do not participate in the goods exchange economy due to their inability to obtain means to participate in the exchange. Unfortunately, organized support provided by the state exposes the system to abuse by individuals who take advantage of their membership status in the group, despite the fact that they would be able to satisfy their needs by their own resource [For more see Olson Mancur,The Logic of Collective Action: Public Goods and the Theory of Groups, 2nd edn, Harvard Economic Studies, Harvard University Press 1971]. Such situations, often referred to as the "free rider effect", are mainly associated with "low-raking" group members, such as the unemployed, disability pensioners, or social welfare recipients. However, abuse of support made available by the group, may occur in a number of other unjustified situations. Assistance offered by the state to support the employment of: individuals facing layoffs, the unemployed, the sick, or the disabled, may be effectively misappropriated by entrepreneurs who could operate their businesses on "regular" terms, but prefer to take advantage of special provisions, which enable them to get direct access to public funds. This poses the question to what extent funds provided by the state serve to improve the situation of individuals who need support, and to what extent they simply add to the profits made by entrepreneurs. In fact, state assistance may actually be obtained by threat, for example, of cuts in employment (an argument used very frequently, and referred to in the justifications of numerous legislative proposals). In other words, entrepreneurs want to avoid the consequences of their business decisions in a free market. Instead, they try to get a free ride, just like those who simulate disabilities in order to obtain benefits. A particularly flagrant example of such behavior was connected with the assistance granted by the U.S. government to American financial institutions. The fact of assistance being provided under the threat of destabilization of the entire economy and massive job cuts did not prevent the executives in charge of the financial institutions from collecting generous salaries and bonuses.

Typically, political parties rarely tackle the issue of eliminating the "free rider effect", also known as the "Ringelmann effect", in their election platforms. This is hardly surprising since measures announced to reduce the free rider effect would have to sound like threats to some extent, which would impact very negatively on the parties' public relations and the image of their platforms. Nevertheless, the Ringelmann effect, unless constrained effectively enough, leads to a loss of confidence in institutions of the rational economic exchange. If gains may be too readily obtained on account of group membership, this considerably reduces the incentives for individuals to make an effort to satisfy their needs by playing according to the rules of the goods exchange economy.

The research question was whether or not a particular studied regulation led to a reduction in undue gains obtained as a result of behaviors earlier described as the "free rider effect", or possibly as a result of the so-called rent-seeking [for a more detailed discussion of the concept see Gordon Tullock 'The Welfare Cost of Tariffs, Monopolies and Theft', *Western Economic Journal* 1976, vol. V, 224–232 and Alan Krueger, 'The political of rent-seeking Society', *American Economic Review* 1974, vol. LXIV, 291–303]. This primarily involves situations when benefits provided for by the state are used by recipients (individuals, groups, or entrepreneurs) whose situation does not make them eligible to use public assistance. The main focus of this research question was on the attention paid by decision makers to eliminating the free rider effect. Positive values were therefore duly assigned in situations when, for instance, stricter criteria were introduced for obtaining transfer payments, or some privileges were withdrawn, while negative values were assigned if the regulation brought about the opposite effect.

The diagram which presents the outcome of the two formalization trends (Fig. 11), i.e., the trend bringing about measures to eliminate the Ringelmann effect, and that stimulating the Ringelmann effect, shows a very characteristic, clear picture of a long-term trend. First, approximately until the year 2000, a majority of the regulations not only did not provide for eliminating the free-rider effect, but they actually encouraged rent-seeking (there is a clear majority of negative values, corresponding to legislative acts which produced regulatory effects contrary to the research assumption of preventing the free-rider effect). After 2000, the trend seemed to slow down, and was reversed for a longer period after

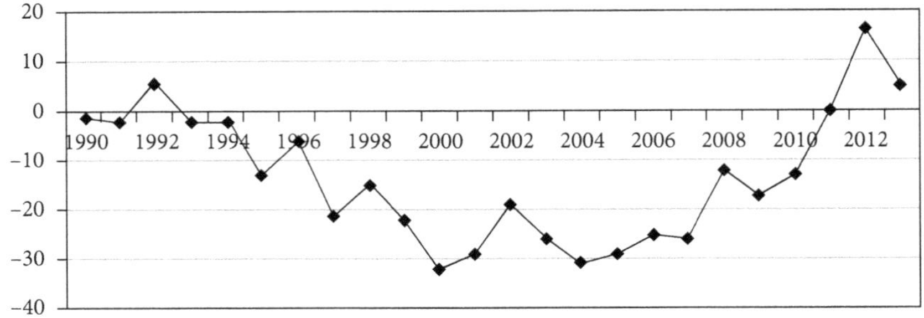

Fig. 11: Diagram based on the aggregate figures for the years 1990–2013. Source: own materials.

2004: a continued interest was observed on the part of law makers in regulations which, more or less directly, discouraged behaviors falling under the category of the Ringelmann effect. In the past years the trend to formalize measures to restrict the free-rider effect has even dominated, which has not been seen for nearly twenty years.

Clearly, until the years 2002–2004, law makers were not particularly interested in analyzing the effects of adopted laws in the context of the Ringelmann effect. Based on an assessment of the actual consequences of legislative acts, it is possible to state that the laws actually rather promoted rent-seeking than eliminated such practices. From 2005 the trend was reversed, with a major surge in the years 2011–2012, which may probably be linked to government pressures on the abolition of group privileges, as the most popular policy of savings in public spending (in order to reduce the government deficit, which was effectively achieved). As soon as the situation of public finances improved (the government deficit in 2012 dropped to 3.9 % of the GDP), the trend to eliminate the Ringelmann effect through appropriate legislative measures was slowed down right away.

The diagram based on the average figures, which show the net result of both the values corresponding to regulations consistent with the assumption that the Ringelmann effect should be prevented and those following the opposite notion (Fig. 12), shows that, not until the government formed by the AWS–UW coalition, did the governments try to reverse the growing negative trend in the development of the institutional order of the economy, which had been persisting for years. After that, efforts oriented towards the same goal were only undertaken during the parliamentary terms 2005–2007 and 2007–2011.

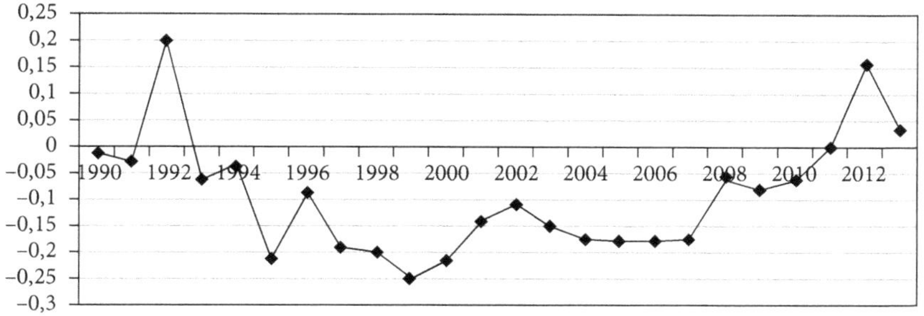

Fig. 12: Diagram based on average figures for the years 1990–2013. Source: own materials.

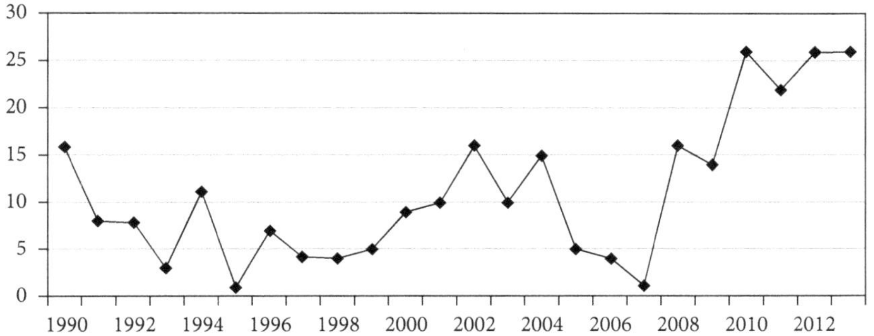

Fig. 13: Diagram based on aggregate figures with a "cut off at 1" for the years 1990–2013. Source: own materials.

The years 2002–2005 generally marked a period when the trend to establish an institutional order free from the Ringelmann effect was not only stopped, but even reversed. On the diagram in Fig. 13 which is based solely on positive valuations (i.e., reflecting legislative initiatives aimed at eliminating the free rider effect), the period 1998–2001 (under the AWS–UD government) shows a clear growth trend fostering the development of a system free from the Ringelmann effect. In the years 2002–2005, there was initially a fluctuating trend which later became a clear regress reflecting a significant decline in interest in preventing the free rider effect.

As shown in the diagram, until the years 2002–2004, law makers were not particularly interested in looking at the adopted legislation from the point of view of the Ringelmann effect. An assessment of the actual effects brought about by legislative acts supports the view that the adopted laws rather promoted rent-seeking than sought to eliminate social loafing. After 2005 the trend was reversed, with a major acceleration in the years 2011–2012, which most likely may be explained by the government's focus on removing group privileges as the most popular policy to cut on public spending (in order to bring down the level of government deficit, which was actually achieved). As soon as the economic figures were better (the government deficit level dropped to 3.9 % of the GDP in 2012), in 2013, the trend to eliminate the Ringelmann effect through appropriate legislative measures was immediately slowed down.

The problem of Ringelmann effect has always led to a loss of confidence in mechanisms determining the rules according to which goods are obtained on account of group membership alone, which provides an ideological argument to those who wish to reduce their costs incurred in relation to maintaining the socio-economic system despite the fact that the existence of the system enables them to prosper and achieve high self-esteem. Unless the Ringelmann effect is controlled efficiently enough, it also depletes trust in institutions based on the rules of exchanging goods for money. When it is too easy to obtain goods on account of membership in a group, individuals have a much lower motivation to work hard in order to satisfy their needs in accordance with the rules of exchange economy. The problem is, that he free rider effect can never be fully eliminated, and the best way to reduce it is by working to achieve a balance within the system between the two categories of patterns followed to obtain goods, and the two basic types of activity: the exchange of goods for money, and the provision of goods on account of membership in the group alone. The system of incentives encouraging conformity with the rules of the institutional order should be shaped in such way, as to ensure that the risk of depleting trust in either of the two categories of activity patterns is minimized.

Therefore, it is necessary to put forward such legislative initiatives which encourage trust in the system and abandon those that weaken this trust. Based on the figures presented in the diagram in Fig. 14, Polish law makers quite quickly, i.e., within less than ten years from the commencement of structural reforms, started to steadily formalize mechanisms consistent with these assumptions. Although there are still quite a number of legislative initiatives which produce the opposite effect, and the data in the diagram reflects these laws, contradictory to the earlier described assumptions of "good legislation", a clear growth trend shown in the diagram from 1999 on does foster some optimism.

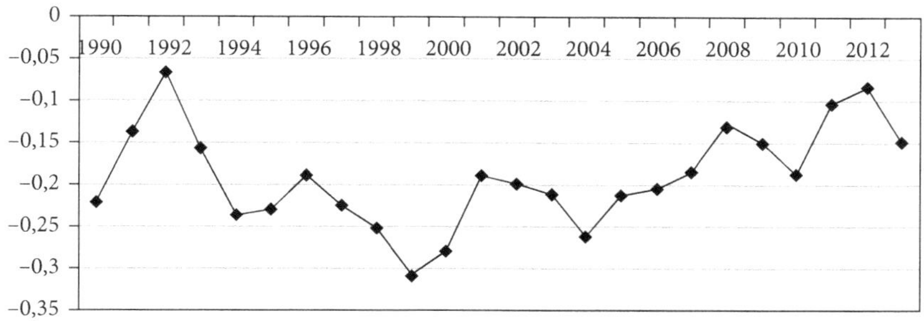

Fig. 14: Diagram based on average figures with a "-1 cut off" for the years 1990–2013. Source: own materials.

2.5 Protection against Dominance

Another factor which clearly has a significant impact on shaping the institutional system is the reinforcement of the ability of vulnerable players to resist the dominance by the powerful ones. Weaker players cannot rely on their own relative power vis-à-vis others, but they also wish to enjoy the safety provided by the society. This may be illustrated by the relationship between employees and employers, small businesses and banks, etc. Therefore, those who are vulnerable press for costs to be imposed on the operations of the powerful ones which seek to take advantage of their relative power in the competition for a place on the social ladder. In a democratic system, the dominated ones are able to succeed in doing so due to their numbers as voters.

The figures presented below, which show the net outcome of the trends in line with the assumptions above, and the opposite trend (based both on positive and negative value assessments), follow a very characteristic pattern. The curve is shaped like a wave rising around the time of Poland's accession to the European Union, with a distinct fall coming thereafter. It is interesting to analyze the factors underlying the evolution of the institutional system of the economy according to this particular pattern.

For a relatively long time, Polish law makers showed a continued interest in this matter, which may be briefly referred to as "protecting the rights of the weakest". The situation clearly changed after 2005, when the Polish politics became dominated by the Law and Justice (PiS) and the Civic Platform (PO). The number of regulations adopted for the purpose of reinforcing the ability of vulnerable market players to resist domination by the powerful ones, has been decreasing noticeably. This does not justify drawing definite conclusions. Such

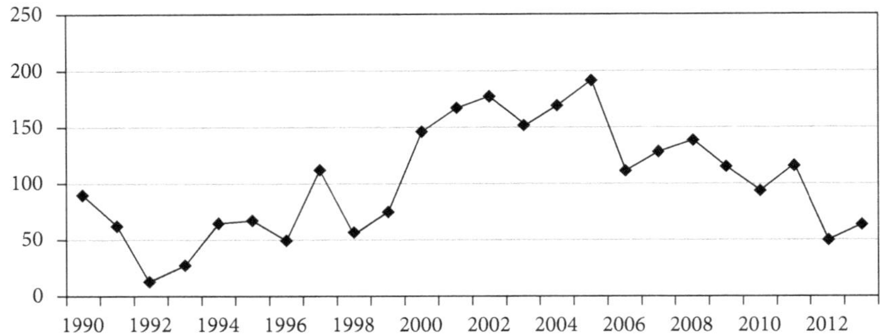

Fig. 15: Diagram based on the aggregate figures for the years 1990–2013. Source: own materials.

situation may be due to the fact that the protection of the rights of the weakest in Poland has reached a level sufficient enough for legislative efforts to be cut down in this area. However, this is only one of the possible interpretations of the figures. Another hypothesis may also be proposed, namely, that the figures indicate a fallback to neoliberal policies by the parties in power, and therefore their support for measures which allow the achievement of economic dominance (less government intervention, free competition leading to utility maximization, etc.), at the expense of dominated market players. Further far-reaching research will be required in order to prove one of the abovementioned hypotheses.

The case discussed here provides a good example of difference in research findings depending on the use of methods based on aggregate vs. average figures. The results of calculations using aggregate figures show that, until 2005, dominated actors were increasingly supported in withstanding the advantageous position of economically stronger actors. Law makers showed a growing interest in the matter, but their interest started to decline after 2005.

As it was earlier mentioned, calculations based on aggregate figures make it possible to establish the total of values assigned to regulations in a particular year and in respect to a particular research question. The diagram based on aggregate figures shows a clear growth trend until 2005 (by approximately a fourfold in the years 1990–2005). This might lead to the conclusion that law makers were more and more interested in matters related to developing this category of legislative measures. However, the graph based on average figures makes it necessary to revise the earlier assessment of legislative initiatives.

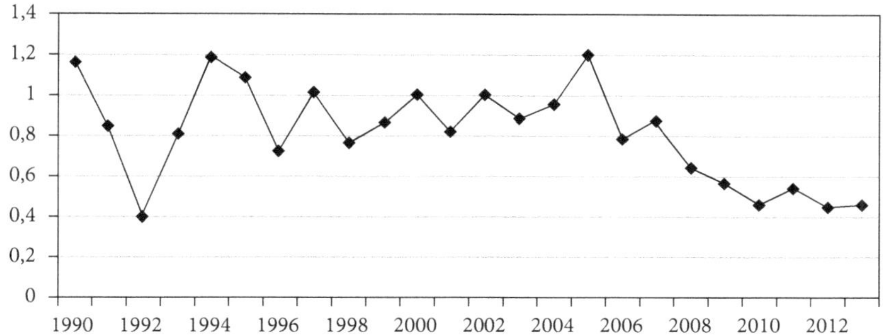

Fig. 16: Diagram based on average figures for the years 1990–2013. Source: own materials.

As already mentioned, the model using average figures is more oriented towards measuring the social and economic significance of adopted regulations. In other words, it shows whether or not the level of law makers' interest in a particular issue in a given year has really increased as compared to the overall volume of adopted regulations. The diagram based on average figures presents the real picture of legislative proposals. It leads to the conclusion that, in reality, legislators did not show a growing interest in matters discussed herein, but their interest remained stable for about fifteen years, while after 2005 even a clear decline trend could be observed.

3. The "Micro" Approach -

3. 1 Normative Set as a Research Tool

This approach differs from traditional research, because the legal norm is studied here as part of a larger whole – a set of formal and informal norms. In this approach, the priority is to determine the impact of individual norms on decisions made by man. It involves the study of functional connections of individual norms of law with other legal norms and with other norms respected in society. The basis for research is the concept of a "**normative set**" (called "activity pattern" either).[5]

5 Further considerations concluding this subsection are based on: Paweł Chmielnicki 'The notion of a normative set' in Paweł Chmielnicki (edt), Anna Dybała, Michał Stachura, *Activity Rules of Economic Man in Society as the Source of Legal Norms*, 1st edn LexisNexis 2010, 133 – 139.

What is the normative set? In short, in order to achieve an objective (satisfy a need) people try to reconstruct the activity pattern, namely identify all the relevant information on activities that is necessary to achieve the assumed objective, irrespective of their origin. This could be information from a category of legal rules, a category of economic rules (exchange of goods and money) or a category of rules for the acquisition of goods due to being a member of a community. Normative set is a set of norms originated from three main basic sets: legal norms, economy rules and other rules of action respected in society (as praxeological, ethical, religious rules), which should be taken into account by a person who wants to achieve a specific aim. The normative set is not an unchanging institution, it must be reconstructed, its content should be determined in accordance with the changes taking place in the system of norms that people use.

Summing up, normative set could be described as a set of relevant information about the conditions for achieving the assumed objective, in particular the activities that need to be carried out. In other words, it is a set of useful information about necessary activities. In this case, by utility we understand the value of the information and which relies on the significance thereof for making a specific decision about an activity (nonfeasance), engaging in an activity (or not completing it – for the sake of simplicity, further in the text, activities will also mean nonfeasance). Such an activity pattern, namely a set of information about specific activities, including activities that are important in the context of pay-offs and the costs related to achieving the assumed objective, originating from three categories of rules: legal norms, rules governing the exchange of goods and money and rules governing the acquisition of goods due to being a member of a community, will be referred to later in as the normative set.

To put it precisely, the information consists of the normative set describe the sequences of defined activities deriving from three different categories (legal norms, rules for the exchange of goods and money and rules for the acquisition of goods due to being a member of a community), that are interrelated and focused on a specific objective, the features and meaning of which are determined by this objective. These rules operate within a given normative set simultaneously and equally, and the importance of individual rules does not result from any levels of influence (hierarchy) existing among the categories from which they originate.

The impact of these activities on the achievement of the activity objective varies. The "core" of the normative set consists of activities which the "user" of the set (the person using the normative set) always has to undertake in order

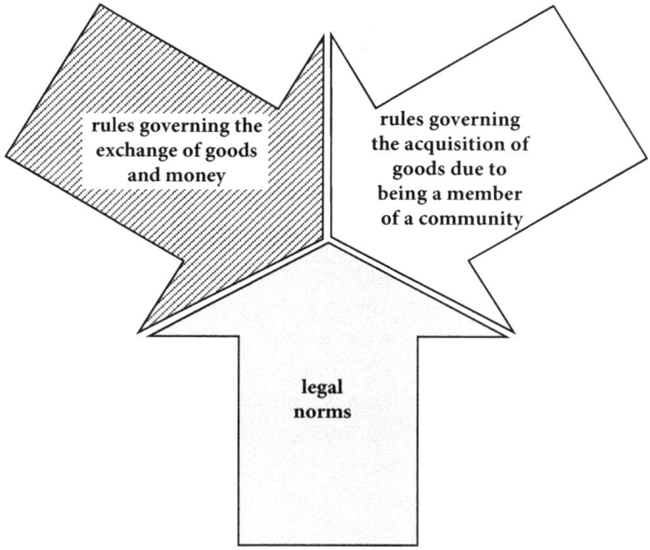

Fig. 17: Categories of rules in the normative set. Source: Paweł Chmielnicki (edt), Anna Dybała, Michał Stachura, *Activity Rules of Economic Man in Society as the Source of Legal Norms*, 1st edn LexisNexis 2010, 65.

to achieve the assumed objective (they are required or necessary), or whose completion will always totally hinder the achievement of the objective. The "soft elements" of the normative set are those activities whose completion is not decisive in achieving the objective, but increase its chances of success, limit the costs, or that have a positive impact on the scope of its achievement (increase the value of the benefit derived, the payoff), as well as those activities whose completion reduces the chances of success, increases the costs or has a negative impact on the scope of achievement of the objective (reduces the value of the benefit derived, the payoff). Let us take note of the fact that the scope of formalization of individual elements of the normative set, or their origin, has no impact on this classification. Admittedly, the "core" elements are often the most highly formalized (most often with the help of law), while the "soft" elements are less formalized; but sometimes it is the other way round – the necessary activities are less formalised (they belong to "unwritten, customary rules", and their key meaning is based on praxeology, but they have not been formally sanctioned), while the soft elements are highly formalized (but their importance, from the point of view of praxeology, is secondary vis-à-vis the activity objective). Consequently, each of the normative set, provides us with three types of information on the necessary activities: the information making up the "core" of the normative set, elements of the "soft" part and information that can be omitted, i.e., information that relates to the situation but which has minimum or even zero impact on the achievement of the activity objective.

The sanctions play a special role among the norms that make up the normative set. Their main considerably consists in inducing to use the schemes of action offered by society. Sanctions should be understood here as any incentive to choose a particular mode of action, both positive and negative. Negative and positive sanctions may be formalized and non-formalized, and may belong to the "core" of the set or to the "soft" elements. Comparing the types of sanctions and the key categories of holders of activity patterns results in the identification of four types of models (this classification is not strongly disjunctive): 1) complied with due to a negative sanction whose holder is a civil or religious authority, or an entity authorized by a body of the authority (highlyformalized sanction; often referred to as a "focused" sanction); 2) complied with due to a negative sanction, the holder of which is a private entity (sanction with different degrees of formalization; "focused" or "diffused"); 3) complied with due to a positive sanction whose holder is a public entity (sanction with different degrees of formalization, but with a significant percentage of highlyformalized sanctions – are expressed mainly in the rights to obtain various benefits; "focused" or "diffused"); 4) complied with due to a positive sanction whose holder is a private entity (usually non-formalized; "diffused").

Finally, it should be emphasized that the elements of the normative set are heterogenic, but are interrelated in a way that determines the form of the elements originating from various information categories. Taking into account the functional aspect, as a whole subordinated to one objective, they make up a set exhibiting emergent properties (mutual influence of the elements of the normative set and their sources result in structured collective phenomena). In other words: combining the activity norms that originate from different sources of norms into one set of rules subordinated to a common objective creates a new quality, and it is not a simple sum of the elements. This is why it is only a reconstruction of the information about elements of the activity pattern based on all the sets of knowledge relevant to the situation that enables us to determine what effects our activity will have on the market of exchange of goods in a social group.

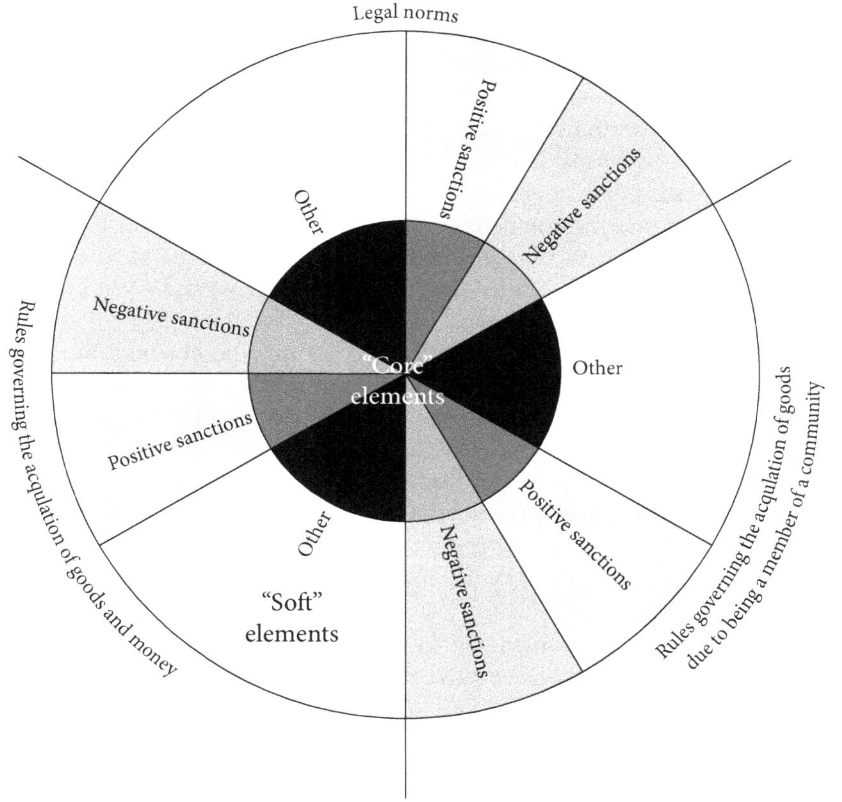

Fig. 18: Normative set (main elements). Source: Paweł Chmielnicki (edt), Anna Dybała, Michał Stachura, *Activity Rules of Economic Man in Society as the Source of Legal Norms*, 1st edn, LexisNexis 2010, 86.

3. 2 Determining the Composition of the Normative Set

3.2.1 Basic Assumes[6]

According to the concept described above, determining the composition of the

6 Sections 3.2.1. and 3.2.2. are based on the article Paweł Chmielnicki 'The Research Method of "Association for the Research on Sources and Functions of Law" *Przegląd Prawa Publicznego* 2015 vol. 3, 95–105.

normative set is a function of ascertaining the nature of interactions of elements of axionormative order, which finding – in turn – is a function of determining the factors influencing the decisions on choosing the way of achieving the aim of action that an individual or a community set for themselves.

It should be determined which formalized norms come into direct relations with informalized norms determining the course of the social-economic interaction and what is their importance for achievement of the assumed aim of this interaction, especially within determining the benefits and costs for the subjects taking part in this interaction. It is necessary to determine the socio-economic sources of legal norms (so-called material sources of law) and socio-economic effects of the researched regulation.

The achievement of these research purposes may be obtained by: distinguishing the category of entities to which the action of a given formal institution relates directly, distinguishing of aims of action that can be realized by these entities, identification of factors that determine the achievement of these aims of action, which include primarily the benefits and costs associated with various stages of action, establishing the ways of realization of individual stages of action and – at the end – distinguishing a set of formal and informal rules that must be taken into account (used) by the entity wishing to achieve the assumed aim of action.

Using the language of methodology of social sciences, the basis of research method described below is a reductive reasoning of special type, referring to the status of axionormative order as a set in the mereological sense, where explanatory statements concern a part of the set, which is the system of law.

3.2.2 The Way of Realization of the Research Objectives

3.2.2.1 Separating of the Analyzed Normative Set (Phase 1)

It consists in initial distinguishing (indicating), from a selected field of research (from an area of legal regulations and informalized norms): 1) the regulations of the law defining the researched legal institution, which regulations are contained in the leading – for this institution – legal act and the regulations, the application of which directly determines the achievement of the aim of action achievable for man due to existence of the analyzed institution (the application of which is directly relevant to the achievement of certain aim of action on the basis of adequate cause and effect relation), contained in other legal acts; 2) informalized norms the use of which directly determines the achievement of the aim of action achievable for man due to existence of the analyzed legal institution (such as the norms of commodity-money exchange concerning a given economic activity).

Correctness of separating of formal and informal norms made in this phase will be verified in subsequent phases of the project and subjected to possible adjustments.

3.2.2.2 Gathering Research Data (Phase 2)

It consists in aggregating the available knowledge of the analyzed institution, both in terms of the sources of its origin as well as its functional relations with other institutions of the socio-economic order, the lines of interpretation of the regulations of the law relating to the analyzed institution, understanding informalized rules relating to the application of the analyzed institution and the socio-economic effects of its functioning. In particular, it is about:

1) collecting of information describing the hitherto existing (or all) course of the legislative process, such as:
   - documents created by public authorities and non-governmental organizations,
   - experts' analyses and opinions,
   - interviews with persons involved in the legislative process,
   - the results of public consultations,
2) preliminary research of scientific literature and trade studies
3) preliminary research of judicial and administrative decisions
4) acquisition (aggregation) of the available data relating to the actual effects of the impact of the analyzed institution, such as:
   - economic data and the results of the economic analysis,
   - statistical data collected by public institutions and private entities,

analyses conducted with the use of the instruments of social sciences (particularly sociology), such as assessments of the effectiveness of the institutions resulting from surveys, questionnaires, etc.

3.2.2.3 Formulating Working Hypotheses (Phase 3)

It concerns the adoption of the initial assumptions both on the basis of information obtained in the preliminary research as well as on the basis of professional knowledge of the project participants as to the category of entities covered by the functioning of the analyzed institution, as to the category of payments (benefits) that these entities can achieve in connection with functioning of the subject institution, as to the category of costs (charges, problems) that are associated with the subject institution for individual entities and as to the aims of action that individual entities may formulate in connection with the subject institution.

As for the formulation of hypotheses concerning the entities affected by the analyzed legal regulation (and actually, the pattern of action within which a given legal institution functions), there can be defined four basic categories of entities of the given activity pattern: the source, the holder (the disposer, the administrator), the beneficiary and the user.

Source is determining the sources of creation of the researched norms (especially legal norms) that will allow drawing conclusions on its effectiveness, especially with regard to the assumptions formally articulated during the legislative process. The source is the actual (real) initiator of introduction into the social circulation of specific norms (solutions, institutions, rules of action). Strictly speaking, it is about the source of the key elements of the normative set. The source are mainly the entities with a significant causative potential (e.g., with a significant ability to project power) as well as large, highly integrated professional groups, large business entities, social organizations, political parties, and – of course – the public authorities, in particular, the center representing the political orientation being dominant in a given moment.

From the psychological perspective, the source of creation of the law is the emergence of the belief that some way of achieving the aim of action (mainly: achieving some benefit) should be propagated within a given community and protected by this community (and, strictly speaking, by the subjects representing this community, as the political power and the apparatus of government subordinate to it). One should therefore ask what triggers this belief? Whose and what aims of action? Aims in line, or opposite? Who profits by the introduction into circulation of a new legal norm? What measures of impact do they have? Who shall bear the costs associated with the establishment of a new formal institution? Do they have measures of impact which can offset the importance of protecting the rule by the apparatus of power? What is the relation between the pressure for the introduction of a legal rule into circulation and the opposition to its formalization? What determines gaining advantage by any of these trends and in what conditions there may occur a turning point in favor of the trend to formalize the rule of an action, and not for the benefit of the reverse trend?

Very often, although not always, the source is the same entity as the beneficiary (the entity benefiting from the use of the norm, for example, a political, social or professional group).

Holderis – most often – a body of public authority (the traditionally understood legislative bodies, courts and tribunals, etc.). It can formalize, modify, supplement and spread the rules and finally derogate them (withdraw from circulation). The roles of the source and the holder can be combined in the

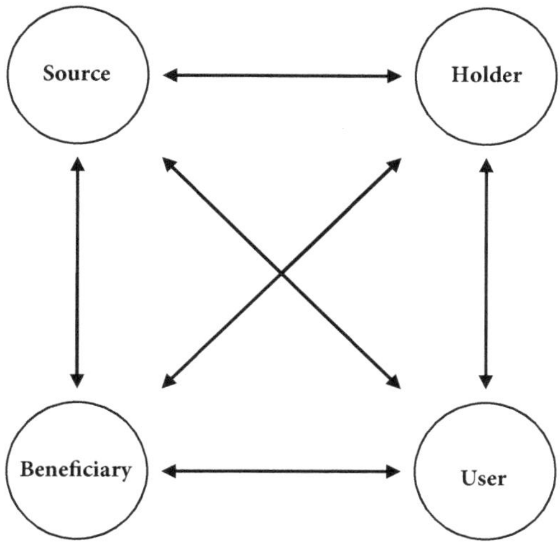

Fig. 19: Subjects of the normative set. Source: Paweł Chmielnicki (edt), Anna Dybała, Michał Stachura, *Activity Rules of Economic Man in Society as the Source of Legal Norms*, 1st edn, LexisNexis 2010, 80.

hand of one entity, but often they are also distributed. As to the role of the holder, apart from the central authorities, it can be any entity that has power locally.

User is a person (collective entity) which functions in a way specified by the analyzed rules incurring, especially the costs of their functioning.

Beneficiary is the person (collective entity) which benefits from the application of the analyzed rules (receives payment).

The roles of the user and the beneficiary does not have to cover – this particularly concerns the patterns of action based on the rules of receiving goods in virtue of belonging to a community, but, in most cases, concerning the separation of these roles there occur relations between the user and the beneficiary that create the reasons for undertaking an action by the user. Similarly, the source's and the holder's roles do not need to cover the user's and the beneficiary's roles, though – undoubtedly – there are strong logical premises for accumulating the roles of the source of the pattern of action and its beneficiary: the entity with the potential for endorsing an element of the pattern does it – as a rule – for its own benefit.

From the point of view of the role played by particular entities in the law-making process, three basic categories of sources can be identified: 1) those that gave direction to the law-making initiative and constantly promoted it with their activities, proposed ideas and specific projects, we can say that these entities are "appropriate" or "original sources of regulation"; 2) those that behaved passively in terms of reporting directions of legislative work and specific projects, but their occurrences were crucial for ending the law-making process, so they played the role of a specific "catalyst" of beginning the law-making process, they were necessary for its creation but they did not affect the content of the regulation (or it was the minimum impact)); 3) those who were involved in the law-making process in spite of their will and only then began to influence the directions of legislative work and submit specific projects. It can be said that these entities are "additional" or "accessory" sources of regulation, that they have become sources in a sense "by the way". In the latter group can be found, among others entities that even attempted to block the law-making process (it can be said that at the initial stage they played the role of "anti-sources", i.e., suspensive sources), however – when its further course became inevitable – they assumed co-participation in this process. Accordingly, the three main categories of sources should be referred:

1) constitutive sources,
2) resolutely sources,
3) accessory sources.

The disposition of a process involving the fixation, by means of legal norms, of a specific normative set is – as a rule – a representative of public authority. He can formalize rules (creating law in the legislative process or decision as a court), modify it, supplement it, distribute it, and derogate (withdraw from circulation). The roles of the source and the holder can be combined in the hands of one entity, but they are often also separated. The sources are entities with significant causative potential (e.g., with significant capacity for projection of force resulting from economic advantage), as economic entities with large capital, integrated professional groups, social organizations, political parties and – of course – public authorities, in particular a center representing the dominant political orientation at a given moment. As far as the role of a holder is concerned, for example – in addition to the central organs of state power – it can be any entity with power in the local sphere.

As in the case of sources, the same categories of holders can be distinguished:

1) constitutive holders,
2) resolutely holders,
3) accessory holders.

A constitutive holder is one that plays a leading role in the process of formalizing the legal solution (it is the "host" of this process), for example, a chamber of parliament or a central public administration body (e.g., a minister). The resolutely holder may be, for example, the Constitutional Tribunal, which indicates the existence of a "legal gap" and the need to establish new solutions (creating a new one, or changing the existing scheme of action). The accessory holder is, for example, the body that participates in the inter-ministerial consultation procedure and submits its own proposals to the legislative proposal.

It should be noticed, that in the context of traditional legal dogmatics, issues related to the intentions of sources and managers of the legislative process, objectives that these entities guided and the forecasted socio-economic impact of the resulting regulation, are considered within the framework of the *ratio legis* concept. Legal argumentation refers to *ratio legis*, primarily as part of a teleological interpretation. Most often, however, it is made in isolation from any scientific findings, based on commonly available knowledge, private views of the author, or – at best – based on the official justification of the draft normative act. This approach to making a teleological interpretation is far from being insufficient, not to say unreliable. One can make credible claims about the *ratio legis* of regulation only after conducting professional scientific research that allows, among others, to know the extent of discrepancies between declarations reported in the official documents of the legislative process, and the real dimension of interests and impact of individual entities on the shape of the regulation, including the goals that can be achieved with it.

As to the benefits and costs, it should be emphasized that it is about costs (losses, burdens, problems) and payments (profits, benefits) in a broad sense, i.e., about every form of benefit or any form of burden, not just payments and costs in a narrow financial sense. The problem of benefits (payment) and costs (problems) related to the functioning of the analyzed institutions usually happens to be either vulgarized or ideologized. Meanwhile, the problem of payments and costs associated with the analyzed normative set should be analyzed in two ways: from the point of view of payments and benefits measurable with economic indicators and from the point of view of payments and costs immeasurable with economic indicators, which payments and costs should include first of all the ones in the understanding of individual psychology, since it is about norms of action and these always, ultimately, serve the realization of aims of human activity which result from the needs specified by the human psyche.

Indication of potential aims of action achievable with the use of the analyzed normative set is possible on the basis of thorough preparation of the cost-benefit balance sheet. These aims may be, for example, the main benefits associated with the analyzed institution or the resulting added value.

3.2.2.4 Reconstruction of Connections between Legal (Formalized) Norms (Phase 4)

These activities concern determining the ways of reaching by individual entities the individual payments/aims of action, possibly avoiding the costs and/or blocking another entity from achieving their aims of action, based solely on the analysis of formalized (legal) norms only. The research effect at this stage is to consist in creation of an incomplete model (pattern) of action, which is to bring to the interested entity the achievement of the intended aim. In other words, it is about the reconstruction of all these elements of the way to achieve the aim of action that can be "reconstructed" on the basis of knowledge of the legal standards alone.

3.2.2.5 Reconstruction of Connections between Legal (Formalized) Norms and Informalized Norms (Phase 5)

These activities concern to supplementing the knowledge of the ways of reaching by individual entities the individual payments/aims of action, possibly avoiding the costs and/or blocking another entity from achieving their aims of action, based on the analysis of informalized norms (e.g., the rules that determine the course of commodity-money exchange). The research effect at this stage is to consist in supplementing an incomplete model (pattern) of action which is to bring to the interested entity the achievement of the intended aim, created within phase 4 (based on the analysis of the status of law), with informal norms relating to the subject institution. To put it colloquially, the essence of these research activities is to find which elements (rules) are missing in the pattern of action reconstructed by a lawyer and to fill the gaps.

3.2.2.6 Verification of Working Hypotheses and Findings from Phases 3–5 (Phase 6)

These activities are intended to verify the working hypotheses (preliminary assumptions) adopted in phases 1 and 3, as to separating of formalized (legal) norms and informalized norms, referring to the analyzed institutions, as to the category of entities affected by functioning of the analyzed normative set, as to the category of payments (benefits) that these entities can achieve in connection with functioning of the subject institution, as to the category of costs (charges, problems) that are associated with the subject institution for individual entities and as to the aims of action that individual entities may formulate in connection with the subject institution. This verification becomespossible due to the identification of connections between formal and informal norms which was made within the two previous research phases, and also due to the analysis of data on the effects of the impact of the analyzed normative set. To put it colloquially, it is about looking again at the problem basing on a significant expansion of knowledge of the analyzed normative set resulting, among other things, from confrontation of different research perspectives represented by the project participants.

3.2.2.7 Assessment of the Nature of Pressure on the Formalization of the Analyzed Institution and the Socio-Economic Effects of Its Impact (Phase 7)

This phase concerns formulating conclusions as to: 1) premises for formalizing the norms that have been identified within the previous research activities, 2) factors that generate real and potential effects of functioning of the analyzed normative set. To put it colloquially, it is about indicating which relations between which considered norms forming the socio-economic order are critical to the establishment of a new formalized normative set, including new legal norms. This indication becomes possible among other things due to preparation, during the previous research activities, the balance of benefits and costs of entities whose aims of action are directly related to the analyzed normative set, which balance allows indicating which of the pressures associated with individual costs and benefits lead to gaining an advantage through the trend aiming at formalization of norms and not through the reverse trend, i.e., aregulation (refraining from formalizing norms) or deregulation (exclusion of a given institution from the system of legal norms), including an analysis of gathered research data concerning the socio-economic effects of functioning of the analyzed normative set.

3.2.2.8 Forecasting and Formulating Recommendations (Phase 8)

It concerns comparing the results of previous research activities with already available knowledge of the essence of the analyzed normative set and the nature of its impact. In short, it is about indicating to what extent the constitutive sources' and constitutive holders' assessments differed from the conclusions reached due to the use of a scientific approach presented here. The possibility to formulate predictions as to the further evolution of the analyzed institution and recommendations within the optimization of legislative policy and related fields (economic policy, social policy, etc.) should be considered as an added value to the research results. For example, it is possible to assess how analyzed normative set, including analyzed legal regulations, correlate with the hitherto existing status of the socio-economic order and what possibilities there are of achieving the effects assumed by the legislator.

3.3 Example: A True Beneficiary of the Act of 16 September 2011 on the Protection of the Rights of a Buyer of a Flat or a Single-Family Home from the Developer[7]

3.3.1 Subject of Research

Officially, the adoption of this law was justified by the protection of financial interests of developer's clients. At some point, the first cases of bankruptcy of development companies appeared (cases had their final by the Constitutional Tribunal). The group of customers remained without money and without a flat. Work on the law in the Polish parliament was marked by haste related to the upcoming election campaign. The purpose of the Members of Parliament's activity was to obtain a favorable election result in the upcoming general elections, including thanks to gaining the favor of a large group of voters, such as developers' clients (about 1,600,000 interested). The question arose on how to provide this protection?

In the justification of the design of the legislative project (RIA), the state of protection the economic interests of the buyers of flat or a home was indicated, as – practically – the only premise of the legislative initiative. The justification for the Act of 16 September 2011 contained an impact assessment of the regulation, which was *in exstenso*, as follows:

"The proposed regulation will not affect the public finance sector, including the state budget and budgets of local government units in the context of the proposed changes, because the change does not cause any additional burdens for these budgets. It is possible, however, to increase budget revenues, indirectly, as a result of the revival of the primary housing market and their purchase at an earlier stage.

The project will have no impact on the competitiveness of the economy and entrepreneurship, including the functioning of enterprises.

The proposed regulation will not affect the situation and development of the regions.

The proposed regulation is not contrary to European Union law."

Therefore, the RIA conclusions were based on the statement that the Act may lead to a revival of the primary housing investment market, while it will have

7 The research results of the project have been extensively discussed in the book Paweł Chmielnicki (edt), Paweł Bała, Anna Chmielnicka, Paweł Chmielnicki, Daria Danecka, Joanna Kozińska, Katarzyna Kurzępa – Dedo, Piotr Ruczkowski, Aleksander Słysz, Przemysław Sporek, Piotr Stec, Igor Styn, Andrzej Szplit, Mariusz Załucki *Nabycie lokalu lub domu od dewelopera. Wykładnia przepisów i efekty ich stosowania*, Difin 2014.

no impact on the competitiveness of the economy and entrepreneurship. The main, actually the only beneficiaries of the new regulations, the authors of the justification for the design of the Act's project they looked for buyers of a flat or a single – family house from a developer.

The research carried out in accordance with the method described above revealed that the catalog of beneficiaries and the effects of the Act, as indicated in the justification of the Act's draft, is very incomplete. Research findings referring to the real beneficiaries of the Act, as well as its real effects, are presented in a nutshell as below.

4.3.2 Main Sources and Their Goals

a) Banks as Constitutive Sources

In the case of normative set formalized by the Act of 16 September 2011 on the protection of the rights of the buyer of a flat or a single-family home (Journal of Laws of 2011 No. 232, item 1377, further: Act of 16 September 2011), the most important constitutive source should be recognize the sector of mortgage banks.

The environment of the mortgage banks had two basic aspects in mind. As the goal of the legislative initiative, particularly exposed at the final stage of the law-making process (2010–2011), protection of the buyer's interest in the premises or house was officially and strong indicated, both in terms of increasing control over the development project during its implementation and in terms of mitigating the effects of its failure.

Their real bank's objective was to be achieved by imposing on developers the obligation to hold a "fiduciary account" for a development project. This solution was postulated for many years, practically from the very beginning of the development industry in Poland, but it was postulated without any success until there were no cases of bankruptcy of entrepreneurs running a development activity. When the first cases of this kind appeared, they allowed for a fundamental enrichment of arguments used by mortgage banks, emphasizing their credibility and social significance.

As the goal that banks wanted to achieve, it should be also mentioned the minimization of credit risk. It is, among others, the fact that the accumulation of funds on the fiduciary account is an additional mechanism that ensures effective satisfaction of the bank's receivables, but not only. The formalization of the normative set in its present form allows the banks to offer "packages" of products including: a fiduciary account (including two options" "open account" and "closed account"), a loan for a developer and loans to buyers. Of course, by selling services in such a "package", the risk associated with granting a loan decreases to a negligible level.

Fees for maintaining a new form of accounts seem doubtful as an important goal (advantage) that banks wanted to achieve, due to the limited number of such accounts and the amount of fees for their maintenance. The point is that the adoption of the described solutions should result in a significant increase in the number of loan agreements concluded.

The essence of the normative set involving the purchase of a flat or a house from a developer in Poland, before 2011 was that the developer could implement the investment from funds paid in gradually by the buyers. In this way, the credit agreement was concluded by the buyer but not by the developer. A large number of development companies acted in such way before 2012.

The effect of creating requirements obliging buyers to collect money on the fiduciary account and to pay them to the developer as the investment is implemented may be – for many (maybe most?) developers – the need to finance a development project first with a loan granted by the bank. This is because the money paid by buyers, in the current legal status, can only be credited to the developer's account after some time, at the earliest after the completion of a certain investment stage. In particular, the agreement with the bank may even provide that the funds accumulated on the fiduciary account will be transferred to the developer only after completion of the investment (in the "closed account" option). This means that the investment will have to be, until the very end, financed by the developer from a loan granted by the bank. The developer will be able to spend the funds paid by the buyers to repay the loan no sooner than after the investment has been completed. To put it simply, currently instead of one loan (for buyers), the bank will be able to provide two, in connection with the same investment (for the buyer and for the developer).

b) Consumers and Media as Resolutely Sources

Consumers, i.e., buyers of a flat or a house from a developer, were the key resolutely source of normative set formalized by Act of 16 September 2011. However, it should be emphasized that this group played only the role of a "catalyst" of the legislative process. They only submitted a request for protection from the State (which resulted in a decision of the Polish Constitutional Tribunal), while they did not intend to adopt any specific solutions. Admittedly, without the active occurrence of consumers, it would probably not have been possible to enact Act of 16 September 2011. However, this group did not play any further role, especially in defining the content of legal norms that should belong to a formally defined normative set. In short, the aim of the consumer's environment – buyers of flat or house from the developer was to minimize the economic and living risks on the part of the buyer.

It should be added that the activity of some media played an important role at certain points in the legislative process, especially at the stage of parliamentary work. The pressure of the media on the adoption of the regulation was of great importance for speeding up legislative work.

c) *MPs and Polish Association of Development Companies as Accessory Sources*

The role of a holder (see above) is a typical role of a parliamentarian in the law-making process. In this case, it is also possible to speak about the role of the source, by some parliamentarians, because the draft of Act was a parliamentary project, and its creation was – in part – dictated in favor of obtaining a favorable electoral result in the forthcoming general election (autumn 2011).

Environment of developers was, in the first place, the "anti-source" of regulation, because – through the organization that represents them – the Polish Association of Development Companies (Polski Związek Firm Deweloperskich – PZFD) – they usually tried to block the adoption of the Act altogether.

PZFD has become an active source since the commencement of work in the Polish parliament (Sejm RP) and since then has had a significant impact on the bill. The aim of PZFD, representing the environment of developers *in gremio*, was to minimize the negative effects of new regulations for these entrepreneurs, primarily taking the form of higher investment costs.

The developer's environment was divided in the impact assessment of the regulation and its part (i.e., the largest companies, especially with the majority shareholding), could perceive the long-term benefits of regulation. Its anticipated effect may be the oligopolization of the real estate development market by eliminating competition of small and medium-sized enterprises. The problem for them is that Act of 16 September 2011 generates such transaction costs that only entrepreneurs with adequate capital may incur that costs.

3.3.3 Main Holders and Their Goals

a) *MPs as Constitutive Holders*

The attitude of the majority of MP's signed under the project can be described as passive. Deputies had little influence on the shape of the act. There are many indications that activating the group of deputies who submitted the project was associated with the pressure of a social factor combined with a media pressure factor. Documents of the legislative process do not allow to reconstruct unquestionably, whether the initiative of running the case at the Sejm RP, actually came from the authorities of the Platforma Obywatelska (PO – political party which had a majority in Sejm RP) club or from a group of deputies, and perhaps only from one member of parliament – with the prior consent of the club's authorities. Work on the act was characterized by a hasty, associated with the election campaign. The aforementioned rush had its impact on the course of legislative work and the substantive solutions contained in the Act. Among others there was no consideration of other forms of protection of the buyer's rights, although there was available knowledge about other options for this protection than just a fiduciary account. However, no analysis of the effectiveness of individual protection models was carried out.

b) Constitutional Tribunal as resolutely holder

The formal premise of undertaking a legislative initiative leading to the adoption of the so-called The developer's Act is a decision of the Constitutional Tribunal of August 2, 2010. The Constitutional Tribunal noted a "gap in the law", in the form of non-regulation of the contract, the object of which would be to oblige the developer to construction of a flat or a home for the purpose of transferring it to the buyer against payment (the so-called developer agreement). In connection with this, he signaled to the Sejm RP and the Council of Ministers the need to initiate a legislative process regarding the regulation of development agreement in order to ensure the protection of the rights of buyers.

c) President of the Office of Competition and Consumer Protection as Accessory Holder

Among the public authorities that participated in the creation of the Act of 16 September 2011 and had a significant impact on his content, it should be mentioned first of all the President of the Office of Competition and Consumer Protection (Urząd Ochrony Konkurencji i Konsumentów – UOKiK). Other public authorities –in particular the Council of Ministers – initially did not show or showed little interest in bringing a legislative initiative aimed at increasing the protection of potential buyers of flats and houses. Apart from representatives of the Minister of Justice, none of the members of the Council of Ministers was rather involved in legislative work.

3.3.4 *Main Beneficiaries*

a) Buyer of a Flat or a House from a Developer

This category includes any person who, under a developer agreement, is entitled to transfer the right to it, referred to in art. 1 of the Act of 16 September 2011.

b) Banks

The effect of the Act will strengthen the position of banks as lenders and institutions controlling the implementation of development projects. It should be pointed out that, formally, all banks can benefit to the same extent. However, only those banks that are strong from the capital and organizational point of view will be able to benefit from the effects of the law,.

c) Developers

Indication of developers among the beneficiaries of the normative set may be surprising, however, the developer's environment may experience the effects of the regulation to a very different extent. Medium and small developers are unlikely to derive any significant benefits due to the Act of 16 September 2011 (mainly they will incur costs), whereas the situation of large companies, especially those created with foreign capital and capital-related with mortgage banks, is different. They can be a significant advantage due to the oligopolization of the developers' market.

d) MPs

Pre-election, quick, legislative process was connected with the goal of obtaining a favorable election result.

3.3.5 *Main Users*

a) Developers

The role of developers as users of the implemented solutions is determined mainly by two factors: the construction of the developer contract and the construction of security measures. They mainly concern the costs of new regulations, while the benefits will be little (only the largest companies can benefit more, but only in the longer term).

It should be noted that some entities currently conducting real estate development activities may try to adapt the profile of their own operations in such a way that statutory requirements may not be covered (change the financing scheme of their ventures in such a way that, for example, only fully completed properties may be sold).

b) Banks

The construction of security measures makes banks one of the main users of the new normative set, not only in the scope of keeping accounts and granting guarantees, but mainly due to the obligation to control the actions of the developer – the banks gained the right to inspect the fiduciary account of the developer and control documentation of the investment. They become jointly responsible for the result of the development venture, which is associated with the increase in the so-called reputational risk.

c) Buyers

The buyer becomes a user of the scheme even before signing the developer agreement, because the developer is obliged to deliver the prospectus with attachments upon the request of the person interested in the development contract – the prospectus must be prepared by the developer who starts selling the given development project. The buyer is a user primarily as a party to the development contract. The costs incurred by the buyers include, above all, the increase in the prices of flats and houses, caused by the increase of operating costs on the part of developers.

d) Public Notaries

Public notaries become the users of the regulation due to – required for the validity of the contract – the form of a notarial contract. By their duties, they participate in the protection of the rights of the parties to the contract. Regulations of the Act of 16 September 2011 introduce a number of solutions that are burdensome for public notaries, which measurable running costs.

3.3.6 Main Benefits and Costs

a) Benefits

Theoretically, the main benefit for a buyer of a flat or a house from a developer is to increase the level of economic security, both in terms of increasing control over the development project during its implementation, as well as in mitigating the effects of its failure.

The protection of buyers' interests is based on the introduction of mechanisms that verify the activities of developers, including through the involvement of the third party to this control (banks).

The increase, in the sense of economic security, for real estate buyers is achieved by legal instruments resulting from the Act of 16 September 2011, such as:

- increasing access to information;
- applying the form of a notarial contract for a development agreement;
- defining the terms of cash delivery and withdrawals from fiduciary account,
- reducing the financial risk of withdrawal from the transaction (in the developer's contract it is not permissible to provide a transfer fee).

Minimizing the risk of economic losses is related to the protection of the buyer's finances against the consequences of the failure of the development project. The increase in the buyer's sense of security is achieved through the conviction that in the event of insolvency or bankruptcy of the developer, it will be possible to complete the investment or recover funds. The development contract is the basis for the buyer's claims in the mortgage register, and the buyer's claim is subject to mandatory disclosure.

Minimizing the risk of losses also results from the obligation to return money to purchasers in the event of a reduction in the area ofa flat or house, in relation to the conditions included in prospectus, which is a part of the notarial contract (!).

In the case of banks, should be paid attention to the difference in the situation when the bank "only" keeps the fiduciary account for the developer, from the situation when the bank runs the account and simultaneously grants the loan to the developer and / or its clients.

As already mentioned, the main benefit of banks should not be seen in the sale of a new product, which is a developer's fiduciary account, but in creating situation that requires the financing of a development project with a loan and not with money paid by buyers. In other words, thanks to the formalization of the new normative set, de facto, one of the source of financing the investment, i.e., the capital of buyers, was "cut off" to the developers.

In the case when the bank offers fiduciary accounts as a "separate product", fees and commissions related to their servicing (foundation, operation) in unitary terms are high, because the bank tries to cover the service costs and the risk associated with their operation. The increase in revenues from fees and commissions of banks maintaining fiduciary accounts based on the provisions of the forefront is not significant for the bank. Also due to the high formal requirements related to the maintenance of these accounts, banks do not pursue an aggressive sales policy.

The benefits that a bank obtains from running a developer's account are not limited to fees for the account. The account-keeping bank has a real impact on the activity of developers and not only developers connected with credit (and / or capital) with a given bank. This means minimizing the risk associated with granting loans to developers for the implementation of investments and for buyers of real estate offered by them, who may be encouraged to use the offer of the same bank that will run a housing account.

Only the bank has the right to terminate the housing contract (both "open" and "closed"), it increases not only the security of influence, stability of cooperation, but also predictability regarding future events.

In the situation when bank is connected with the developer, both the account maintenance contract and the loan agreement, the main bank's benefit is gains from the increase in the volume of loans granted to developers by bank. The need to accumulate buyers' money on the account is a security for the loan, reduces the risk on the part of the bank and opens the possibility of granting loans to a greater extent than before (developers will be forced to reach for loans more often than before, because the obligation to hold a trust account makes it impossible for the developer to get a loan at the "expense of the buyer"), thus increasing the profit of mortgage banks. This is far greater than the profits resulting from the mere operation of a fiduciary account and in general the main financial benefit that any entity may derive from the entry into force of the legal solutions. Increasing the profits of individual banks results, therefore, mainly due to the simultaneous granting of loans to developers (and – possibly – buyers), and keeping an account for them. The sale of a "package" of services also means minimizing the risk associated with granting loans to developers and purchasers of their real estate.

As for developers, the situation of the so-called average developer (small and medium developers) is different from the situation of the largest companies in the industry, including companies with foreign capital and capital related with mortgage banks. First, the situation of small and medium-sized developers will be discussed, including issues common to the entire development industry.

Among the main benefits raised by developers, should be indicated:

- Increased buyers' confidence in property development investments, which results mainly from the need to draw up a development contract by a public notary and to transfer funds to a fiduciary account;
- Improving the image of the developer community as fully professional;
- Increased sense of responsibility for the effects of activities carried out on developers, and thus the overall stability of the industry.

At present special consequences for large development companies, companies with good access to crediting (e.g., companies with capital links with mortgage banks, companies with foreign capital) will be indicated. The benefits that these companies can derive may appear as a long-term effect of market consolidation, i.e.:

- To increase the flexibility of supply in relation to the demand needs of the market;
- Decreasing price competitiveness on the market (resulting in low price drops in case of economic downturn and large price increases in case of economic recovery).

It should be stipulated that both phenomena may also depend on a number of other factors, which makes it difficult to forecast them.

The mastering of the development market by the largest companies, especially with the overwhelming share of foreign capital, means the oligopolization of the market. The discussed normative set is therefore the most advantageous for large developers who sell flats on a mass scale. The Act of 16 September 2011 may reward these developers (reduction of costs by cheaper financing) who operate within financial groups, with well-developed mortgage financing and knowledge of the specifics of the real estate market in Poland.

b) Costs

The economically measurable costs of the discussed normative set, in the long run, are primarily the increase in the prices of flats or houses. In particular, this will take place in the event of forecasts regarding the oligopolization of the development services market resulting in an increase in the price and the liquidation of small and medium-sized developer companies.

Among negative (for the buyer) the Act of 16 September 2011's effects is weakening of protection of the buyer's interests due to the greater importance of the arrangement between the bank and the developer (than between the developer and the buyer) and due to the lack of connection between the developer agreement (concluded between the developer and the buyer) and the content of the fiduciary account (concluded between the developer and the bank). Another consequence is the weakening of protection of the buyer's interests due to the advantage of measures securing the interests of banks (mainly: securing the bank's mortgage debt, but also general information advantage of banks) holding a fiduciary account and granting loans, worsening the ability to satisfy a claim against the developer.

We can even talk about the apparentness of protecting the rights of buyers. Formally, in the light of the Act of 16 September 2011the interests of the buyer are protected by the accumulation of funds on the fiduciary account in the event of the bankruptcy of the developer. Nevertheless, the Act of 16 September 2011 is silent on the resolution of conflicts of interest between various creditors of the developer, which are in particular the buyer and the bank. Therefore, this collision is settled on general principles, and these give an advantage – de facto – to banks. The thing is that the protection of buyers' rights at the expense of the mortgagee (bank) would mean that banks would resign from financing the investment (due to the impossibility of obtaining a satisfactory loan security for the bank).

Among the main costs incurred by the bank that maintains the fiduciary account for a development project, the following should be mentioned:

- Obligations of banks related to the control of a development project (co-responsibility for the correct implementation of a development project, e.g., costs of assessing the state of the investment);
- The risk of the bank losing credibility due to the failure of the development venture controlled by the bank (risk of joint responsibility for the improper implementation of the development project) – due to the need to make the decision to launch the funds deposited on the fiduciary account, there is a very significant risk of reputation on the bank's side, making an incorrect decision;
- Loss of clients (and therefore profits) as a result of poor assessment of the development project and lowering the position in the industry ranking – as a result of deteriorating the bank's reputation;
- The labor-intensive servicing of the aforementioned solutions in relation to the obligations for the bank resulting from the provisions of the Act, particularly concerns the obligations related to the control of the investment and generation of documentation regarding the financial condition of the developer.

In the case of a problem of costs resulting for the developer from the discussed regulations, it is both an increase in transaction costs (in the understanding of the economics of transaction costs), and the appearance of entry barriers for entities wishing to start a property development business.

In general, the costs of the entire industry are the weakening of the economic position of small and medium-sized developer films, oligopolization or monopolization of the market and the resulting increase in property prices.

As a result of the regulation being set up, some developers may have problems related to:

- Obtaining credit (insufficient creditworthiness);
- Economic profitability of investments in new projects, with the necessity of incurring other costs resulting from Act of 16 September 2011.

The economic unprofitability of the investment will result mainly from higher unit costs per m^2 of the newly built (usable) area of the flat. The aforementioned phenomena will be additionally strengthened by the crisis in the construction industry and the residential real estate market.

As a result of the decrease in competitiveness, development companies will either be forced to merge into larger enterprises, or they will go bankrupt or change their business profile and leave residential real estate from the development market. In the event of bankruptcy, classic bankruptcy costs will arise, such as:

- loss of job by the developer's employees and its co-operators,
- loss of creditors due to write-offs of overdue receivables that cannot be recovered from the bankruptcy estate.

The issues discussed above create "entry barriers" for those who want to undertake property development. Therefore, there is a real risk of the developer's market decreasing, mainly due to the small profitability of the venture itself (too high costs with a low margin), difficulties in gaining access to banking instruments (fiduciary account, loan). Increasing the complexity of development activities may result in smaller companies, without proper legal and financial resources, even with adequate capital, who decide to re-arrange or withdraw from the market. As a result, the market may be oligopolized – developers without proper capital will be able to enter the market without easy access to bank loans or other forms of bank financing. Increasing the entry barrier for new companies will limit the number of development companies on the market in the future, which will greatly facilitate the control of property prices.

Meanwhile, the analysis of the expected benefits and costs leads to the conclusion that the economic benefits will be primarily related to banks, especially mortgage banks, as well as the largest development companies, in particular companies with foreign capital and affiliated companies with banks. The economic costs will be borne mainly by consumers, small and medium-sized developers and entities cooperating with them, mainly from the construction industry.

3.3.7 Summing Up of the Project

Abovementioned legislative actions were to lead to the adoption of solutions that should protect the interests of buyers and "order" the developer's market.

Fig. 20: The normative set based on the Act of 16 September 2011 on the protection of the rights of a buyer of a flat or a single-family home from the developer (basic stages).

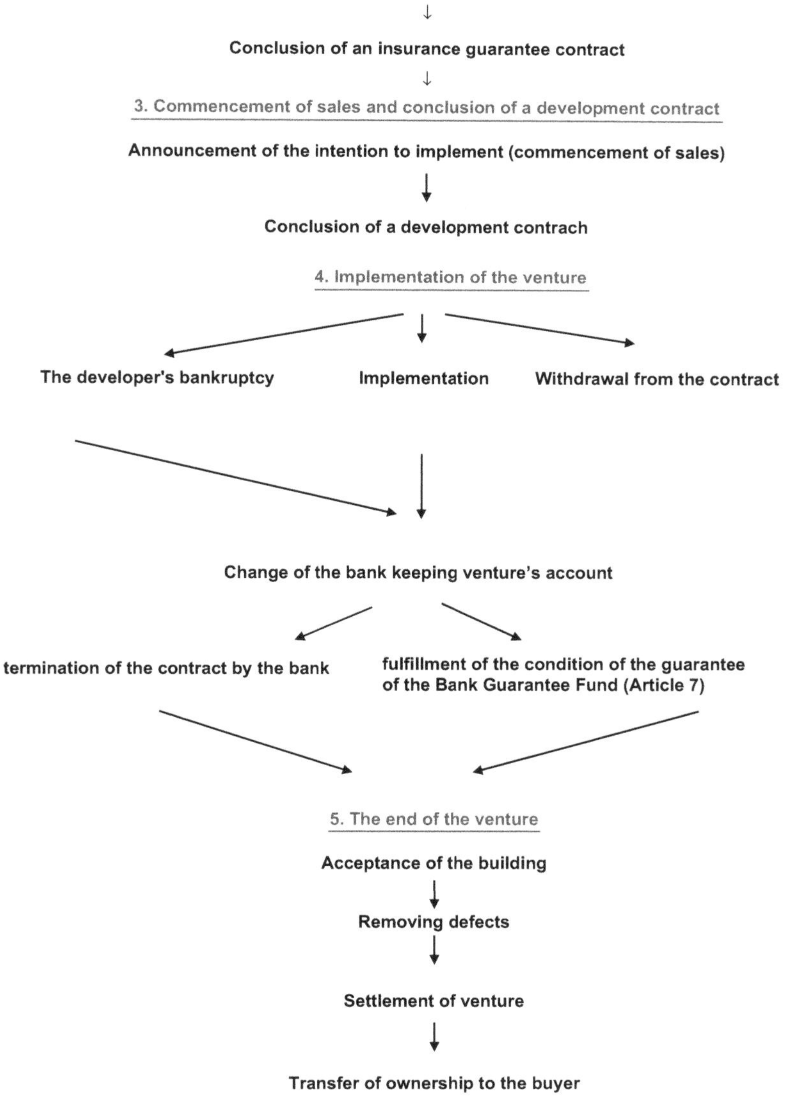

However, already on the basis of the information available during the legislative process, it was possible to conclude that the proposed solutions may lead to the elimination of small and medium-sized development companies from the market, while placing barriers to new entities wishing to enter the market, which increases the risk of increasing the cost of purchasing premises. In addition, the solutions already adopted at the stage of legislative work raised doubts as to the effectiveness of the proposed measures to protect the interests of buyers (including the adopted methods of securing bank claims, the bankruptcy of the developer).

Banks providing mortgage loans have long been proposing to regulate the principles of financing a development project by introducing the obligatory accumulation of funds paid by buyers on the so-called "fiduciary account". As the main objective of such regulation, banks declared the minimization of economic risk on the part of developers' clients.

However, the result of creating norms that requiring the buyers to collect money on the fiduciary account and to pay them to the developer once in a while (as the investment progresses), would be – for many developers – to finance the development project with a loan granted by the bank, not directly from the money paid by the buyers. In short, the compulsory accumulation of funds on a fiduciary account would mean the abolition of the option of "crediting the developer at the expense of the buyers". Simply put, by formalizing the mentioned solution, instead of one loan (for buyers), the bank would provide two, for the same investment (for the developer's client and for the developer). The bankruptcy of a well-known development company has credited the proposal of banks, which became the basis of the act.

From the economic point of view, it was of great importance. As according to the estimates of the "Employers of the Republic of Poland" organization, in mid-2011 (i.e., during the legislative works), approximately53 % of development investments were carried out without a bank loan in the "project finance" formula. The Act of 16 September 2011did not significantly improve the protection of buyers' rights, because banks can still satisfy their claims against developers faster than the buyer. On the other hand, it significantly increased the cost of implementing a development project and created the possibility of a significant increase in profits by banks that grant mortgage loans.

General Conclusions

The reorientation of the current lawyers' research approach must therefore relate to: identification of the subject of research, the purposes of the cognitive process and methods of scientific research that are considered to be adequate for the assumed research objectives. The question about the sources and the effectiveness of the law means giving up the research of the law as if it was an autarkic phenomenon or some kind of autopoietic system and reporting – in this place – a desire to the research the law as a part of social relations (interactions, processes). A very important stage, since – in a particular aspect – finalizing (at a given moment) the course of social interactions, but, however, only one stage of these processes. The adoption of this point of view entails the need for changes in the traditional setting of cognitive objectives. The traditionally (i.e., according to the paradigm of legal positivism) formulated cognitive objective, which is the exegesis of legal rules, should become a partial aim: an intermediate stage of the research process, one of the tools for achieving the fundamental objective which is to determine the relations between the process of creating and applying the law and other interactions taking place in the community. In this connection, the cognitive method, which is now considered by the majority of lawyers active in the field of science to be the only appropriate scientific method, i.e., the method of exegesis based on linguistic-logical knowledge corresponding to the assumptions of legal hermeneutics, should become only one of the methods used. At this point, there appears a necessity to develop new research methods adapted to new definitions of the object and purpose of the research.

References

Chmielnicki, Paweł (eds), AnnaDybała, MichałStachura, *Activity Rules of Economic Man in Society as the Source of Legal Norms*, 1st edn Warsaw, LexisNexis 2010.

Chmielnicki,Paweł (eds), PawełBała, AnnaChmielnicka, PawełChmielnicki, DariaDanecka, JoannaKozińska, KatarzynaKurzępa - Dedo, PiotrRuczkowski, AleksanderSłysz, PrzemysławSporek, PiotrStec, IgorStyn, AndrzejSzplit, MariuszZałucki,*Nabycie lokalu lub domu od dewelopera. Wykładnia przepisów i efekty ich stosowania*, 1st edn Warsaw, Difin 2014.

Chmielnicki, Paweł,'The Research Method of Association for the Research on Sources and Functions of Law",*Przegląd Prawa Publicznego* 2015, vol. 3, 95–105.

Gaweł, Tomasz, Klimczak, Michał, 'Pojęcie instytucji w prawie i ekonomii' in *Ład instytucjonalny w gospodarce*, Barbara Polszakiewcz, Jerzy Boehlke (eds), Toruń 2005.

Hayek, Friedrich August v., 'The Results of Human Action but Not of Human Design' in *Studies in Philosophy, Politics and Economics*, 1st edn, Simon and Schuster 1967.

Hechter, Michael, *Principles of Group Solidarity*, 1st edn, Berkeley CA University of California Press 1987.

Jakubowski, Rafał M., 'Efektywność gospodarcza w ujęciu ekonomicznej teorii prawa własności – wybrane zagadnienia' in *Ład instytucjonalny w gospodarce*, Barbara Polszakiewcz, Jerzy Boehlke (eds), Toruń 2005.

Karpiński, Jakub, *Trzecia niepodległość. Najnowsza historia Polski*, 1st edn, Bertelsmann Media Warsaw 2001.

Krueger, Alan, 'The political of rent-seeking Society', *American Economic Review* 1974, vol. LXIV,291–303.

Magiera, Ryszard, *Modele i metody statystyki matematycznej*, 3rd edn, Oficyna Wydawnicza GiS Warsaw 2002.

Michalak, Ryszard, Piasecki, Andrzej K., Historia polityczna Polski 1952–2002, *„Akapit" Jolanta Piasecka* 2003.

Morawski,Wojciech, *Dzieje gospodarcze Polski*, 2nd edn, Difin Warsaw 2011.

Olson, Mancur, *The Logic of Collective Action: Public Goods and the Theory of Groups*, 2nd edn, Harvard Economic Studies Harvard University Press 1971.

Sobczyk, Mieczysław, *Statystyka*, 1st edn, Państwowe Wydawnictwo Naukowe Warsaw 1991.

Szarzec, Katarzyna,*Racjonalny podmiot gospodarczy w klasycznej myśli ekonomicznej i jej współczesnych kontynuacjach*, 1st edn, Fundacja Promocji i Akredytacji Kierunków Ekonomicznych: Polskie Towarzystwo Ekonomiczne Warsaw 2005.

Sztompka, Piotr, *Socjologia. Analiza społeczeństwa*, 1st edn, Znak Cracow 2002.

Tullock, Gordon,'The Welfare Cost of Tariffs, Monopolies and Theft', *Western Economic Journal*1976, vol. V,224–232.

Turek, Michał, 'Ekonomiczne podstawy zmiany instytucjonalnej, zmiana mikroekonomiczna i makroekonomiczna' in *Dokonania współczesnej myśli ekonomicznej. Ekonomia instytucjonalna – teoria i praktyka*, Urszula Zagóra-Jonszta (ed.), Wydawnictwo UE Katowice2006.

Woźniak Michał,Gabriel, 'Niesprawności kapitalizmu globalnego w świetle podejścia ekonomii instytucjonalnej. Wnioski dla Polski' in *Dokonania współczesnej myśli ekonomicznej. Ekonomia instytucjonalna – teoria i praktyka*, Urszula Zagóra-Jonszta (ed.), Wydawnictwo UE Katowice2006.

Alexandra C. Evans

5 Some Examples and Experience from Australian Income Tax Law

Abstract: The chapter discusses the gap between the standards of law making and theoretical design and what is implemented in real life in Australia with a focus on income tax legislation. The chapter uses two main examples. The first is Australia's project of rewriting the old income tax act into a new piece of legislation during the 1990s. The aim was simplification and to make the act more coherent and comprehensible. This project was never completed, so the legislation continues to straddle the two acts. The second example is the use of "principles-based" drafting. The chapter outlines what this approach means in English and Australian literature, and then critically analyses the use of this technique in Australia and its shortcomings. The chapter discusses the Australian Treasury's most recent approach in using principles-based drafting. The chapter then briefly suggests some recommendations and discusses broader challenges. Challenges include that: legislative adjustments are often made in reaction, to correct unintended consequences or address avoidance behaviour; and while we have had wide-ranging economic reviews of the tax system, these often prove hard to implement for a range of reasons, including a lack of consensus of interested parties during consultation, complexity of the subject matter and because most of the changes needed are politically unpalatable. The author gratefully acknowledges the generosity of the Law Design Office of the Australian Department of Treasury (Australian Treasury) in discussing the coherent principles approach and the drafting process with the author in September 2018. The views expressed in this chapter are the author's and do not reflect those of the Australian Treasury.

Keywords: Legislative drafting, plain English drafting, principles-based drafting, Australia, Australian income tax

I Introduction

This chapter is designed to explore the gap between the theoretical, organisational and practical levels and dimensions of the law-making process that was raised during the conference on "Theory, organisation and the practice of the law-making process". This chapter focuses on the Australian federal income tax legislation, and it is practically oriented. This focus was selected because Australia began experimenting with the drafting and expression of the rules in the Australian income tax legislation. To the outside observer, income tax legislation might seem like an odd venue for drafting experiments. That observation is well founded. This was, in fact, unusual in Australia.[1] However, as described below, it was largely driven by necessity, based on the idea that "changing the choice and organisation of words within the tax Acts would [can] deliver significant benefits to the community."[2]

In 1918, the Australian federal income tax legislation was short – it was printed on 20 pages – and the provisions were drafted using a simple structure and simple language. The legislation then was fairly easy to navigate and understand. If we fast forward one hundred years later, to 2018, the situation is dramatically different. In 2019, the primary income tax legislation spans 7,473 pages, and it is complex.[3] That complexity exists both in the ideas that underlie the provisions and the way in which they are written. This is part of a broader phenomenon as federal income tax legislation in other countries, such as the United States of America (US), is similarly saturated with complexity. An important question to ask is – how did we get here?

This chapter argues that, in Australia, this situation was created by the interaction of several different problems. The chapter outlines the problems and then describes two approaches Australia has used in an attempt to remedy it. The two approaches are: plain English drafting and principles-based drafting. An important part of the principles-based drafting project was an article written by Greg Pinder from Australian Treasury in 2005.[4] This was written after consultation with staff from both Treasury and the Australian Taxation Office. To date, Australian academic literature has not pursued whether the approach set out in that article was able to be implemented in practice, how successful it was and whether there were any shortcomings. This chapter fills this gap.

This practically oriented chapter is intended to supplement and enhance the points made in the theoretically oriented papers of the other international authors.

---

1 Graeme S Cooper, 'Text, Style and Presentation – Assessing the Drafting Experiment in Australian Tax Laws' (Legal Studies Research Paper No 08/92, Sydney Law School, 2008) 1.

2 ibid.

3 See Table 2 below, provided by the Law Design Office of Australian Treasury.

4 Greg Pinder, 'The coherent principles approach to tax law design', Australian Government, The Treasury, Economic Roundup, Autumn 2005 <http://archive.treasury.gov.au/documents/987/HTML/docshell.asp?URL=07_coherent_principles.asp> accessed 25 May 2019.

II The Problems That Led to the Current Situation

The state of the Australian federal income tax legislation described above was the result of a number of different but often interwoven problems. These can broadly be grouped into seven loose groups.

II.A Unstructured Growth in the Legislation

The first group is unstructured growth in the legislation. The first part of this point is growth simply in terms of length. As the graph below shows, the legislation grew fairly steadily until the mid-1970s. There was then a gradual acceleration until the mid-1990s, followed by a very significant acceleration from the late 1990s to around 2006.[5] There are various reasons for this. For example, a number of anti-avoidance provisions were inserted during the 1970s and early 1980s,[6] and a series of new and complex regimes were introduced from the end of the 1990s.[7] The significant drop during the 2000s was due to the repeal of a number of provisions that were seen to be inoperative, but the general trend, at least 2006, has been an increase in length.[8]

---

5 Commonwealth Parliament, House of Representatives, Committee of Taxation (2006) Report, Chapter 3, 51 [3.11].

6 Including: the introduction of rules to prevent parents' income splitting to their minor children through trusts: Income Tax Assessment Act 1936 (Aust) (ITAA 1936) div 6AA.

7 Including: the consolidation rules for groups of wholly owned companies; rules to classify an instrument as either debt or equity; and the taxation of financial arrangement rules.

8 Committee of Taxation's Report (2006) (n 5) 51–2 [3.12,3.13]. Practically at least one of these named inoperative provisions is still required to interpret remaining provisions, e.g., the holding period requirement to obtain the benefit of a franked dividend (the person must be a qualified person): Income Tax Assessment Act 1997 (Aust) (ITAA 1997), subdiv 207-F brings back to life the former ITAA 1936, div 1A of pt IIIA. Refer also to Table 2 below.

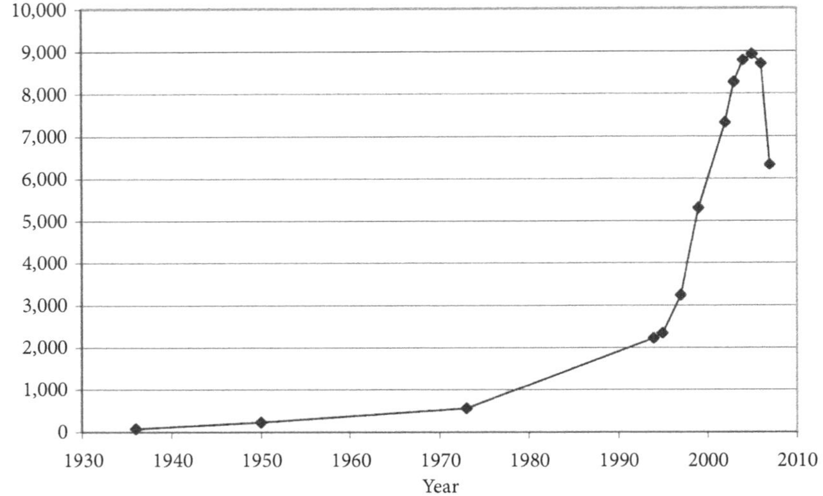

Graph showing number of pages in the Australian income tax legislation, 1936 to 2006[9]

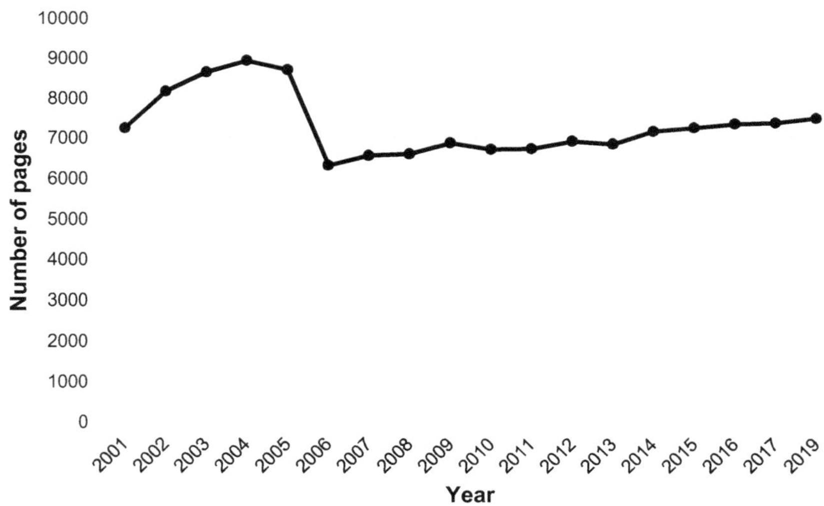

Graph showing number of pages in the Australian income tax legislation, 2001 to 2019[10]

9 Committee of Taxation's Report (2006) (n 5) 52 citing M Kobetsky and Michael Dirkis, *Income Tax* (Federation Press, 1997) 40.

10 Data sourced from legislation.gov.au and covers the primary income tax legislation. Data was provided to the author in a more comprehensive table compiled by the Law Design Office of Australian Department of Treasury.

The second point is that the changes were drafted at different times based on different policy agenda and using different drafting approaches.

The combination of these two points is that the legislation is voluminous.

II.B "Poorly Conceived Policy Choices"[11]

The second group has been described as "poorly conceived policy choices."[12] It is noted that Cooper used this label in a list of a number of different reasons to explain the complexity of the Australian income tax legislation, but he did not describe what this meant. This chapter argues that it covers several issues.

The first issue is that generally in tax, there is often no one ideal solution. This is evidenced by the fact that different countries often experience common problems but develop different ways of resolving them. This often due to legal parameters and the environment beyond tax, such as the competitive relationships between states in the US. Further, a perennial issue in tax is that often what economists view as an ideal solution is not able to be implemented because it is not practically feasible.[13] In other words, the ideal economic solution may not be the ideal legal or practical one. Another problem is that what is ultimately settled on may be designed only as a short term measure to address a particular problem but then, once it is in the legislation, the solution is extremely difficult to remove.[14]

A second issue is that, even if an ideal solution is developed, in Australia it is often challenging for the government to shepherd that solution (in the form of a bill) through Federal Parliament so that it forms part of Australian law. This is

---

11 Cooper, 'Text, Style and Presentation – Assessing the Drafting Experiment in Australian Tax Laws' (n 1) 2.

12 ibid.

13 One example is the allocation model for flow through taxation put forward by the Carter Commission which has not been adopted there or in another developed country: See also, Canada, Royal Commission on Taxation, *Report of the Royal Commission on Taxation – Volume 4: Taxation of Income* (Queen's Printer, Ottawa, Canada, 1967) (***Carter Commission Report 1967***) 6–7, 83–84. Another example is the cash flow tax model for corporations: e.g. Alan J Auerbach, Michael P Devereux, Michael Keen and John Vella, 'Destination-based Cash Flow Taxation' (February 6, 2017) Oxford Legal Studies Research Paper No 14/2017 <https://papers.ssrn.com/sol3/papers.cfm?abstract_id=2908158> accessed 25 May 2019.

14 Examples include the introduction of negative gearing and also the 2011 streaming measures for trusts: ITAA 1936, div 6E; ITAA 1997, subdiv 207-B (dividends) and subdiv 115-C (capital gains) – these were inserted by Tax Laws Amendment Act (2011 Measures No 5) Act (Aust) 2011, sched 2.

because tax measures involve both nuanced economic and technical arguments. These are not easily understood in lay terms. It is often extremely challenging for the government of the day to explain, let alone sell, the solution to the general (voting) public, particularly if the measure involves increasing the government's power of taxation and the government requires support from minor parties to secure the change. More sceptically, the technical nature of tax measures also creates the opportunity for the differing political parties to develop narratives about the solution to suit their broader political agenda. This problem is exacerbated where the government's popularity is important, for example, in the lead up to a tightly contested federal election. Further, historically, there has been a tendency for Australian governments to avoid or defer embarking on fundamental tax reform to implement solutions that would be hard to sell politically. So the issue here is not only that what is in the legislation is often based on poorly conceived policy choices, but also what is missing can based on similarly questionable policy choices. Often there are other factors, such as politics, at play.

II.C Reviews but Recommendations not Implemented

Between 1915 and 2018, the federal government initiated more than five reviews of the Australian tax system.[15] The review panels often comprised economists, members of academia and industry. These reviews often considered significant issues where it was challenging to find a robust solution. The reviews also tended to be focused on the longer term, so the reports they produced often considered proposals that would have involved significantly changing the existing system.[16] Despite the merits of those proposals and the arguments made in support of them, the governments of the day often either declined to implement them, deferred their consideration (which practically left the issue open for successive governments) or attempted to implement them but needed to abort

---

15 Including the Warren Kerr Royal Commission (1921–1922); Ferguson Royal Commission (1932–1934); Asprey Committee (1975); Treasury Draft White Paper (1985); Henry Tax Review (2008–2009): C John Taylor, 'Australian Corporate Tax Reform in the best of times and the worst of times'. There are other reviews (e.g., instigated by the tax advisory group to the government, the Board of Taxation) but the ones listed above are the most relevant to the current topic.

16 There are too many examples to list here, but one is that the Henry Tax Report questioned whether the imputation system for income derived through an Australian company was valuable to retain long term: Commonwealth of Australia, Treasury, 'Chapter B, B2–3: The Future of Dividend Imputation', Australia's Future Tax System (Australian Government Publishing Service 2009) (***Henry Tax Report***).

the attempt because the measure proved to be politically unpalatable to the general public.[17] This problem connects back with the previous one described in Section II.B., because this meant that often well-considered reform proposals that were supported by sound policy objectives never made it into the legislation. Consequently, problems that were identified and well-known often continued unremedied in the legislation. This chapter argues that these problems often are at the centre of foundational problems in many of the complex regimes.[18] So these identified but unresolved problems continue to affect many different parts of the legislation.

II.D Different Drafting Styles

Over time, the Australian federal income tax legislation was written using different drafting styles. Due to the number of changes between 1915 and 2018 and the range of agenda driving them, it is too arduous to track the rationale for the drafting style that was used for each tax measure. However, this chapter observes that there are several likely explanations.

One explanation is simply that drafting style changed over time. The legislation is evidence of the fact that, over time, there came to be a preference for detailed rules, and "certainty through detail",[19] over a sparsely and clearly written simple rule. Anecdotally, this appears to have been driven by the fear that a more abstractly written and general rule would not encompass the range of current and future situations that a more detailed rule would (**coverage**). Put another way, the fear was that the rule would be interpreted in a static not ambulatory way.

Another explanation is that the drafting practice in other areas of Australia law or in income tax law in other countries changed and that style began to influence drafting practices in Australia.

17 For example, the Coalition's proposal to introduce the uniform entity tax regime. This was discontinued in 2001 due to powerful lobbying from the National Farmers' Federation and the small business community: Peter Costello, 'Entity Taxation' (Media Release No 8, 27 February 2001) <http://www.petercostello.com.au/press/2001/2445-entity-taxation-a> accessed 25 May 2019.

18 An example is the problem of income splitting. This was considered in detail by the Asprey Committee: Commonwealth of Australia, Taxation Review Committee, *Full Report: 31 January 1975* (Australian Government Publishing Service, Canberra, Australia) (***Asprey Report***) 150–8. This issue recurs as a problem in relation to closely held private vehicles, namely discretionary trusts.

19 John Avery Jones, 'Tax Law: Rules or Principles' [1996] *British Tax Review* 580, 581.

A further explanation is that, as the income tax legislation came to cover more complex ideas that did not have a basis in economics and came be written more reactively to address particular practices, it was harder to express such rules as succinctly and clearly as the rules had been expressed in 1915.

II.E Reaction for Integrity Reasons

As stated in Part II.A. above, the primary motivator behind the growth in the legislation from the 1970s was the attempt to curb various avoidance practices that had developed. The technical bases of those practices are set out elsewhere. It is sufficient to appreciate that the 1970s and 1980s was a "heady period of avoidance" in Australia.[20] The legislative reaction was often time sensitive to prevent the offending behaviour continuing as soon as possible. Whether it was due to the drafting timeframe or a concern that the remedy would capture as many situations as possible, the style of these provisions tended to be fairly long, detailed and complex.[21]

When the general anti-avoidance rule was rewritten in 1981, it was also longer than its predecessor.[22] It is interesting that a much later addition to that rule, to clarify the limits of the Commissioner's ability to apply it in practice, was in line with that initial approach – it was fairly long and necessitates complex analysis. Brabazon argued that that recent addition was difficult to understand, the language was unclear and "it is as if some particular idea is hovering above the page, not quite achieving expression."[23] There is an argument that such ambiguity could favour the Commissioner. Because, from the information that was

---

20 Alex C Evans, 'Why private trusts are used in Australia: The income tax dimension explained' (2019) 41(2) *Sydney Law Review* 217 citing Richard Vann, Richard J Vann, 'Structural Issues in the Taxation of Small Business' [unpublished] (Draft dated 8 June 2015) 11; Trevor P W Boucher, *Blatant, Artificial and Contrived: Tax Schemes of the 70s and 80s* (Australian Taxation Office, 2010) chs 12, 26 and 54.

21 Examples include: the regime that was designed to prevent parents splitting income to their minor children through trusts in ITAA 1936 div 6AA; and the regime that deemed some transactions between a private company and their shareholders to be an assessable dividend: ITAA 1936 div 7A.

22 Part IVA replaced s 260 in the ITAA 1936 in 1981.

23 Mark Brabazon, 'The Hatter's Watch: Tax Benefit in Part IVA' (2014) 43(3) *Australian Tax Review* 150, 161, 153 (discussion of s 177CB, and its interaction with s 177C, of ITAA 1936).

publicly available, there appears to have been no urgency in drafting this change, it is unclear why it was not written more succinctly and captured with greater clarity. However, drafting such rules is challenging, so perhaps what appears in the legislation is the best that could be written.

II.F Other Reasons

The length of the legislation, use of different drafting styles and the complexity of the legislative provisions could also reflect other broader factors. For example, Avery Jones argued that "changes and increased sophistication in commercial practices" and "evolution in general law" could have been factors that contributed to the same phenomenon in the United Kingdom (UK).[24] However, Avery Jones also posed the question whether business practice was four times more sophisticated than it was ten years ago.[25] This is what he thought would be required to justify the growth in the income tax legislation. In the 1990s, the Tax Law Review Committee in the UK cited other systemic factors, including: the common law system itself, "the courts, the Parliamentary process, Parliamentary counsel, lack of time" and inaction over a very long period of time.[26] This is a fairly long list of external factors and they are likely to interact. It would be very challenging, if not impossible, to determine how much of the problem of the length and complexity in the legislation is due to any one of these factors.

III The Way Australia Has Approached This Problem

Part II above argued that the current state of the Australian income tax legislation was likely the result of the interplay between a number of factors. There is concern about both the length and complexity of the legislation. That concern has been expressed by judges in relation to particular provisions or areas (such as in the rules for taxing trusts) and that concern was reiterated in the most recent wide-ranging review of the Australian tax system. For example, the report of the Henry Tax Review stated that the "Trust tax rules are complex, uncertain and result in inappropriate outcomes"[27] and recommended that the "general. . .rules should be updated and rewritten".[28]

---

24 Avery Jones, 'Tax Law: Rules or Principles' (n 19) 581.

25 ibid.

26 ibid.

27 *Henry Tax Report*, Part 2 – Detailed Analysis (n 16) 189–91.

28 ibid 191.

A more general level of concern about the complexity of the entire income tax legislation was apparent in two drafting approaches that the Australian government at the time initiated as corrective measures. Those approaches are: a rewrite using plain English drafting and setting a path forward to use principles-based drafting. This section outlines each of these approaches.

Before turning to the two approaches, it is important to note that a recurring theme in Australian debates about how to fix the length and complexity of the income tax legislation is the tension between simplicity and certainty. Abreu stated:

> If taxes had existed in the Garden of Eden, the serpent would not have needed an apple; the promise of a simpler tax system alone would have seduced Eve.[29]

Anecdotally, simplicity is generally very appealing in Australian tax reform debates, seemingly on the assumption that it improves compliance.[30] Dean outlined that many "inspired politicians" in the US campaign promising to simplify the income tax law, but none have really achieved lasting change in this respect.[31] Dean argued therefore that "simplification becomes tax law's equivalent of a perennially ill-fated New Year's Eve resolution."[32]

In contrast, there is a considerable amount of fear around rules that are expressed in the abstract. Pinder described this as fear about the law's failure to cover enumerated situations. He stated:

> How can there be certainty about cases that the law does not deal with expressly?[33]

The analysis below shows that this was the central tension inherent in each approach. This chapter argues that it is also the core tension in Australian legislative drafting more generally.

IV Attempt 1: A Rewrite Using Plain English Drafting

A minor recommendation in the Joint Committee on Public Accounts' report into the performance of the Australian Taxation Office in 1993 was

---

29 Alice Abreu, 'Untangling Tax Reform: Simpler Taxes, Complex Choices' (1996) 33 *San Diego Law Review* 1355 as cited in Graeme S Cooper, 'Legislating Principles as a Remedy for Tax Complexity' (2010) 4 *British Tax Review* 334.

30 E.g. including Chris Evans and Binh Tran-Nam, 'The Development and Testing of a Diagnostic Tool for Assessing VAT Compliance Costs: Pilot Study Findings' (2019) *e Journal of Tax Research* 1.

31 Steven Dean, 'Attractive Complexity: Tax Deregulation, the Check-the-Box Election and Future Tax Simplification' (2005) 34(2) *Hofstra Law Review* 405, 406, 413.

32 ibid 406.

33 Pinder, 'The coherent principles approach to tax law design' (n 4).

that Australia's income tax legislation should be redrafted.[34] That became the Tax Law Improvement Project (**TLIP**). The explanatory memorandum to the Tax Law Improvement Bill of 1996 stated that the draft legislation contained rewritten provisions in several areas that included "30 enhancements in the operation of the rewritten provisions which will make the law simpler, clearer and less burdensome for taxpayers."[35] One of the key goals was to help compliance.[36] As part of this process, provisions from the old act (*Income Tax Assessment Act 1936*) were gradually migrated into the new act (*Income Tax Assessment Act 1997*).

TLIP involved "several innovations" in the use of language.[37]Cooper described that these were:

> The text was said to be written in 'plain language' and many provisions were drafted in the second person – the text addressed the reader as "you". Defined terms were preceded by an asterisk and sometimes the term was printed in a different typeface.[38]

TLIP also used broader drafting changes. These included "the use of descriptive material, for example, 'Guides' to parts of the law, charts showing 'Key Concepts', diagrams, explanatory notes to the text and examples showing how the provisions worked."[39] The legislation also used a new structure – "the so-called pyramid in which 'core provisions' were followed by 'general provisions', then 'specialist provisions', provisions dealing with collection and administration and finally, the definitions, located in a 'Dictionary'."[40] This section and this chapter focus on the use of plain English drafting, that is, using ordinary language that laypeople (that is, people with no legal training) can understand.

The TLIP project was never completed. In 1998, the Australian Liberal Party announced that it would enact a new integrated tax code if elected. This promised great change, with the Treasurer announcing that this project would bring:

---

34 Joint Committee on Public Accounts, *An Assessment of Tax: A Report on an Inquiry into the Australian Taxation Office* (Report 326) (1993) ch 5.

35 Parliament of the Commonwealth of Australia, House of Representatives, *Tax Law Improvement Bill 1996*, Explanatory Memorandum, 6<http://classic.austlii.edu.au/au/legis/cth/bill_em/tlib1996245/memo_0.html> accessed 25 May 2019.

36 ibid 5–6.

37 Cooper, 'Text, Style and Presentation - Assessing the Drafting Experiment in Australian Tax Laws' (n 1) 4.

38 ibid 4.

39 ibid 5.

40 ibid.

> The tax laws together in a code...that is designed from the taxpayers' perspective, has internal consistency, uses general principles in preference to long and detailed provisions, and is easy to understand and difficult to avoid.[41]

The TLIP project was absorbed into the project of developing the new income tax code. There was some discussion of a principles-based approach but this and other aims got lost as the government focused on the reform of business taxation within the income tax law. The business tax reform ended up being challenging for the government to implement as proposed. For example, as discussed above, it needed to abort a plan to tax trusts as companies under the Uniform Entity Taxation proposal due to strong lobby pressure, particularly from the National Farmers' Federation and small business.

The literature that analysed Australia's experience with plain English drafting was fairly scathing about its success. For example, Cooper debated whether this initiative was "improvement or just change?"[42] Factors and criticisms included the following. Although the provisions were written in more accessible non-technical language, the provisions were longer and less succinct. Cooper argued that in this regard plain English did not make the law clearer.[43] Avery Jones argued that the whole process made the situation more complicated.[44] His main observation was that the practice of interpreting the provision in the new act by referring back to the wording and interpretation of the old act did not provide clarity or make the law simpler.

Returning to the recurring theme of simplicity versus detail, the plain English approach did not seem to resolve the issue of the legislation's coverage. Rather, Cooper argued that the entire exercise posed an "unhappy trade-off" for the drafters.[45] He stated:

> If the drafting uses technical language it will be harder for a broad audience to grasp but admit fewer ambiguities; if the drafting uses plain language, it will be likely to be easier for a broader audience to grasp initially but will admit more possibilities.[46]

Although other dimensions of TLIP, such as the use of a clearer structure with signposting, were helpful, the body of literature that analyses the plain English

41 ibid 6.
42 ibid 13.
43 ibid 20.
44 Avery Jones, 'Tax Law: Rules or Principles' (n 19) 582.
45 Cooper, 'Text, Style and Presentation – Assessing the Drafting Experiment in Australian Tax Laws' (n 1) 20.
46 ibid.

drafting approach is very critical of it.[47] As noted above, the other challenge in relation to the perception of this approach was that the TLIP project was never completed.

V Attempt 2: Principles-Based Drafting

A second approach that Australia attempted was principles-based drafting. This section: outlines the origins of this approach and what it involved; the path that Australian Treasury adopted in 2005; and analysis of how successfully Treasury has been able to implement this approach in practice.

V. A The Origins of the Principles-Based Drafting Approach and What it Involved

The idea for principles-based drafting in the tax context began in 1996 when Professor Avery Jones from Oxford University gave a lecture that raised the distinction between rules and principles. In making that distinction, Avery Jones drew heavily on Ronald Dworkin's 1967 University of Chicago Law Review article called 'The Model of Rules', which was later written into *Law's Empire* (1998).[48] In referring to principles, Avery Jones was contemplating something external to the rules that helps with construction.[49] He thought of a principle as a statement at a level of abstraction, but not one that was inaccessible, broad or vague.[50] Further, he contemplated that "principles can have exceptions; can conflict with one another" in a way that underlying rules could not.[51] At the time, Avery Jones contemplated that UK law would need to be more aligned with the European legal system.[52]

Avery Jones' article referred to two models. The first was to have a framework of principles in the primary legislation with detail in secondary legislation.[53] This model contemplated that a secondary parliamentary committee would be

---

47 Including ibid.

48 Ronald M Dworkin, 'The Model of Rules' (1967) 35 University of Chicago Law Review 14. It is noted that there has been some contention about Avery Jones' definition of principles, see for example Cooper, 'Legislating Principles as a Remedy for Tax Complexity' (n 29) 341.

49 Avery Jones, 'Tax Law: Rules or Principles' (n 29) 341.

50 ibid.

51 ibid.

52 ibid 593.

53 ibid 593–4; Judith Freedman, 'Improving (Not Perfecting) Tax Legislation: Rules and Principles revisited' (2010) 6 *British Tax Review* 717, 719.

created to oversee the creation and detail of the secondary legislation.[54] Although this model had some support in the UK,[55] Avery Jones was critical of it. He considered that using secondary legislation would not fix the problem, it would only move it into secondary legislation. He thought this would only perpetuate the "rule madness."[56] The American tax law is an example of this. The *Internal Revenue Code* 1986 is supplemented by the US Treasury Regulations, which are often very detailed and complicated, even on fairly straightforward issues.[57]

The second model was a two-tier system based on the model common in European legal systems. In the UK, this is sometimes referred to as European drafting.[58]Avery Jones contemplated that the top level would contain:

> more abstract principles corresponding to those found in the EC Treaty applying generally, and the more specific principles found in the preamble to the Community legislation.[59]

The second level would contain:

> legislation itself which is interpreted with the aid of the higher level principles as well as the explanatory memoranda.[60]

Avery Jones argued that this second model would reduce the amount of detail necessary and would provide greater certainty than a very detailed provision.[61]

The broad aim of principles-based drafting was to reduce the complexity and length of the legislative provisions. Literature describes that this approach was argued to bring four main benefits. The first was that it would result in legislative provisions that were more precise and provided greater certainty.[62] This was based

---

54 ibid.

55 This model was proposed in the Final Report of the UK Tax Law Review Committee on Tax Legislation, see Avery Jones, 'Tax Law: Rules or Principles' (n 19) 592; ibid.

56 Avery Jones, 'Tax Law: Rules or Principles' (n 19) 592. Avery Jones attributed the term to Richard J Vann, "A Rose is a Flower is a Plant – Tax Simplification south of the equator" (1995 Conference Report, Report of Proceedings of the 47th Conference, Canadian Tax Foundation) 222.

57 For example, US Treasury Reg 301.770102 (Business entities) which defines when an entity is classified as a corporation for US federal income tax purposes.

58 E.g., I Turnbull, 'Legislative drafting in plain language and statements of principle' (1997) 18 *Statute Law Review* 21; B Hunt, 'Plain language in legislative drafting: Is it really the answer?' (2002) 202 *Statute Law Review* 24, 37.

59 Avery Jones, 'Tax Law: Rules or Principles' (n 19) 593.

60 ibid.

61 ibid.

62 Cooper, 'Legislating Principles as a Remedy for Tax Law Complexity' (n 29) 343ff.

on the argument that a principle could be more clearly articulated and would cover more situations than a rule. The second argument was that principles-based drafting was less complex and would be more flexible.[63] The third argument was that the approach would promote fairness.[64] The idea of fairness here is particular. It referred to the fact that, in the abstract, disputes at the principles level are easier to resolve and give judges more clarity about choosing between different criteria of tax policy (e.g., equity or economic efficiency). Further, it was argued that it would be easier for judges to interpret principles because, rather than being buried in the extrinsic material, the legislation's intent would be clear on its face. The fourth argument was that this approach would promote economic efficiency.[65] This referred to the fact that, in theory, the approach involved fewer words so this would reduce the work for the government and legislative drafters in monitoring and maintaining the legislation. But it was also argued to give the benefit of reduced complexity and therefore lower compliance costs for taxpayers. Freedman also later argued that a further benefit of this approach is that it limited the opportunity for taxpayers to create schemes which satisfied the detail of the provisions (the letter of the law) but not the intent. This is sometimes called "creative compliance" in tax and generally falls within avoidance.[66]

V.B The Path Adopted by Australian Treasury in 2005

While there has been some literature written about the UK's experience with principles-based drafting, this section focuses on Australia's approach.[67]

Principles-based drafting in Australia came about following Australian Treasury's 2004 review of the self-assessment system,[68] and the plan to develop an income tax code.[69] This approach was selected based on the realisation that, although taxpayers expressed a strong desire for detailed legislative provisions, the detail was obscuring the underlying policy intention.

63 Pinder, 'The Coherent Principles Approach to Tax Law Design' (n 4).

64 Cooper, 'Legislating Principles as a Remedy for Tax Complexity' (n 29) 343ff.

65 ibid.

66 Freedman, 'Improving (Not Perfecting) Tax Legislation: Rules and Principles revisited' (n 53) 719–20.

67 Judith Freedman, Geoff Loomer and John Vella, 'Analysing the Enhanced Relationship between Corporate Taxpayers and Revenue Authorities: A UK Case Study' in Lynne Oats (ed), *Taxation: A Fieldwork Research Handbook* (Routledge, Taylor & Francis group, 2012).

68 Cooper, 'Text, Style and Presentation – Assessing the Drafting Experiment in Australian Tax Laws' (n 1) 10.

69 Pinder, 'The Coherent Principles Approach to Tax Law Design' (n 4).

In 2005, Greg Pinder from the Australian Treasury published an article setting out what was referred to as the "coherent principles approach."[70] This reflected some level of discussion and consensus between Australian Treasury and the Australian Tax Office. In the article, Pinder articulated what he meant by a principle. Pinder stated:

> A principle is a statement about an intended outcome in a general field…it is a statement about the essence of all outcomes intended within its general field…
> When a principle works, it does so because the essence it captures appeals to readers at other than an abstract intellectual level; it means something to readers because it relates to their understanding of the real world.[71]

It also stated that a principle "expresses the outcome at the highest possible level rather than itemising a list of outcomes for every conceivable case."

Pinder described that using a principles-based approach was not new. He argued that even though they had not previously appeared in the legislation, they had been the backdrop to provisions. In advocating for this approach, he argued that principles could provide greater certainty because they focus on the law's intended outcome, rather than setting out the detail of the law's application to a variety of different situations.

Pinder's article included a diagram setting out the "hierarchy of steps" that were contemplated as being involved in the process of using the coherent principles approach to create legislation. The diagram is set out below.[72]

Policy outcome	Policy
Policy means	
Legislative purpose	Law
Coherent principle/s	
Lower level detail (unfolding)	
Interpretation/systems	Admin

Diagram showing the hierarchy of steps involved in the "Coherent principles approach"

The Policy strata comprised two steps: policy outcome and policy means. The policy outcome was simply a statement at an economic, political or social

70 ibid.
71 ibid.
72 ibid.

level of what the government intended to achieve. The policy means articulated what means the government wished to use to achieve the policy outcome. In other words, how the government intended to give effect to the policy outcome.

The Law strata comprised three steps: legislative purpose; coherent principle/s; and lower level detail (unfolding). The legislative purpose was a clear identification of the purpose of the legislation. The aim was for all new law to capture this purpose in an objects clause. The coherent principles step involved developing the principles that would form the operative rules for implementing the legislative purpose. This step has the potential for some very interesting analysis. It essentially was the stage of settling on an articulation of the principle and then stress testing it. Pinder envisaged that this would be done by: looking at the possible situations that are intended to be covered by the law; identifying patterns in the characteristics of the situations covered and seeing what the results are; transforming what was identified as the pattern into a principle; and then applying the principle to a range of new situations to see whether they were covered and then what the result was. Pinder's vision was pragmatic. He envisaged that there may be a need for carve outs and add-ons to be created. He realised that the principle that was settled on could cover more or fewer of the situations than the government intended. Working on the assumption that the principle had been carefully crafted, it would be better to keep the principle and adjust its application, either by expanding it (by add-ons) or reducing it (through carve outs), rather than changing the principle. The coverage could be monitored and refined (if necessary) post-implementation through formal and periodic reviews. Such reviews are conducted as a matter of course by the Australian government's tax advisory body, the Board of Taxation. If the application of the principle was unclear or ambiguous, the legislation could contain a description or provide detailed guidance about its application. This was the lower level detail (unfolding) step. Pinder described that to tell if unfolding was required, the principles would be tested against known situations to ensure that it was within the principle's coverage. If the principle didn't cover the situation, then unfolding would be necessary.

The Administrative stratum comprised just one step. Pinder viewed that, even if legislation was created using the coherent principles approach, further guidance may need to be provided about its content, coverage and application. In the tax context, the Australian Treasury contemplated that this would be done through rulings published by the Commissioner of Taxation.

V.C Analysis of How Successfully Australian Treasury Has Been Able to Implement the Coherent Principles Approach in Practice

Since Pinder's article, neither the Australian Treasury nor the Australian Taxation Office has made any information publicly available on how easily the coherent principles approach has been to use and whether there are any significant problems with it. This chapter covers first the evidence of the approach in practice, and then examines the critical analysis of the approach in academic literature.

i The Experience since 2005

Background about the Australian Treasury

Broadly, Australian Treasury develops the policy that underpins the economic dimensions of Australian law. The concentrates heavily on tax law, business law and superannuation (the Australian system that requires employers to make contributions to a fund for each employee that can only be accessed once the employee meets certain conditions, namely retires and reaches a certain age). The Australian Treasury accounts for about 25 % of the bills (pieces of draft legislation) that are presented to Australian Parliament each year, and about half of those are on the subject of tax.[73]

The Australian Treasury has recently implemented an internal structural change. This change was a movement towards the development of an expert law design function: the Law Design Office.[74] Creating a separation between policy development and law design is novel for the Australian Treasury. As this change was fully implemented only in 2017, it will take time to see what affect this has on the legislation that is produced.

What Australian Treasury has said publicly and what legislation drafted since 2005 shows in relation to the Law steps of the coherent principles approach

Publicly, the Australian Treasury has not expressly stated that it has altered its approach since 2005. This suggests that it still follows the coherent principles approach when drafting legislation. This approach is most evident in legislation created since 2006 from scratch. The best examples are therefore outside the

---

73 Australian Government, *Treasury Annual Report 2017-18*, Overview and Report on Performance <www.treasury.gov.au/publication/annual-report-2018> accessed 25 May 2019.

74 Australian Treasury, 'Directory' <www.directory.gov.au/portfolios/treasury/department-treasury/central-office/revenue-group/law-design-office> accessed 25 May 2019.

income tax legislation and include the *Fuel Tax Act 2006* (Cth) and the *Australian Charities and Not-For-Profits Commission Act 2012* (Cth).

The coherent principles approach is very clear on the face of the *Fuel Tax Act 2006* (Cth). Section 2-1 provides an "overview" of the legislation and states its purpose. It clearly states that the legislation is designed to create a single system for fuel tax credits, and the section then broadly outlines the situations when fuel tax credits will be given. The section also articulates that the administrative dimension of the fuel tax system is aligned with how other taxes are administered to reduce the compliance burden for taxpayers. This statement of objects then recurs, as a structural feature, at the start of each part before the relevant operative sections.[75] The statement of objects is either called "Statement of Objects" or "What this Division is about". This structure is a very obvious demonstration of the legislative purpose step in the coherent principles approach and it seems to be effective in the sense that the operative rules that follow the statement of objects in each part can be easily traced back to those objects at a conceptual level.[76] It is therefore likely that the statement of objects would provide a useful conceptual anchoring guide when applying the operative provisions in practice. However, whether this is true and whether this clear use of this aspect of the coherent principles approach has actually translated into any clear measurable and positive benefits for taxpayers is hard to determine as this point has not yet been covered in academic literature.[77] The benefits contemplated here are those outlined above as broad aims of using principles based drafting in the tax context,

---

75 *Fuel Tax Act 2006* (Cth), ss 40-5, 41-1, 42-1, 44-1, 46-1, 47-1,60-1, 61-1, 65-1, 70-1, 75-1 and 95-1.

76 E.g. the entitlement to fuel tax credits to fuel used in the course of carrying on an enterprise in section 41-5(1) of the *Fuel Tax Act 2006* (Cth) is easily connected back to the requirements set out in the statement of objects in section 41-1. Reid stated previously that "historically, the main way of explicitly stating legislative purpose in an Act has been through an objects clause. . .the objects clause in the coherent principles approach is an important link between the principles in the law and the principle-based policy outcome and the policy means.": Tom Reid, 'Interpreting the GST Law: Tax Law based on Coherent Principles' (2005) *Australian GST Journal* 239, 242.

77 It is noted that academic literature has referred to and discussed the *Fuel Tax Act 2006* (Cth) but not in relation to the drafting of the relatively new act and its impacts: e.g. Megan Vine, 'Energy Security, Oil and the Transport Sector: Is Australia's Policy Adequate, Reliable and Affordable?' (2012) 29(5) *Environmental and Planning Law Journal* 401; Dale Pinto and Prafula Pearce, 'The Role of Motor Vehicle Taxes in Shaping Australia's Oil Policy' (2013) 17(2) *Tax Specialist* 75.

namely: providing greater certainty and more flexibility; promoting fairness; being more easily interpreted, and reducing manipulation.

The *Australian Charities and Not-For-Profits Commission Act 2012* (Cth) employs a very similar structure, using a "Guide to this Act", the "Objects of this Act", the "Object of this Part" and then a series of "Simplified Outline"[s] before the relevant operative parts.[78] Again, while this is a clear example of the legislative purpose step in the coherent principles approach, the available literature does not indicate what measurable benefits this has had in applying the legislation.[79]

A corollary of the point above that the coherent principles approach appears to be most obvious and arguably most successful when used in legislation being written from scratch is that it appears to be very difficult to use this approach when inserting new parts into or rewriting existing legislation (i.e. the drafting equivalent of retrofitting). This chapter argues that four key themes are visible in examples from the Australia's income tax legislation, stripped of their technical detail.

The first theme is whether it is appropriate to use the coherent principles approach, or for the provisions to show outward signals of the approach, when

78 *Australian Charities and Not-For-Profit Commission Act 2012* (Cth), ss 10-5 (Guide to this Act), 15-5 (Object of this Act), 20-5 (Object of this Part) and 25-1 (Simplified Outline). A "Simplified Outline" is then mostly provided at the start of each subsequent part.

79 Academic literature has analysed the main institution and the system established by the *Australian Charities and Not-For-Profits Commission Act 2012* (Cth), but to date that analysis has not focused on the drafting and its effectiveness: e.g. Nicholas Aroney and Matthew Turnour, 'Charities are the New Constitutional Law Frontier' (2018) 41(2) *Melbourne University Law Review* 446; Fiona Martin, 'Tax Deductibility of Philanthropic Donations: Reform of the Specific Listing Provisions in Australia' (2018) 33(3) *Australian Tax Forum* 533; Marina Nehme, 'Australian Charites and Not-For-Profits Commission: Enforcement Tools and Regulatory Approach' (2017) 45(2) *Australian Business Law Review* 159; John Vaughan-Williams, 'The Future of Charity Regulation in Australia: Complexities of Change' (2016) 37(1) *Adelaide Law Review* 219; Marina Nehme, 'Regulation of the Nor-For-Profit Sector: Is Another Change really needed?' (2014) 39(1) *Alternative Law Journal* 24. It is noted that Australian Treasury suggested some "additional" legislative amendments in its 2018 review, but these were related to implementing its 30 recommendations (broadly the need for a national scheme, referral powers from the States to the Commonwealth and reducing red tape: Department of Treasury (Australia), *Strengthening for Purpose: Australian Charities and Not-For-Profits Commission Legislation Review 2018* (August 2018), Part D.

amendments are being written into existing parts of the income tax legislation. This is best illustrated by the recent package of amendments to address stapled structures.[80] To achieve the desired objective, amendments were required to be made to several different dimensions of the income tax legislation.[81] Each part of the package of amendments contains a clear structure. For example, one part sets out the four different types of income that are excluded from the concessional treatment and the following sections then set out detail on what falls into certain of those types of income, a de minimis threshold and an exception.[82] However, despite that structure, there is no obvious demonstration of any of the steps from the coherent principles approach. For example, the operative sections in each part are not preceded by an objects or purpose section stating the guiding principle in relation to stapled structures. This is interesting because the parts into which the amendments were inserted do exhibit signs of the coherent principles approach, for example, in the use of a beginning guide section in one part,[83] and the use of a beginning guide section in combination with objects sections in the other part.[84] The reason for this difference in approach is not outwardly clear. It may have been because it was judged to be too cumbersome to insert a

---

80 These amendments were contained in the Treasury Laws Amendment (Stapled Structures and Other Measures) Bill 2018, which later became Treasury Laws Amendment (Making Sure Foreign Investors Pay Their Fair Share of Tax in Australia and Other Measures) Bill 2018. The latter bill was passed by both Houses of Federal Parliament and obtained Royal Assent on 3rd April 2019. This package contained integrity measures that were broadly designed to prevent income from active business being converted into passive rental income by stapling a company to a managed investment trust, because such income can then be taxed concessionally (typically 15% not 30%): Department of Treasury (Australia), *Stapled Structures: Details of Integrity Package* (March 2018). As background, a stapled structure "is an arrangement where two or more entities that are commonly owned (at least one of which is a trust) are bound together, such that they cannot be bought or sold separately.": ibid, 1, 1.

81 Including the withholding tax rules for managed investment trusts and the thin capitalisation rules: ibid.

82 Taxation Administration Act 1953 (Aust) (TAA 1953), ss 12-435, 12-436, 12-437 (MIT cross staple arrangement income), 12-438, 12-439 (approved economic infrastructure facility exemption).

83 TAA 1953, s 12-375 (this is in the part that requires amounts to be withheld from distributions made by eligible managed investment trusts to certain entities).

84 ITAA 1997 ss 820-1 ("What this division is about") and 820-30 ("Object of Division").

sub-principle into the middle of the existing part that already contained a statement of principle.

The second theme is that in some places where amendments are made, the existing provisions were drafted using a style that predated the coherent principles approach.[85] In this situation, consistency requires that the amendment is made without the stylistic signals of the coherent principles approach, such as a statement of the guiding principle in an objects section. As discussed in Part II. E. above, this can give rise to ambiguity around the legislation's meaning and therefore also its target and capture.

The third theme is that recent legislative amendments tend to reveal a preference for detail, in the sense of including all known possible situations, over trust that those situations will be covered by an ambulatory interpretation of a general statement of principle. This is likely to be the result of lobbying and consultation with stakeholders (e.g. the Australian Taxation Office, practitioners and interest groups) with concerns about coverage of particular situations. It is expected that such concerns would be particularly high in exercises of rewriting provisions which are in themselves and where the ideas underlying them are complex.[86]

The fourth theme, which may overlap with some of those above, is that in some situations complex legislative solutions are required to be written rapidly to meet extremely tight deadlines for political reasons.[87] In these situations, the solutions tend not to show clear signs of the coherent principles approach. This is likely to be because creating provisions using that approach takes time and also, because in these situations, due to the political pressures, the legislation is often subject to a significant amount of consultation.

Comments in relation to the final two Law steps of the coherent principles approach

Australian Treasury has not yet publicly released any information on the coherent principles step (how it comes to the articulation of the principle and the stress testing of it) and the unfolding step in Pinder's coherent principles approach. It would be very valuable for the Australian Treasury to be transparent about the extent to which these steps have been used and challenges that have

85 A key example is the drafting of the 2013 amendment to the general anti-avoidance provision that was discussed in Part II. E. above.

86 E.g. if ITAA 1936, div 6 was ever rewritten.

87 A key example is the 2011 measures for streaming franked distributions and capital gains through a trust, see (n 14).

been encountered when applying it to both legislation created from scratch and retrofitting into existing and well-established pieces of legislation. It is likely that both steps would require some interagency co-operation, for example, in the income tax context, it is expected that Australian Treasury would need to work with the Australian Taxation Office. It is not clear whether and to what extent this has been done.

Comments in relation to the Administrative steps of the coherent principles approach

In relation to the final Administrative step in Pinder's articulation of the coherent principles approach, there has recently been some experimentation with the location of detail. For example, to supplement the material that is provided in the explanatory memoranda that accompany Australian income tax bills (**EMs**), the Australian Tax Office has recently started to release guidance documents called Law Companion Rulings (**LCRs**) around the same time as the EM. As it has become practice for EMs to paraphrase the law, the LCRs attempt to provide broader guidance on how the law will operate in practice, including how it applies to specific and more complex situations. As LCRs are fairly new, it will take time to determine how useful they are and how well they can function to keep detail out of the legislation.

ii The Academic View of the Use of the Coherent Principles Approach to Date

There has been some analysis of how successfully the coherent principles approach has been implemented in practice. The most valuable analysis is detailed and highly specific to Australia's income tax legislation.[88] However, that analysis does make some broader points that are valuable to this discussion.

First, Cooper argued that, to date, the ostensible use of the coherent principles approach had created a "targeting problem".[89] Cooper argued that the exercise of "try[ing] to capture the substance of a matter – rather than to define a precise target clearly" indicated a "deliberate decision not to be precise about a target."[90] Cooper critically analysed several critical technical regimes to show examples of this.[91] The broad argument was that the coherent principles approach appears

88 Cooper, 'Text, Style and Presentation – Assessing the Drafting Experiment in Australian Tax Laws' (n 1); Cooper, 'Legislating Principles as a Remedy for Tax Complexity' (n 29).

89 Cooper, 'Legislating Principles as a Remedy for Tax Complexity' (n 29) 28.

90 ibid.

91 The single entity rule, the debt / equity rules and the taxation of financial arrangements (TOFA) rules: ibid 28–37.

to involve a certain level of ambiguity that can become problematic when trying to apply the provisions involving the principle to complex situations in practice.

Secondly, Cooper argued that the approach faced a key process problem.[92] This was because, although much time and care could be taken to develop a perfect principle in the abstract, the government, and in turn, Australian Treasury, could come under pressure from lobbyists to massage the principle to meet specific interest concerns. This could result in a principle that is less pure and therefore one that is less robust as a pillar for designing the tax legislation around.

Thirdly, Cooper argued that there was a real problem around "principle-creep."[93] This seems to relate to Hart's point that laws have "furry edges" and are "open textured."[94] Cooper's argument was that where principles are created and placed into existing legislation, often we do not want that principle to have an effect in an already existing regime or series of regimes as it could cause undesirable unintended effects. When implementing a new principle, this forces drafters to ask questions including: where do the implications of a principle naturally stop? And where do we want them to stop?[95] Once those questions are asked, if it is necessary to adjust the principle's natural scope, then drafters need to put in place drafting that can switch the principle on and/or off. This brings a level of complexity into the drafting process and the legislation.

Finally, while the coherent principles approach was developed for use in the broader tax context, Reid argued in 2005 that it may be a more appropriate approach going forward for Australia's Goods and Services Tax (GST) legislation, not Australia's Income Tax Legislation, because it is more closely aligned with both the architecture and style of the GST legislation.[96]

iii Overall Assessment

The above analysis of the practical experience in implementing the coherent principles approach and the identification of key issues that result from using that approach in academic literature indicates that Australia is still in need of a guiding approach that can be used universally across Australian legislation.

One observation that threads together the recent approaches to tax law drafting in Australia and the academic literature echoes a comment that the

---

92 Cooper, 'Text, Style and Presentation – Assessing the Drafting Experiment in Australian Tax Laws' (n 1) 45.

93 Cooper, 'Legislating Principles as a Remedy for Tax Complexity' (n 29) 347.

94 Dworkin, 'The Model of Rules' (n 48) 22.

95 Cooper, 'Legislating Principles as a Remedy for Tax Complexity' (n 29) 347.

96 Reid, 'Interpreting the GST Law: Tax Law based on Coherent Principles' (n 76) 245.

Confederation of British Industry made in 2008. That comment was that a principles-based approach can work effectively where the principle itself is capable of drawing a clearly understandable and appropriate line. The author's experience in practice is that where a principles-based approach is used in contexts where this is not the case, despite what the legislation states, the principle does not provide a "central operating principle" that can provide the basis for construing and interpreting all provisions in that regime.[97]

VI Conclusion

A key limitation in relation to the coherent principles approach is that, where the bulk of drafting is revising existing legislation, in practice that approach is extremely hard to apply. The question then becomes – what is the way forward for Australia in legislative drafting that will help to improve the quality of the legislation? This chapter argues that the solution is not straightforward. However, given the significant limitations outlined above with the coherent principles based approach, it would be wise for Australia to have some realistic expectations in determining the path forward.

The first reality that is important is an acceptance that there will always be a certain level of complexity in income tax legislation. As Cooper stated, "a complex system may be clearly expressed and yet it will remain a complex system."[98] His point was that, while it is possible to embark in drafting exercises to simplify the language and terminology that is used in the legislation, if the provisions are based on complex ideas, whether they are nuanced legal distinctions or economic ideas, it will not be possible to remove complexity completely. But there is also an added dimension to this in the tax area, which has been observed in the US. That is that there appears to be something more than a tolerance of complexity in the legislation. In fact, taxpayers actually seem to have an appetite for what Dean termed "attractive complexity."[99] The basic idea here is that a

97 This is a specific comment regarding Australia's regime to classify an instrument as either debt or equity for tax purposes: ITAA 1997, div 974. This is an important distinction because returns on debt (i.e., interest) are generally deductible, while returns on equity investments (i.e., dividends) are not deductible.

98 Graeme S Cooper, 'A Rose is a Flower is a Plant: Tax Simplification South of the Equator' in *Report of the Proceedings of the 47th Conference* (Canadian Tax Foundation, 1995) 3:4. See also Adrian Sawyer, 'Rewriting Tax Legislation – Can Polishing Silver Really Turn it into Gold?' (2013) 15 *Journal of Australian Taxation* 1.

99 Dean, 'Attractive Complexity: Tax Deregulation, the Check-the-Box Election and Future Tax Simplification' (n 31) 413–416.

danger of a simplification process in rewriting legislation is that benefits, such as concessions and deductions (referred to as preferences), can be stripped out of the legislation so, for example, there can be common rules across taxpayer types. Dean described that, in economic terms, rational taxpayers prefer more complex tax systems because such systems tend to give them more.[100] The assumption is that this ultimately results in a lower income tax liability for the taxpayer. So the taxpayer is prepared to tolerate the complexity for the benefits that the complexity provides.

The second point is the importance of reflecting on the question of who the legislation is written for. There was some discussion of this between the speakers during the question and answer section of the author's part of the conference schedule. Avery Jones argued that, ultimately, if all else fails, the purpose of the legislation is to provide a means of communication between Parliament and the courts. He stated:

> The important issue is the interaction between Parliament...and the courts...What really matters is that the courts should come up with the right answers, not whether the rest of us have an easy time reading the statutes...[101]

While this can be debated, an important point is that an essential part of the Australian legal process is that legislation, and the Parliament's intention, can be interpreted by the judiciary when points of law are litigated.[102] Australia has clear rules for how statutory interpretation must be done and this currently includes limiting reference to extrinsic material.[103]

Whatever path we adopt to move forward, this chapter argues that it would be best to take into account the learnings about the limitations of the coherent principles approach that are set out in this chapter as well as the two points above. While it may be possible to continue to use the coherent principles approach strategically, for example, when writing new legislation from scratch, this

100 ibid citing Deborah Schenk, 'Positive Account of the Realization Rule' (2004) 57 *Tax Law Review* 355, 376 ("Taxpayers are quite willing to accept a large number of complex rules that encourage transactional complexity (so long as they perceive that they will benefit from their use)").

101 Avery Jones, 'Tax Law: Rules or Principles' (n 19) 583.

102 See also Reid, 'Interpreting the GST Law: Tax Law based on Coherent Principles' (n 76) 240.

103 An important limitation in this regard is in the Acts Interpretation Act 1901 *(Aust)*, s 15AB.

chapter indicates that this cannot be the whole solution going forward. Other more robust and long-term options will be examined in future work.

References

Abreu, A., 'Untangling Tax Reform: Simpler Taxes, Complex Choices' (1996) 33 San Diego Law Review 1355.

Aroney, N. and Turnour, M., 'Charities are the New Constitutional Law Frontier' (2018) 41(2) Melbourne University Law Review 446.

Australian Government, Treasury Annual Report 2017-18 (October 2018).

Avery Jones, J. F., 'Tax Law: Rules or Principles' [1996] British Tax Review 580.

Boucher, T. P. W., Blatant, Artificial and Contrived: Tax Schemes of the 70s and 80s (Australian Taxation Office 2010).

Brabazon, M., 'The Hatter's Watch: Tax Benefit in Part IVA' (2014) 43(3) Australian Tax Review 150.

Canada, Royal Commission on Taxation, Report of the Royal Commission on Taxation – Volume 4: Taxation of Income (Queen's Printer1967).

Commonwealth of Australia, Joint Committee on Public Accounts, An Assessment of Tax: A Report on an Inquiry into the Australian Taxation Office (Report 326) (1993).

Commonwealth of Australia, Taxation Review Committee, Full Report: 31 January 1975 (Australian Government Publishing Service1975).

Commonwealth of Australia, Treasury, Australia's Future Tax System (2009).

Commonwealth Parliament of Australia, Report (House of Representatives – Committee of Taxation 2006).

Cooper, G. S., 'A Rose is a Flower is a Plant: Tax Simplification South of the Equator' in Report of the Proceedings of the 47th Conference (Canadian Tax Foundation, 1995).

Cooper, G. S.,'Text, Style and Presentation – Assessing the Drafting Experiment in Australian Tax Laws' (Legal Studies Research Paper No 08/92, Sydney Law School, 2008).

Cooper, G. S.,'Legislating Principles as a Remedy for Tax Complexity' (2010) 4 British Tax Review 334.

Costello, P., 'Entity Taxation' (Media Release No 8, 27 February 2001) www.petercostello.com.au/press/2001/2445-entity-taxation-a.

Dean, S., 'Attractive Complexity: Tax Deregulation, the Check-the-Box Election and Future Tax Simplification' (2005) 34(2) Hofstra Law Review 405.

Dworkin, R. M., 'The Model of Rules' (1967) 35 University of Chicago Law Review 14.

Evans, C. and Tran-Nam, B., 'The Development and Testing of a Diagnostic Tool for Assessing VAT Compliance Costs: Pilot Study Findings' (2019) e Journal of Tax Research 1.

Evans, A. C., 'Why Private Trusts are Used in Australia: The Income Tax Dimension Explained' Sydney Law Review (2019) 41(2) Sydney Law Review 217.

Freedman, J., Loomer, G. and Vella, J., 'Analysing the Enhanced Relationship between Corporate Taxpayers and Revenue Authorities: A UK Case Study' in Lynne Oats (ed), Taxation: A Fieldwork Research Handbook (Routledge, Taylor &Francis 2012).

Hunt, B., 'Plain Language in Legislative Drafting: Is it Really the Answer?' (2002) 202 Statute Law Review 24.

Kobetsky, M. and Dirkis, M., Income Tax (Federation Press1997).

Martin, F., 'Tax Deductibility of Philanthropic Donations: Reform of the Specific Listing Provisions in Australia' (2018) 33(3) Australian Tax Forum 533.

Nehme, M., 'Regulation of the Nor-For-Profit Sector: Is Another Change really needed?' (2014) 39(1) Alternative Law Journal 24.

Nehme, M., 'Australian Charites and Not-for-Profits Commission: Enforcement Tools and Regulatory Approach' (2017) 45(2) Australian Business Law Review 159.

Pinder, G., 'The Coherent Principles Approach to Tax Law Design' (Australian Government, The Treasury, Economic Roundup, Autumn 2005) http://archive.treasury.gov.au/documents/987/HTML/docshell.asp?URL=07_coherent_principles.asp.

Pinto, D. and Pearce, P., 'The Role of Motor Vehicle Taxes in Shaping Australia's Oil Policy' (2013) 17(2) Tax Specialist 75.

Reid, T., 'Interpreting the GST Law: Tax Law based on Coherent Principles' (2005) Australian GST Journal 239.

Sawyer, A., 'Rewriting Tax Legislation – Can Polishing Silver Really turn it into Gold?' (2013) 15 Journal of Australian Taxation 1.

Schenk, D., 'Positive Account of the Realization Rule' (2004) 57 Tax Law Review 355.

Taylor, C. J., 'Australian Corporate Tax Reform in the Best of Times and the Worst of Times' (unpublished paper).

Turnbull, I., 'Legislative Drafting in Plain Language and Statements of Principle' (1997) 18 Statute Law Review 21

Vann, R. J., 'Structural Issues in the Taxation of Small Business' [unpublished] (Draft dated 8 June 2015).

Vaughan-Williams, J., 'The Future of Charity Regulation in Australia: Complexities of Change' (2016) 37(1) Adelaide Law Review 219.

Vine, M., 'Energy Security, Oil and the Transport Sector: Is Australia's Policy Adequate, Reliable and Affordable?' (2012) 29(5) Environmental and Planning Law Journal 401.

Joanna Kuźmicka-Sulikowska

6 Problems Arising in Connection with Implementation of the Product Liability Directive (85/374/EEC) into Polish Law[1]

Abstract: The article presents practical problems that have emerged in connection with implementation into Polish law the Council Directive 85/374/EEC of 25 July 1985 on the approximation of the laws, regulations and administrative provisions of the Member States concerning liability for defective products. Taking into account the legal nature of the directive and the possibility for individual countries of using the options reserved in it, there has been made confrontation with allegations of irregularities in the implementation of this directive to the Polish legal system made by some lawyers. Attention was also paid to the specific way of implementing this directive to the Polish law and it has been shown how far this has affected the substantive interpretation of the provisions on liability for damage caused by dangerous products. Attention was also paid to real imperfections in the implementation of the above-mentioned directive to Polish civil law.

Keywords: defective products, liability, producer, innovation risk, damage, implementation of directive

1 Introduction

Implementation into the Polish legal regime of **Council Directive 85/374/EEC of 25 July 1985 on the approximation of the laws, regulations and administrative provisions of the Member States concerning liability for defective products**[2] was performed by way of the Polish parliament adopting the Act of 2 March 2000 on the protection of some consumers' rights and on liability for damage caused by defective products[3], under which provisions regulating such liability were incorporated into the Polish Civil Code[4] (Art. 449^{1} – 449^{11}

1 The publication presents results of research project No. 2017/27/B/HS5/00897 financed by the National Science Centre, Poland.

2 Published in: *Official Journal L 210 of 7 August 1985, p. 0029 –0033, hereinafter referred to as* Directive 85/374.

3 Dz. U. No. 22, item 271 with amendments; this Act entered into force 1 July 2000.

4 Civil Code of 23 April 1964 (consolidated text: Dz. U. 2019 , item 1145 with amendments), hereinafter referred to as CC.

CC [5]). It should be emphasized that this step was taken prior to Poland's accession to the European Union. However, it was felt at the time that Poland was already under international obligations to implement the regulations under Art. 68 and 69 of the Europe Agreement of 16 December 1991 establishing an association between the European Communities and their Member States, of the one part, and the Republic of Poland, of the other part[6]. The former of those two articles held that an important initial condition of Poland's economic integration with the Community was convergence of existing and future Polish legislation to laws in effect in the Community. Poland had committed itself to engaging in all possible efforts so as to ensure compliance of its future legislative output with the legal regulations enacted in the Community. Article 69 of the aforementioned Agreement, in turn, indicated the areas in which particular emphasis would be placed on achieving convergence of legal regulations; these included protection of human life and health, as well as consumer protection. Furthermore, adaptation of Polish regulations to those of Directive 85/374 as early as in 2000 was felt to be justified as it facilitated materialization of the norms contained in Art. 76 of the Polish Constitution[7], which assigns public officials with the task of adopting legislation protecting consumers, renters and users from actions that may threaten their health, privacy and safety, as well as from unfair market practices. The practical realization of implementation into Polish law of the solutions contained in Directive 85/374 led to significant doubts and reservations as to the manner in which it was performed, with controversies remaining unresolved through the present day as to the adequacy of Polish legal provisions and their application in judicial rulings.

2 The Legal Character of the Directive, the Use of the Options It Affords, and Charges of Improper Implementation

In light of the issue explored in the present text, it should first be emphasized that the legal character of Directive 85/374, similarly to other such acts, necessitates acceptance of the view that it is binding upon every Member State of the European Union in respect of the result to be achieved, while leaving national

---

5 It should be observed, however, that Art. 449^{11}CC was revoked on 16 May 2011 under Art. 69 of the Private International Law Act of 4 February 2011 (consolidated text: Dz. U. 2018, item 1792), at present the relevant regulation is contained in 449^{1}–449^{10}CC.

6 Dz. U. 1994, No. 11, item 38 with amendments.

7 Constitution of the Republic of Poland of 2 April 1997 (Dz. U. No. 78, item 483 with amendments).

authorities discretion to select the means and measures by which this is accomplished. A Directive is therefore an instrument for harmonization, rather than unification, of Member States' laws. Within the EU, Member States are required in a timely and comprehensive manner to introduce appropriate domestic legislation in order to approximate their legal solutions with one another[8]. Directive 85/374 is no exception in this regard, and is therefore designed not to unify legal solutions regarding product liability, but rather to render them more similar (the preamble to the Directive leaves no doubt, containing such statements as "the harmonization resulting from this cannot be total at the present stage, but opens the way towards greater harmonization"). The directive thus neither determines what method is to be applied, nor what place in the hierarchy of laws the legislation used to achieve that aim must occupy[9]. Furthermore, individual Member States were afforded a measure of discretion in substantive matters, including in particular the adoption of clauses declaring the optionality of certain solutions. To be precise, the initial version of Directive 85/374 envisioned three such possibilities. The first of them concerned the freedom of Member States to adopt or reject producer liability for innovation risk. Taking advantage of this option, the legislature in Poland opted to exclude such liability (which applies to situations in which it was not possible to foresee the dangerous characteristics of a product taking into account the state of science and technology at the moment it was marketed - Art. 449^3 § 2 second sentence CC). The second such option permitted legislatures to establish a domestic limit on damages that a producer could be required to pay in the event of so-called serial loss caused by a product for which the producer is liable; this is understood as mass incidents of personal injury caused by the same products with the same flaws; the minimum for this limit, however, could not be lower than EUR 70,000,000 (prior to 1 January 1999 – ECU).The Polish legislator opted not to take advantage of this limit. Finally, the third of the aforementioned options consists in allowing domestic legislatures to decide whether unprocessed agricultural and husbandry goods would be considered "products"[10] (more precisely, natural agricultural products and fishery

8 Stanisław Biernat, 'Źródła prawa Unii Europejskiej' in: Jan Barcz (ed.), *Prawo Unii Europejskiej – zagadnienia systemowe*, (Wydawnictwo Prawo i Praktyka Gospodarcza 2003) 190–192.

9 Monika Jagielska, *Podstawy odpowiedzialności za produkt* (C.H. Beck 2004) 26.

10 Strictly speaking, such products were initially excluded from the subjective scope of the directive under Art. 2, but in Art. 15(1)(a) each Member State was permitted to exclude the application of Art. 2 and to apply the concept of product to unprocessed goods as well.

products, with the exclusion of those subjected to any degree of processing). This last examined discretion in decisions afforded to domestic legislatures was, however, revoked on 4 December 2000 under Directive 99/34[11], amending Directive 85/374. As a result of this change, the present dangerous product liability regime in every Member State must encompass all crops and products of husbandry, including unprocessed goods. This did not, however, lead to changes in the Polish Civil Code, as the relevant provisions from the very beginning did not include any exclusions for unprocessed agricultural and husbandry products.

The foregoing directly counters the inaccurate charges sometime raised in the Polish legal literature that the domestic legislature has given agricultural producers the opportunity to relieve themselves of liability for defective products by invoking innovation risk, as well as that no upper limit has been imposed on damages sums in the event of serial loss. Indeed, this was an example of the use of discretion in this scope granted by Directive 85/374 itself, similarly to the encompassing by Polish regulation of unprocessed agricultural and husbandry products with the product liability regime, particularly considering that at present – as has already been mentioned – it is already mandatory to do so.

There also do not deserve the acceptance the proposals sometimes put forward by legal scholars , that in implementing Directive 85/374 the Polish legislator should depart in some places from its wording even where the regulations of the Directive do not foresee such a possibility, in order to make allowances for the specificity of Polish law and the situation of Polish consumers and producers[12]. The application of exclusions from solutions adopted in Directive 85/374 in the process of its implementation would seem acceptable only when a choice in a particular matter is foreseen in this Directive (examples of which have been discussed above). It is also considered that the independent regulation of a particular issue by the domestic legislator is permissible in matter which are not addressed in the Directive, or when the legal solutions in effect in a given country prior to implementation of the Directive provide more rights to the injured party than the Directive itself[13]. This last reservation results from the fact that, on the one hand, the objective of the Directive and its implementation into domestic legal

11 Directive 1999/34/EC of the European Parliament and of the Council of 10 May 1999, published in: Official Journal L 141 of 4 June 1999, pp. 20–21.

12 Monika Jagielska, 'Odpowiedzialność za produkt w prawie polskim – uwagi *de lege ferenda*' (1995) 9 Rejent 179, 196.

13 Ewa Łętowska, *Europejskie prawo umów konsumenckich* (C.H. Beck 2004) 108; Bogusława Gnela, 'Uwagi na temat projektów uregulowania w prawie polskim odpowiedzialności za produkt' (1998) 4 Kwartalnik Prawa Prywatnego, 674.

regimes is to ensure a minimum standard for protection of victims of dangerous products[14], while on the other hand, it is stated that following the Directive's issue and the arising of the duty to implement it, no deviations from its wording are permissible even with a view to improving the situation of the injured party[15] (save for the exception of cases where some discretion has been granted by the Directive itself). The Polish legislature, however, has in some aspects exceeded the limits of this discretion, introducing other solutions in some questions that are regulated unequivocally in Directive 85/374. Furthermore, less than satisfactory use has been made of the aforementioned discretion concerning the method for the incorporation of product liability regulations into the Polish legal system, which has resulted in a number of interpretative difficulties, themselves leading to problems with the practical application (more precisely, the absence thereof, something which will be discussed further on) of those regulations. The most significant problems arising out of these circumstances will be explored below.

3 Significance of the Manner of Implementation for Substantive Interpretation of the Regulations Concerning Liability for Damage Caused by a Dangerous Product

As has already been mentioned, implementation into Polish law of the regulations contained in Directive 85/374 was performed by amending the Polish Civil Code through Art. 449[1] et seq. Nevertheless, this was done in a very unusual manner, specifically by creating out of the aforementioned rules for liability for damage caused by a faulty product a set of regulations encompassed by the separate Title VI[1] in Book Three of the Civil Code, immediately after Title VI addressing torts, and before Title VII addressing the performance of obligations and failure thereof[16]. This inevitably gave rise to doubts concerning the legal character of this particular liability regime.

Theoretically, this editorial extraction within the Polish Civil Code of regulations addressing liability for damage caused by unsafe products could, at first glance, suggest that we are dealing with an entirely new liability regime, distinct from the others contained therein. However, the substantive content of

14 Bogusława Gnela, *Odpowiedzialność za szkodę wyrządzoną przez produkt niebezpieczny (tak zwana odpowiedzialność za produkt)* (Kantor Wydawniczy Zakamycze 2000) 108.

15 Jagielska (n 8) 39.

16 For the sake of brevity and to avoid redundancy, I shall refer to liability in tort on the one hand, and contractual liability on the other, with the latter understood to mean liability associated with failure to perform or improper performance of an obligation.

those regulations (which should be regarded as incomparably more important from the secondary issue of the legislative technique applied) leads us to a very different conclusion; namely, that liability for damage caused by a dangerous product should be qualified as tort liability owing to its being possessed of all of the characteristic elements for this liability regime which differentiate it from other types of liability distinguished under Polish civil law, such as contractual and guarantee liability.

Proceeding to more detailed arguments in support of the position presented above, it should first be observed that Art. 449[1] et seq CC implies the obligation to remedy damage arising out of an event specified in legislation in reference to which a provision of law established a duty for a specified entity to remedy the injury caused by that event. Thus, the emergence of this duty within the framework of the regime governing liability for damage caused by a dangerous product is independent of the existence of any previous legal relations (*id est* existing prior to the occurrence of the event responsible for causing injury) between the entity bearing liability and the injured party[17]. These are typical characteristics for tort liability, and thus exclude the classification of product liability as contractual.

This conclusion also finds support in the fact that in cases of liability for damage caused by a dangerous product, neither the liable entity nor the victim are defined in advance (individually specified), but rather their identification occurs *post facto*, following the infliction of injury by a specified event, on the basis of statutory regulations determining who is liable in the event of damage arising in a specified manner[18]. This is also typical of liability in tort; here simply with another source of damage, but also constituting a tort, the legislature has imposed a duty to remedy injury on a particular entity, for example this duty may be imposed on an entrepreneur or the possessor of a motorized form of transport; when the source of the injury is a dangerous product, liability is assigned to entities associated with it, such as the producer, *quasi*-producer, producer of materials, raw materials or component part, importer, and retailer. At the same

17 Andrzej Śmieja in: Adam Olejniczak (ed.), *System Prawa Prywatnego, vol. 6, Prawo zobowiązań-część ogólna* (C.H. Beck 2009) 342–343.

18 For more detail see Joanna Kuźmicka, 'Zakres podmiotowy obowiązywania przepisów o odpowiedzialności za szkodę wyrządzoną przez produkt niebezpieczny' in: Piotr Machnikowski (ed.), *Odpowiedzialność w prawie cywilnym,* (2006) 2897 Acta Universitatis Wratislaviensis no. 2897, Prawo CCC, 199–210. See also: Paweł Granecki, 'Odpowiedzialność za szkodę wyrządzoną przez produkt niebezpieczny – charakter i miejsce w systemie odpowiedzialności odszkodowawczej' (2001) 1 Przegląd Legislacyjny, 32.

time, this mechanism for assigning liability to a defined entity is quite different from that which functions *ex contractu*, under which the parties of specified legal relations are individualized at the moment of establishment of the contractual bond between them; thus, only one of them may be responsible for improper performance or failure to perform a duty that would be of legal relevance within those relations, thereby limiting to those parties the scope of potentially liable entities.

It should also be observed that, within the framework of liability for loss caused by a dangerous product, damages are of a main and primary nature, similarly to other cases of liability in tort. Due to the fact that this is the nature of the damages here and in other cases of tort liability, this is another strong argument in favor of categorizing product liability as tort liability. This characteristic distinguishes that last liability regime from contractual liability, where compensation in damages is merely a substitute or complement to the debtor's primary contract performance[19]. Compensation in damages, however, is of a primary nature in respect of liability in insurance. However, it must be kept in mind in respect of that form of liability, the source of the debtor's duty to remedy loss is a contract concluded prior to the occurrence of the damage[20], which excludes the possibility of liability for loss caused by a dangerous product being deemed liability in insurance.

There are many other arguments in favor of categorizing liability for dangerous product as a form of tort liability[21], including the invocation by Art. 449^6 CC of appropriate application of Art. 441 § 2 and 3 CC (the provision regulating recourse claims in the event of remedying loss resulting from a tort by one of two or more entities liable for the loss). It should also be acknowledged that the construction of Art. 449^{10} CC prejudges the tort nature of product liability, that regulations for dangerous product liability do not exclude liability in tort under general principles, nor for damage resulting from improper performance or non-performance of an obligation, nor in respect of statutory warranty and quality guarantees. These last two categories are related to contractual liability regimes – the former of a general nature, while the latter refers in particular to warranty against defect and quality guarantees; if this is the case, the "liability

19 Śmieja (n 16) 342–343.

20 Śmieja (n 16) 342–343.

21 There is insufficient space for a detailed discussion of them here, the reader is therefore referred to the relevant literature (see e.g., Joanna Kuźmicka-Sulikowska, *Zasady odpowiedzialności deliktowej w świetle nowych tendencji w ustawodawstwie polskim* (Lex a Wolters Kluwer Business 2011) 427–434).

pursuant to general principles" referred to in the referenced Art. 449^{10} CC must also refer to liability other than contractual. It would seem that the legislator had in mind liability in tort, and treated as a special case of it the liability for dangerous product, similarly to how he separately treated the liability in warranty and guaranty considered in relation to the contractual liability[22].

Also of importance is reference to the important legal consequences resulting from the classification of liability for damage caused by a dangerous product as a form of tort liability. Namely, it opens the injured party the possibility of claiming financial redress for the harm suffered. According to the dominant view of representatives of Polish civil law science, due to the location of art. 445 CC constituting the basis for seeking redress under the provisions of tort liability, only under the latter it is possible to seek such redress [23] (however, it should be observed that other opinions have been expressed in this issue[24]).

In light of the foregoing remarks, it should be considered that the previous move by the legislator, who, instead of including regulations for loss caused by dangerous product in Title VI, Book III of the Polish Civil Code (which regulates liability in tort), has given them a separate place in Title VI^1 of the same book of CC made it, because this solution was dictated by practical considerations, primarily the breadth of product liability regulation and thus preventing it from being mixed up with other tort provisions , which could lead to significant

22 Monika Jagielska in: Adam Olejniczak (ed.), *System Prawa Prywatnego, vol. 6, Prawo zobowiązań-część ogólna* (C.H. Beck 2009) 891–892.

23 Per *inter alia*: Mirosław Nesterowicz, 'Odpowiedzialność kontraktowa i deliktowa (Uwagi de lege ferenda i o stosowaniu prawa)' (1999) 1 Państwo i Prawo 17, 21; Andrzej Cisek, Piotr Machnikowski in: Edward Gniewek, Piotr Machnikowski (eds.), *Kodeks cywilny. Komentarz* (6th edn, C.H. Beck 2014) 891; Gerard Bieniek in: Gerard Bieniek (ed.), *Komentarz do kodeksu cywilnego, Księga trzecia, Zobowiązania, vol. 1* (6th edn, LexisNexis 2005) 463; Andrzej Janik, 'Nowe tendencje w dziedzinie odpowiedzialności za produkt (uwagi prawnoporównawcze)' (1984) 8 Państwo i Prawo 71, 72–73.

24 Marek Safjan, 'Naprawienie krzywdy niemajątkowej w ramach odpowiedzialności ex contractu' in: Małgorzata Pyziak-Szafnicka (ed.), *Odpowiedzialność cywilna. Księga pamiątkowa ku czci Profesora Adama Szpunara* (Wydawnictwo Zakamycze 2004) 264–267; Jan Rezler, *Naprawienie szkody wynikłej ze spowodowania uszczerbku na ciele lub zdrowiu (według prawa cywilnego)* (Wydawnictwo Prawnicze 1968) 32–34; Andrzej Stelmachowski, 'Recenzja pracy J. Rezlera pt. Naprawienie szkody wynikłej ze spowodowania uszczerbku na ciele lub zdrowiu (według prawa cywilnego)' (1969) 11–12 Nowe Prawo 1751.

interpretation difficulties[25]. However, this solution, essentially an editorial device, should not be read as an attempt to carve out a new liability regime.

In addition, this view is strongly supported by the fact that the tort nature of product liability is not questioned in the legal scholarship of other European Union Member States obliged to implement Directive 85/374[26]. The dominant position in the Polish legal literature is identical[27].

---

25 However, it should be observed that the editorial maneuver as applied did not entirely facilitate their avoidance. Indeed, it led to other legal acts offering separate treatment of liability for loss caused by a dangerous product from liability in tort. For example, Art. 1(2) of the Mass Claims Act of 17 December 2009 (Dz.U. 2018, item 573 with amendments) begins with "The Act is applicable to court cases for claims under liability for damage caused by a dangerous product and for liability in tort, (. . .)". It does not, however, seem reasonable to reach the conclusion that the legislator has qualified liability for loss caused by a dangerous product as an entirely separate regime from tort liability when considering that the provision invoked above is contained in legislation addressing procedural issues, and thus the separate recitation of liability for loss caused by a dangerous product and tort liability is rather merely the result of a mechanical reflection of how those liability regimes are captured in separate titles of Book Three of the Polish Civil Code, as has already been discussed.

26 Philippe Malinvaud, *Droit des obligations* (Litec 2002) 469; Jacques Flour, Jean-Luc Aubert, Eric Savaux, *Droit civil. Les obligations. 2. Le fait juridique* (Sirey 2005) 321; Rolf Schmidt, Schuldrecht. BesondererTeil II, (Dr. Rolf Verlag 2006) 315; Josef Esser, Hans L. Weyers, *Schuldrecht, Band II, Besonderer Teil* (Heildelberg 1991) 578; HansBrox, *BesonderesSchuldrecht* (C.H. Beck 1999) 358; W.V.H. Rogers, Winfield and Jolowicz on Tort (Sweet and Maxwell 2002) 357; Chris Turner, *Tort* (Hodder & Stoughton 2005) 85; Vivienne Harpwood, *Principles of Tort Law* (Cavendish Publishing Limited 2000) 334.

27 *Inter alia* Ewa Bagińska, 'O odpowiedzialności za produkt' (2009)9 Państwo i Prawo, 34; Bogusława Gnela, 'Odpowiedzialność przedsiębiorców za szkody wyrządzone przez produkt niebezpieczny' in: Andrzej Śmieja (ed.), *Odpowiedzialność cywilnoprawna w obrocie gospodarczym* (2011) 203 Prace Naukowe Uniwersytetu Ekonomicznego we Wrocławiu 39, 41; Gnela (n 13) 280; Ewa Łętowska, *Ochrona niektórych praw konsumentów. Komentarz* (C.H. Beck 2001) 124; Kuźmicka-Sulikowska (n 20) 427–434; *ibid*, Odpowiedzialność za szkodę wyrządzoną przez produkt niebezpieczny a odpowiedzialność deliktowa na zasadach ogólnych i odpowiedzialność kontraktowa-wybrane zagadnienia, Radca Prawny 2013, no. 133, dod. naukowy, pp. 7–9; P. Granecki, Odpowiedzialność. . ., p. 32; F. Mohmand, Pojęcie produktu niebezpiecznego w rozumieniu przepisów kodeksu cywilnego o odpowiedzialności za produkt [in:] Odpowiedzialność cywilna. Księga pamiątkowa ku czci Profesora Adama Szpunara, ed. M. Pyziak-Szafnicka, Kraków 2004, p. 142. Taking the opposite view and perceiving a new type of liability, neither contractual nor in tort: Marian Kępiński, 'O zakresie odpowiedzialności za produkt niebezpieczny' in: Leszek Ogiegło, Wojciech Popiołek, Maciej Szpunar (eds.), *Rozprawy prawnicze. Księga pamiątkowa Profesora*

However, the majority of authors correctly points out that liability for loss caused by a dangerous product is risk-based liability in tort; this is the leading perspective among both civil law scholars in Poland[28] and in other EU Member States[29].This conclusion is also supported primarily by the conception which forms the basis of the solutions adopted in Directive 85/374, finding support in the fact that in the case of the product liability regime there are clearly legislative motives that typically support the introduction of liability based on this principle , that is, the principle of *cuius commodum eius perriculum* (the person who benefits from something should also bear the burdens of it – losses), as well as the increased level of danger that others may incur loss[30]. The application of the elimination method also supports the view that the form of liability analyzed here constitutes risk-based liability under the Polish civil law. There is insufficient space to discuss it here, thus the reader is referred to the source in respect of the concept at the heart of this method and the manner in which it is executed[31]. Declaring at the outset that the following remarks are quite general and incomplete, it may be pointed out that in respect of product liability there are no grounds for perceiving a fault-based obligation to remedy loss, as the legislator does not mention fault at all in product liability regulations, does not refer to it using descriptive means, and does not state that liability here is to be borne under general principles, which in the Polish civil law means fault-based liability as set forth in the general liability clause in Art. 415 of the Civil Code. Given that the Polish legislator imposes fault-based liability exclusively through one of those three methods, and does not apply any of them in respect of product liability, one cannot conclude that product liability is fault-based. In turn, its classification as equity-based liability is excluded by the absence of a link between the imposition of a duty to remedy loss and considerations resulting from the principles of social co-existence or equity *per se*. There is also no link

Maksymiliana Pazdana (Wydawnictwo Zakamycze 2005) 1036; Zbigniew Strus, 'Odpowiedzialność za szkodę wyrządzoną przez produkt niebezpieczny' (2001) 1 Palestra 23, 25.

28 For an in-depth justification of this perspective see Kuźmicka-Sulikowska (n 20) 434–436. Arguing that this is risk-based liability *inter alia*: Jagielska (n 21) 873 and 911; Bagińska (n 26) 35; Gnela (n 26) 41; Sebastian Sikorski, 'O odpowiedzialności za szkodę wyrządzoną przez produkt niebezpieczny' (2003) 12 Prawo Spółek 33, 37.

29 Flour, Aubert, Savaux (n 25) 321; Schmidt (n 25) 315; Esser, Weyers (n 25) 578; Brox (n 25) 358; Rogers (n 25) 357–358; Turner (n 25) 85; Harpwood (n 25) 334.

30 For more: Kuźmicka-Sulikowska (n 20) 194–208.

31 See Kuźmicka-Sulikowska (n 20) 268–280 and 434–437.

between the arising of liability for unlawful conduct on the part of the producer, which excludes the conclusion that liability is based on unlawfulness. However, the existence of a number of exonerating circumstances allowing for the avoidance of product liability excludes its qualification as absolute liability, additionally supporting its classification as risk-based liability[32].

4 Actual Flaws in Respect of Implementation of the Directive

With the preceding remarks in mind, it should, however, be observed that in some aspects the Polish legislator may be accused of improper implementation of Directive 85/374. In some places, there are departures from the Directive's wording that do not seem to be explicitly permitted by its regulations and which do not afford Member States with any level of discretion, as the norms of the Directive do not provide for freedom in their application by Member States. The most significant of these improprieties will be discussed below.

4.1 Naming the Liability Regime

It should be pointed out that the provisions of the Civil Code implementing Directive 85/374 into the Polish legal order do not use the term "defective" as applied in the Directive's title, but rather uses the term "dangerous". This is not the result of improper translation of the Directive, but rather a deliberate move by the Polish legislator to differentiate the product liability regime from regulations governing liability for defect in a product under statutory warranty. The latter comes into play when a given product is faulty (either physical or legal defect). Such arguments referring to the need to adapt regulations for the implementation of Directive 85/374 to solutions already in effect in the Polish legal regime, including efforts to avoid suggesting normative links between product liability and warranty or guaranty liability, are frequently felt to justify the Polish legislator's use of a separate term for defining the liability regime from that invoked in the aforementioned Directive[33]. It should, however, be pointed out that voices opposed to this approach claim it was unnecessary to go so far as to select a different name for the liability regime than that used in Directive 85/374 for the sole purpose of preventing associations with the warranty and guaranty regime. It would have been sufficient to refer in the Polish legislation to "dangerous product defect", and defining it in a manner consistent with the solutions

32 For more: Kuźmicka-Sulikowska (n 20) 268–280 and 434–437.

33 Per e.g., Łętowska (n 26) 121.

applied in the Directive; according to some authors, the Directive is meant to apply to this type of defect as well[34].

In respect to the above, it should primarily be observed that the aforementioned maneuvre, used by the Polish legislator consisting in the use of a name different from that in Directive 85/374 for the liability regime in the Polish Civil Code which is intended to be an implementation of that Directive, is in fact a clear departure from the Directive suggesting that the regulations of the Polish Civil Code regulate different matters than those governed by Directive 85/374 (that is to say, they have not been implemented). This conclusion would, however, be unjustified in the light of those provisions in the code which are explicitly intended to reflect solutions from the Directive (here the term "intended to reflect" has been used rather than stating that they do, in fact, reflect those solutions, as it is not necessarily the case in all aspects, as we will discuss later on). The Directive clearly concerns liability for loss caused by defective products, both in its title and in the wording of the regulation contained therein. Some authors attempt to rescue the situation by explaining that, contrary to their name, the provisions of the Polish Civil Code do nor concern liability for every dangerous product, only liability for products with dangerous defects[35]. This interpretation, however, obviously contradicts the clearly-worded provisions of the Polish Civil Code regarding product liability, including the name of the Title in which they are contained (Title VI^1 of Book Three), as well as the definition of a dangerous product (Art. 449^1 § 3 CC). With this in mind, the claim that these regulations address only dangerous defects in a product, and not liability for loss caused by a dangerous product, is revealed as flatly contradicting the actual content of the Polish regulation. Additionally, those representing such a position seem to be unaware of the important distinction that exists between the concepts of defect and danger. It consists mainly in that a product which is free from defect and fit for purpose can, however, be dangerous for its surroundings, such as owing to the use of toxic substances in its production[36].Furthermore, some products available for purchase are dangerous *per se*, that is, certain potential dangers are imminent features of such products (e.g., chemicals, medicine, paint, rat poison), but because of the purposes for which these products are created, there

---

34 Gnela (n 13) 276. In a later publication the same author stated directly that this difference is a clear-cut example of improper implementation of Directive 85/374 (Gnela (n 26) 42).

35 Gnela (n 13) 277.

36 Which is rightly pointed out by Sikorski (n 27) 35–36.

is a certain level of acceptable risk necessary for them to be used in accordance with their purpose; this disallows us from treating them as defective (insofar as they fulfil safety requirements resulting from legal regulations).

Apart from the foregoing, it should also be emphasized that not only did the Polish legislator apply its discretion in departing from the regulations of the Directive by introducing liability for loss caused by a dangerous product rather than a defective one, leading to the aforementioned controversies regarding discrepancies between the Polish regulation and that of the Directive coupled with a range of interpretative concepts, but that it also did so in a rather inconsistent manner. In spite of Title VI[1] of Book Three of the Civil Code being named "Liability for loss caused by a dangerous product", with the majority of its provisions invoking the concept of a dangerous product, in some of them the legislator applies language referring to defective (not dangerous) products, either directly (e.g. in Art. 449^5 § 1 CC, which mentions "defective construction of the product"), or indirectly (by indicating in the cited provision that the producer's instructions may be the cause of loss).

4.2 The Concept of Producer. The Legal Status of the Manufacturer of Material, Raw Material or Component Part of a Product

First and foremost, it should be noted that the Polish legislator applied a different normative construction concerning the identification of entities potentially liable for damage caused by a dangerous product. Specifically, the definition of a producer contained in Art. 3(1) of Directive 85/374 encompasses not only the producer of the finished product, but also of raw materials, component parts and so-called *quasi*-producers, meaning those who advertise themselves as the producer of a product by placing their name, trademark or other distinguishing feature on the product. What is more, under Art. 3(2) of the Directive, the importer of a product is also considered to be its producer. However, the concept of producer as applied in regulations governing product liability in the Polish Civil Code encompass only the producer of the finished product, whereas in respect of other entities, the term "liable as the producer" is employed (in Art. 449^5 § 2 CC in respect of a *quasi*-producer, meaning one who places their name, trademark or other distinguishing feature on the product to present themselves as the producer, while in Art. 449^5 § 2 CC it does the same regarding the importer of a product) or "as if the producer" (Art. 449^5 § 1 CC concerning the producer of the material, raw material or component part of a product). Particularly in respect to the last group, attention is drawn by the use of a term suggestions that they are not considered to be a producer, but that their liability is constructed in an analogical manner to that of the producer. The accompanying separate presentation in a separate provision of the norm addressing the producer of a product's material, raw material or component part leads some Polish civil law scholars to the conclusion that the aforementioned entities are not equated with producers, but are rather considered additional entities obliged to remedy loss[37]. What is more, it should be observed that the aforementioned editorial separation in the Civil Code of a norm addressing the producer of the material, raw material or component part of a product leads to particular legal consequences; it is difficult to determine whether these consequences were intended, but it would seem they were not. More precisely, in defining circumstances which will allow the vendor to shield himself from product liability, Art. 449^5 § 5 CC reserves that if the vendor is unable to indicate the producer or any of the individuals listed in § 4, he can be relieved of liability by indicating the person from whom he acquired the product. In Art. 449^5 § 4 CC, to which the legislator refers us, there is mention of the vendor's liability when it is unknown who the producer of a given product is, or one of the people listed in Art. 449^5 § 2 CC, unless within a month from the day on which notice is given of the loss, the vendor provides the injured party with the identity and address of the producer or one of the people listed in 449^5 § 2 CC. That said, the wording of the cited provision refers only to the *quasi*-producer (thus one who purports to be the producer by placing his name, trademark or other distinguishing feature on the product), as well as the importer of the product which has caused loss in a given case. From the foregoing it results that the Polish legislator does not envision the possibility of avoiding liability by the vendor of a product by providing the injured party with the identity and address of the manufacturer of the material, raw material or component part of the product, as there is mention made of that manufacturer in Art. 449^5 § 1 CC, to which there is no reference in the aforementioned do Art. 449^5 § 4 and 5 CC. This is no small matter and cannot be dismissed as just a legislative "oversight", as this is a question of normative material, the construction of liability therein is legally significant and should be applied exactly as the statute sets out. As a consequence, it must be held that the Polish Civil Code does not provide a vendor with the possibility to free himself from liability in respect of the injured party by providing that party with the identity and address of the manufacturer of the material, raw material or component element used in the product, which flatly contradicts Art. 3(3) of Directive 85/374[38]. It would

37 Gnela (n 13) 292.
38 Kuźmicka (n 17) 204.

seem that this is an unintended consequence of the Polish legislator's improperly composed definition of "producer". Under the last cited provision, liability of a product's vendor comes into play when it is impossible to identify the producer, but the broad definition of "producer" in the Directive should be kept in mind, which – as we have already mentioned – also encompasses the manufacturer of the product's materials, raw materials or component parts. This manufacturer is not, however, considered a producer under the concept as applied for product liability in the Polish Civil Code; for this reason as well, rendering it impossible for the vendor under Art. 449^5 § 4 CC to relieve himself of liability through providing the injured party with the identification of the producer does not at all imply the possibility of escaping liability by informing the injured party of the manufacturer of the material, raw material or component part of the product. This solution, however, finds no justification, neither axiological nor by way of any systemic concept of Polish law; rather, what we are dealing with here is an example of sloppy legislative technique which effectively has led to improprieties in respect of implementation of Directive 85/374. The Polish legislator must intervene to correct this error by amending the relevant provisions in accordance with the above remarks.

4.3 Understanding of the Term "Importer"

An amendment of the regulations from the Polish Civil Code under analysis is desirable as well in other respects. It should be observed that the definition of "importer" applied by the Polish legislator is inadequate. Specifically, this concerns the definition of the term given in Art. 449^5 § 2 CC as one who markets domestically a product of foreign origin within the scope of his commercial activity. This is inconsistent with Art. 3(2) of Directive 85/374,which, for understandable reasons, defines "importer" as one who brings a product into the territory of the Community. Insofar as the present distinctiveness in the Polish regulation can be justified to a certain degree in the context of implementing regulations on dangerous product liability into the Polish legal order in 2000, before the country joined the European Union, maintaining this distinction today is no longer reasonable. Thus, Art. 449^5 § 2 CC should also be adapted to the present legal policy and legal reality, to take account of Poland's membership in the European Union. This leads to the postulate of amending the latter regulation in order to ensure that, under the regulations of the Polish Civil Code concerning product liability, the concept of importer is understood to mean the one who brings a product into market of the European Union area. As it stands, we are faced with the unusual situation in which a norm of Polish law, designed to be an implementation of Directive 85/374, holds an importer to be one who brings a product to Poland from another European Union country; this is not only inconsistent with the logic underlying the definition of "importer" in the Directive, but also indirectly violates the fundamental assumptions inherent in the common market designed to include Member States.

Besides the aforementioned, there is another discrepancy that can be observed in respect of the definition of the term "importer" within the analyzed regulations. Specifically, in Art. 3(2)Directive 85/374,which refers to the concept "importer", treats it as the individual who introduces a product for sale, hire, leasing or any form of distribution in the course of his business, while the relevant Polish regulation (specifically Art. 449^5 § 2 CC) does not indicate the types of legal relations that should be entered into for the purposes of importing a given product; rather, there is only a general mention of a product being brought onto the domestic market. This discrepancy does not, however, seem to result in any substantive differences, as it should be noted that the formula applied in the cited provision of the Directive is not an exclusive one, as the particular types of legal relations listed therein are explicitly stated to be examples, and that others may apply as well. With this in mind, it would seem that the solution contained in the Polish Civil Code, employing an entirely open formula, would seem consistent with the European regulations.

4.4 *Quasi*-Producer

Other discrepancies can be identified in the manner in which other entities liable for damage caused by a dangerous product are identified. In particular, when specifying the concept of a *quasi*-producer in Art. 3(1) Directive 85/374, mention is made of one who purports to be the producer by placing his trade mark on the product, whereas the analogous Polish regulation (Art. 449^5 § 2 CC) mentions placement of a given entity's brand on the product. This does not appear to be a mistake on the part of the Polish legislator, who clearly intended to account for existing Polish legal terminology and a particular legal act then in force – at the moment the discussed regulations were adopted, the Brand Act of 31 January 1985 was still in effect[39], which was shortly thereafter superseded by the Industrial Property Act of 30 June 2000[40]. However, in this case it does not seem that this difference would justify amending the Polish product liability regulations to substitute the term "trade mark" applied in Directive 85/374 for

39 Dz. U. No. 5, item 17 with amendments.

40 Consolidated text: Dz. U. 2017, item 776 with amendments.

"brand". Essentially, the manner in which Polish law defines and understands the latter term is consistent with the sense and the essence of what the Directive's authors had in mind using the term "trade mark"[41].

4.5 Animals

Other differences which attest to the improper implementation of Directive 85/374 into Polish law can be pointed out not only in respect of its subjective scope of product liability (examples of which have been provided above), but also in its objective scope.

For example, in accordance with the regulations of the Polish Civil Code concerning the aforementioned type of liability, an animal is also considered to be a product (Art. 449^1 § 2 CC). Many authors state that categorization of animals as a product here is an "unfortunate" solution[42].What is more, there are some who argue that recognition of a product within the aforementioned regulation from the Polish Civil Code is baseless, because loss caused by an animal should not be encompassed by product liability, which should only apply to damage arising as a result of dangerously defective products made or derived from animals; those products should then be classified as movables[43]. B. Gnela, a representative of this school of thinking, invokes in support of the argument that product liability does not apply to living animals the reasoning that in the opposite case it would clash with other regulations in place, particularly Art. 431 CC[44], which, in her opinion, also encompasses loss resulting from an animal made aggressive

41 Under Art. 120(1–2) of the Industrial Property Act: "1.A trade mark can be every symbol that can be presented graphically if such symbol is suitable for distinguishing the goods of one enterprise from those of another enterprise. 2. As understood by par. 1, a trade mark can in particular be an expression, drawing, ornament, colour scheme, spatial form including the shape of a product and/or packaging, and also a melody or other sound".

42 See e.g., Jerzy Rajski, 'Odpowiedzialność za produkt niebezpieczny w świetle nowych przepisów kodeksu cywilnego' (2001) 100 Przegląd Prawa Handlowego 23, 25; Gnela (n 26) 43.

43 Bogusława Gnela, 'Odpowiedzialność za produkt (uwagi o polskiej regulacji)' (2009) 9 Państwo i Prawo 33, 37; Gnela (n 26) 43.

44 Under Art. 431 § 1 of the Civil Code, he who keeps or uses an animal is obliged to remedy damage caused by the animal regardless of whether it was under his oversight, or whether it had gone missing or run away, unless neither he nor a person for which he is liable is not at fault (in turn, § 2 sets out a particular case of liability for damage caused by an animal based on the principles of social co-existence).

as the result of genetic modification[45]. This statement is vigorously opposed by Z. Zaporowska, who claims that liability under Art. 431 CC does not exclude the application of product liability regulations. She argues that liability under Art. 431 CC will be borne by the individual who keeps or uses the animal rather than its breeder or producer, and while it could be the case that the same individual will bear liability resulting from the aforementioned provision as well as from product liability regulations, this will be liability based on different legal grounds. What is more, liability on the part of a range of entities may come into play, such as when the breeder has already sold the animal and another person is now keeping or using it; in such cases the former will bear liability for the product, while the latter incurs it under Art. 431 CC[46].

In reference to the issue of animals in this context, when discussing the Polish legal regime it is necessary to pay close attention to Art. 1 of the Animal Protection Act of 21 August 1997[47]. Pursuant to this regulation, an animal, as a living being capable of suffering, is not a thing, and only in matters not regulated by the provisions of that particular statute are provisions concerning things to be applied as appropriate. This serves as the background for the observation that analogical regulation incorporated into the portion of the Civil Code concerning product liability would be a more adequate solution[48]. This is not, however, the only position represented in the debate; one may also encounter the opinion that the clearly separate indication contained in Art. 449^1 § 2 CC holding that animals are also encompassed by the concept of a product was entirely unnecessary, because product liability in this scope will apply most frequently to

---

45 Gnela (n 13) 270.

46 Zofia Zaporowska, 'Odpowiedzialność za zwierzę jako produkt niebezpieczny' (2009) 1 Rejent 130, 144–145. It is worth pointing out that the author also claims that the view of B. Gnela is correct, that it was unnecessary for the legislator to indicate that an animal is also held to be a product. In Zaporowska's opinion, to establish that animals are encompassed by regulations for product liability, the wording of Art. 1(2) of the Animal Protection Act (previously referred to) is sufficient. This statement may be called into question, as it refers to regulation contained outside the Civil Code, in a special act. For this reason, any amendment at all to that Act in the scope under consideration here would imply a change in the manner in which the related regulation in the Civil Code was interpreted, which in turn would not be favorable to developing a stable interpretation of the matter.

47 Consolidated text Dz. U. 2019, item 122 with amendments.

48 Per, it would seem, J. Rajski, but he has certainly committed a mistake in writing of a solution on whose basis "animals would be covered by regulations addressing animals" (Rajski (n 41) 25).

products of animal origin, which are things, and a separate indication that animals are also considered to be products was unnecessary as it would in any case be encompassed by the definition of a product by way of interpretation of the referenced provision[49]. However, some authors feel that referring *expressis verbis* to animals in the aforementioned provision was justified on grounds of preventing potential doubts as to whether or not loss caused by them is regulated under Title VI[1] Book Three of the Civil Code addressing liability for loss caused by a dangerous product[50].

It should also be emphasized at the end that, in the subject literature, we may come across the charge that "holding an animal to be a product doubtlessly runs contrary to the current trend towards ensuring broader possibilities for protection of animals against abusive treatment, and is in conflict with Art. 1(1)of the Animal Protection Act of 21 August 1997, under which an animal, as a living being capable of suffering, is not a thing"[51]. This statement, however, should be approached critically[52]. There are no grounds for perceiving any discrepancy with regulations and solutions associated with the principle of protection of animals. The regulations addressing liability for dangerous product do not at all concern the issue of treatment of animals. Furthermore, as has already been mentioned and should in this context be emphasized, in Art. 449[1] § 2 CC animals are not acknowledged as things. Just the opposite – the fact that the legislator has perceived the need for a clear, separate indication that under regulation concerning product liability animals are also considered a product attests to the fact that they were not classified as things as referred to in Art. 449[1] § 2 CC; otherwise, a norm within the framework of that regulation establishing the status of animals would be redundant[53].

---

49 This is pointed out by Gnela (n 13) 288.

50 Wojciech Dubis in: Edward Gniewek (ed.), *Kodeks cywilny. Komentarz* (C.H. Beck 2006), 827.

51 Cezary Czech-Śmiałkowski, 'Dobra intelektualne jako produkt niebezpieczny' (2006) 6 Radca Prawny 51, 90.

52 Also: Zaporowska (n 45) 142.

53 For more on the subject see Joanna Kuźmicka-Sulikowska, 'Pojęcie produktu niebezpiecznego na gruncie przepisów kodeksu cywilnego dotyczących odpowiedzialności za szkodę wyrządzoną przez produkt' in: Jacek Mazurkiewicz (ed.),*Księga dla naszych kolegów. Prace prawnicze poświęcone pamięci doktora Andrzeja Ciska, doktora Zygmunta Masternaka, doktora Marka Zagrosika* (Prawnicza i Ekonomiczna Biblioteka Cyfrowa 2013) 245, 250–252.

4.6 Limitation of Claims

Under the present wording of Art. 449[8] CC, claims for loss inflicted by a dangerous product are subject to a limitation of three years from the day on which the injured party learned of the loss and the individual obliged to remedy it, or, assuming the exercise of due caution, could have done so. In every case, the maximum limitation period for claims expires 10 years after the initial marketing of the product.

This regulation gave rise to particularly serious doubts concerning its compatibility with Directive 85/374, particularly in its initial version, which did not contain a fragment from the Directive concerning the running of the limitation period from the moment when the injured party acting with due diligence could have learned about the damage and about the person obliged to remedy it. This incompatibility of the Polish legislation with EU regulation has already been eliminated, as the aforementioned fragment was added to Art. 449[8] CC in 2004[54]. Nevertheless, the manner in which the issue of limitation of claims arising out of loss caused by a dangerous product is regulated in CC remains inconsistent with Directive 85/374, because, as has been mentioned above, the Polish legislator imposes a ten-year limitation period calculated *a tempore facti*, that is from the initial marketing of the product, whereas the Directive in Art. 11 establishes this not as a limitation period but as a preclusory one. Under the latter norm, claims of the injured party expire upon the passage of 10 years from the initial marketing of the product which caused the loss, unless that party previously brought an action against the producer. For this reason as well, the regulation contained in Art. 449[8] CC remains inconsistent with the Directive, and a change in the construction of this solution is proposed by stating that the ten-year period is preclusory rather than a limitation period[55]. The Polish legislator has not, however, taken any steps to do this, and thus the matter remains one of theoretical divagations.

54 Under the Act of 20 April 2004 on changes and abrogation of some laws in conjunction with the Republic of Poland's accession to the European Union (Dz. U. No. 96, item 959).

55 Gnela (n 26) 54; Jagielska (n 21) 920; Zbigniew Radwański (ed.), Zielona Księga. Optymalna wizja Kodeksu cywilnego w Rzeczypospolitej Polskiej (Oficyna Wydawnicza Ministerstwa Sprawiedliwości 2006) 126.

4.7 The Issue of the Relation between Art. 449^{9} and 449^{11} CC and Directive 85/374

The Polish legislator has determined in Art. 449^{9} CC that regulations concerning liability for damage caused by a dangerous product are binding in all cases and cannot be excluded or limited. This leads to significant consternation resulting from the content of Art. 449^{11} CC, which states that the aforementioned liability cannot be excluded or limited by way of agreement, including in the event of selection of foreign law. The first part of this provision is a redundant repetition of Art. 449^{9} CC, whereas the second concerned an issue generally not addressed by the content of Directive 85/374, that is choice of law and limitations in that respect. With this in mind, the Polish legislator's decision to repeal Art. 449^{11} CC should be acknowledged as proper[56].

5 Summary

While approval should be voiced for efforts undertaken to adapt the Polish legal order to Directive 85/374 before the obligation to implement that Directive formally arose, the manner in which this was performed gives rise to far-reaching doubts. As the article has indicated, the editorial decision itself consisting in placing product liability regulations in a separate Title VI^{1} in Book Three of the Civil Code, just after Title VI addressing liability in tort and before Title VII concerning the performance of obligations and effects of non-performance, led to a dispute about the legal character of that particular grounds for liability. However, as has been shown, by way of interpretation it can be demonstrated that product liability is liability in tort grounded in the risk principle. Yet the legal literature continues to feature voices claiming that the normative material alone should be the basis for conclusions rather than complex legal interpretation efforts. In connection with this, it is proposed to transfer the regulation for dangerous product liability to the aforementioned Title VI of Book Three of the Civil Code in order to definitively demonstrate that the liability at hand is in tort[57].

Furthermore, as has been demonstrated in the article, a significant number of regulations adopted in the Polish Civil Code differ in substance from those contained in Directive 85/374. It should be emphasized in this context that the European Court of Justice is firm in its position that Directive 85/374 does not

---

56 Under Art. 69 of the Private International Law Act of 4 February 2011 (consolidated text: Dz. U. 2018, item 1792).

57 B. Gnela (n 26) 58.

constitute minimal legislation – domestic law may not introduce regulations that depart from its content[58]. As a result, it is necessary to amend the provisions of the Polish Civil Code as quickly as possible in order to adapt its contents to the regulations set out in Directive 85/374. As the line of reasoning undertaken in this article has shown, the appropriate modifications should concern such aspects as the manner in which the definition of the concept of "producer" is stated by including in it the *quasi*-producer, importer, and manufacturer of materials, raw materials and component parts of a product; this would also have the benefit of solving the problem indicated in the article and consisting in the inability of a product's vendor to relieve himself of liability through indicating the aforementioned manufacturer. It is also necessary to amend the manner in which the concept of "importer" is understood – it should clearly be stated that this is the entity bringing the product into the European Union, and not Poland. Another urgently needed change in the regulations of the Polish Civil Code relates to the expiration of claims for product liability, as the inconsistencies between the Code and Directive 85/374 have not been entirely corrected by the revision to those provisions (as has already been mentioned). Indeed, it remains necessary to modify the regulations concerning the ten-year period from the day of marketing the product so that this period, rather than being a limitations period, constitutes a preclusory period as in Directive 85/374 leading to the claim's exclusion, unless the claimant brings an action to recover damages from loss caused by the product[59].

---

58 See rulings of the European Court of Justice: of 10 January 2006 in Skov/Eg versus Bilka Lavprisvarehus A/S and Bilka Lavprosvarehus A/S versus Jette Mikkelsen and Michael Due Nielsen (C-402/03, http://curia.europa.eu/juris/liste.jsf?td=ALL&language=pl&jur=C,T,F&num=C-402/03, access: 10 April2019) and of 25 April 2002: Commission of the European Communities versus France (C-52/00, http://curia.europa.eu/juris/liste.jsf?td=ALL&language=pl&jur=C,T,F&num=C-52/00, access: 10 April 2019), Commission of the European Communities versus Greece (C-154/00,http://curia.europa.eu/juris/liste.jsf?td=ALL&language=pl&jur=C,T,F&num=C-154/00, access 10 April 2019) and in Maria Victoria Gonzáles Sánchez versus Medicina Asturiana S.A. (C-183/00,http://curia.europa.eu/juris/liste.jsf?td=ALL&language=pl&jur=C,T,F&num=C-183/00, access10 April 2019).

59 This is also why I disagree with Marek Safjan, who proposes amending Art. 449^8 CC concerning expiration of claims arising out of damage from dangerous products, but in order to maintain the institution of expiration, and also to adapt the provision to general regulation concerning expiration of claims in tort, particularly Art. 442^1§ 3 CC (Marek Safjan in: Krzysztof Pietrzykowski (ed.), *Kodeks cywilny, vol. I, Komentarz. Art. 1–449^{10}* (C.H. Beck 2015) 1482). This proposal should be rejected as one that would

The article naturally engages in discussion of some of the most important inconsistencies between Directive 85/374 and the Polish regulations constituting its implementation. That said, there is a large number of such discrepancies, some less important, others more so. The present article's limited scope does not allow for all of them to be examined, thus it must suffice to point out that urgent changes should also be made to Art. 449^1 § 3 CC. This particular provision states that a dangerous product is one that does not provide the level of safety that should be expected when taking into account normal use of the product. Such criteria for assessment of a product differs from that put forth in the Directive, where it is said that in assessing whether a product is defective, account must be taken not only of normal use of the product, but also of use which could rationally be expected. The Directive's solutions thus also demand that consideration be given to use of the product which is foreseeable, meaning use of the product which can be reasonably be assumed, even if this is not the exact use that the producer intended. This demonstrates how important the distinctions between these formulae are in establishing the criteria by which a given product is assessed as dangerous or defective, depending on whether the criteria applied are taken from Polish law or Directive 85/374. As has already been noted, the very terminology applied in Polish regulations is different from that in the Directive. While the latter mentions defective products, the Polish Civil Code refers to dangerous products; as has been demonstrated in the conducted considerations , such differences lead to further substantive discrepancies, necessitating further revision of the Polish legislation.

In the course of the conducted analyses it has, however, been shown that while certain solutions adopted in the Polish Civil Code are said to be inconsistent with Directive 85/374, they should not be judged particularly harshly. This especially concerns those cases in which the Polish legislator has taken advantage of the discretion offered by the Directive to national legislatures. For this reason, the Polish law may not be criticized as inconsistent with the Directive because the Polish Civil Code allows a producer to relieve himself of liability by invoking innovation risk, nor because it does not establish an upper limit on damages for so-called serial loss, while in turn it encompasses with liability damage caused by non-processed plant and animal products (especially, as has been mentioned, that this has been obligatory since 2000).

---

not only fail to eliminate the aforementioned incompatibility with Directive 85/374, but would even serve to worsen it.

Nevertheless, many regulations contained in Polish law require adaptation to the provisions of Directive 85/374. The improprieties in implementation signaled above are among the most important reasons why the dangerous product liability regime is not practically applied by Polish courts. Another contributing factor is uncertainty on the part of courts resulting from the particular location of provisions regulating such liability in the Polish Civil Code; it is unclear whether and to what extent provisions concerning liability in tort can be applied in respect of areas not addressed directly by product liability regulations. As a result, in cases where the application of product liability regulations could come into play, courts typically resort to seeking grounds within norms addressing warranty for physical defects under contracts of sale, or they dismiss claims on grounds of the complainant failing to demonstrate fulfilment of conditions for liability due to dangerous product[60]. It goes without saying that this is not a desirable state of affairs; what we have is merely formal implementation without any reflection in the real practice of applying the law. This negative trend can be reversed with the appropriate amendments to the provisions of the Polish Civil Code implementing Directive 85/374, specifically through a clear definition of the legal character of the regulation and its relationship to other provisions on liability in tort.

References

1. Bagińska, Ewa, 'O odpowiedzialności za produkt' (2009) 9 Państwo i Prawo.
2. Biernat, Stanisław, 'Źródła prawa Unii Europejskiej' in: Jan Barcz (ed.), *Prawo Unii Europejskiej – zagadnienia systemowe* (Wydawnictwo Prawo i Praktyka Gospodarcza 2003).
3. Brox, Hans, *Besonderes Schuldrecht* (C.H. Beck 1999).

---

60 As in e.g., verdict of the Court of Appeals in Szczecin of 29 May 2014 (I ACa 377/13, http://orzeczenia.szczecin.sa.gov.pl/content/$N/155500000000503_I_ACa_000377_2013_Uz_2014-05-29_001, access10 April 2019), where the complainant's claim was dismissed and the verdict of the Regional Court in Szczecin upheld rejecting a claim for remedy of loss caused by a dangerous product due to the claimant's failure to demonstrate the standing of the respondents (because the claimant failed to produce proof of purchase of the telephone charger that shocked her with electricity), and for failure to indicate the entity that brought the specific product causing the damage to market. Significantly, in the opinion accompanying the verdict, the Court of Appeals also emphasized the absence of rulings by Polish courts awarding claims arising out of damage caused by dangerous products.

4. Cisek, Andrzej, Machnikowski, Piotr in: Edward Gniewek, Piotr Machnikowski (eds.), *Kodeks cywilny. Komentarz* (C.H. Beck 2014).
5. Czech-Śmiałkowski, Cezary, 'Dobra intelektualne jako produkt niebezpieczny' (2006) 6 Radca Prawny 51.
6. Dubis,Wojciech in: Edward Gniewek (ed.), *Kodeks cywilny. Komentarz* (C.H. Beck 2006).
7. Esser, Josef, Weyers, Hans L., *Schuldrecht, Band II, Besonderer Teil* (Verlag C.F. Müller 1991).
8. Flour, Jacques, Aubert, Jean-Luc, Savaux, Eric, *Droit civil. Les obligations. 2. Le fait juridique* (Sirey 2005).
9. Gnela, Bogusława,'Uwagi na temat projektów uregulowania w prawie polskim odpowiedzialności za produkt' (1998) 4 Kwartalnik Prawa Prywatnego.
10. Gnela, Bogusława, *Odpowiedzialność za szkodę wyrządzoną przez produkt niebezpieczny (tak zwana odpowiedzialność za produkt)* (Kantor Wydawniczy Zakamycze 2000).
11. Gnela, Bogusława, 'Odpowiedzialność za produkt (uwagi o polskiej regulacji)' (2009) 9 Państwo i Prawo 33.
12. Gnela, Bogusława, 'Odpowiedzialność przedsiębiorców za szkody wyrządzone przez produkt niebezpieczny' in: Andrzej Śmieja (ed.), *Odpowiedzialność cywilnoprawna w obrocie gospodarczym* (2011) 203 Prace Naukowe Uniwersytetu Ekonomicznego we Wrocławiu 39.
13. Granecki, Paweł,'Odpowiedzialność za szkodę wyrządzoną przez produkt niebezpieczny – charakter i miejsce w systemie odpowiedzialności odszkodowawczej' (2001) 1 Przegląd Legislacyjny.
14. Harpwood, Vivienne, *Principles of Tort Law* (Cavendish Publishing Limited 2000).
15. Jagielska, Monika, 'Odpowiedzialność za produkt w prawie polskim – uwagi *de lege ferenda*' (1995) 9 Rejent 179.
16. Jagielska, Monika, *Podstawy odpowiedzialności za produkt* (C.H. Beck 2004).
17. Jagielska, Monika in: Adam Olejniczak (ed.), *System Prawa Prywatnego, vol. 6, Prawo zobowiązań-część ogólna* (C.H. Beck 2009).
18. Janik, Andrzej,'Nowe tendencje w dziedzinie odpowiedzialności za produkt (uwagi prawnoporównawcze)' (1984) 8 Państwo i Prawo 71.
19. Kępiński, Marian, 'O zakresie odpowiedzialności za produkt niebezpieczny' in: Leszek Ogiegło, Wojciech Popiołek, Maciej Szpunar

(eds.), *Rozprawy prawnicze. Księga pamiątkowa Profesora Maksymiliana Pazdana* (Wydawnictwo Zakamycze 2005).

20. Kuźmicka,Joanna,'Zakres podmiotowy obowiązywania przepisów o odpowiedzialności za szkodę wyrządzoną przez produkt niebezpieczny' in: Piotr Machnikowski (ed.), *Odpowiedzialność w prawie cywilnym*, (2006) 2897Acta UniversitatisWratislaviensis no. 2897, Prawo CCC.
21. Kuźmicka-Sulikowska, Joanna, *Zasady odpowiedzialności deliktowej w świetle nowych tendencji w ustawodawstwie polskim* (Lex a Wolters Kluwer Business 2011).
22. Kuźmicka-Sulikowska, Joanna,'Pojęcie produktu niebezpiecznego na gruncie przepisów kodeksu cywilnego dotyczących odpowiedzialności za szkodę wyrządzoną przez produkt' in: Jacek Mazurkiewicz (ed.), *Księga dla naszych kolegów. Prace prawnicze poświęcone pamięci doktora Andrzeja Ciska, doktora Zygmunta Masternaka, doktora Marka Zagrosika* (Prawnicza i Ekonomiczna Biblioteka Cyfrowa 2013) 245.
23. Łętowska,Ewa, *Ochrona niektórych praw konsumentów. Komentarz* (C.H. Beck 2001).
24. Łętowska,Ewa, *Europejskie prawo umów konsumenckich* (C.H. Beck 2004).
25. Malinvaud, Philippe, *Droit des obligations* (Litec 2002).
26. Nesterowicz, Mirosław, 'Odpowiedzialność kontraktowa i deliktowa (Uwagi de lege ferenda i o stosowaniu prawa)' (1999) 1 Państwo i Prawo 17.
27. Radwański, Zbigniew in: Zielona Księga(ed.),*Optymalna wizja Kodeksu cywilnego w Rzeczypospolitej Polskiej* (Oficyna Wydawnicza Ministerstwa Sprawiedliwości 2006).
28. Rajski, Jerzy, 'Odpowiedzialność za produkt niebezpieczny w świetle nowych przepisów kodeksu cywilnego' (2001) 100 Przegląd Prawa Handlowego 23.
29. Rezler, Jan, *Naprawienie szkody wynikłej ze spowodowania uszczerbku na ciele lub zdrowiu (według prawa cywilnego)* (Wydawnictwo Prawnicze 1968).
30. Rogers, W.V. H., *Winfield and Jolowicz on Tort* (Sweet and Maxwell 2002).
31. Safjan, Marek, 'Naprawienie krzywdy niemajątkowej w ramach odpowiedzialności ex contractu' in: Małgorzata Pyziak-Szafnicka (ed.), *Odpowiedzialność cywilna. Księga pamiątkowa ku czci Profesora Adama Szpunara* (Wydawnictwo Zakamycze 2004).

32. Safjan, Marek in: Krzysztof Pietrzykowski (ed.), *Kodeks cywilny, vol. I, Komentarz. Art. 1—449[10]* (C.H. Beck 2015).
33. Schmidt, Rolf, *Schuldrecht. Besonderer Teil II*, (Dr. Rolf Verlag 2006).
34. Sikorski, Sebastian, 'O odpowiedzialności za szkodę wyrządzoną przez produkt niebezpieczny' (2003) 12 Prawo Spółek 33.
35. Stelmachowski, Andrzej, 'Recenzja pracy J. Rezlera pt. Naprawienie szkody wynikłej ze spowodowania uszczerbku na ciele lub zdrowiu (według prawa cywilnego)' (1969) 11–12 Nowe Prawo 1751.
36. Strus, Zbigniew, 'Odpowiedzialność za szkodę wyrządzoną przez produkt niebezpieczny' (2001) 1 Palestra 23.
37. Śmieja, Andrzej in: Adam Olejniczak (ed.), *System Prawa Prywatnego, vol. 6, Prawo zobowiązań-część ogólna* (C.H. Beck 2009).
38. Turner, Chris, *Tort* (Hodder & Stoughton 2005).
39. Zaporowska, Zofia,'Odpowiedzialność za zwierzę jako produkt niebezpieczny' (2009) 1 Rejent 130.

Part Three Legislation and Lawyers

Sanita Osipova

7 "The Borders" of the Legislator's Freedom in the Legislation

Abstract: The law is used in society as an effective social tool to provide regulatory protection of values. With the development of society, also the understanding of the law or the sources of law changes. During the second half of the 19th century – the first half of the 20th century, the representatives of the school of legal positivism provided the substantiation for the legislator's discretion in creating the law. However, in examining the institute of legislator, it must be kept in mind that whoever the legislator might be: the national or the supranational parliament, the source of the sovereign power constantly is the people. Therefore, each legislator exercises the power of the people, not that of its own. Hence, only an appropriately authorized body of state power has the right to issue norms of conduct that are binding upon society. The legitimisation must be direct, and the people's authorisation cannot be transferred; however, in an exceptional case, in doing so, the limits set in the constitution and the law must be strictly observed.

Keywords: contemporary society, legislator, fundamental rights, constitutional justice

The limits of the legislator's discretion in adopting conceptually new regulation binding upon society is a very stimulating issue. Namely, how free the legislator is in its actions in a democratic state governed by the rule of law, where the separation of powers rules, a person's fundamental rights binding upon the State exist, where the legislator is bound by the authorisation granted by electors, the constitution and the international agreements entered into. To reach a complex answer to this question, it could be examined from the vantage point of both history of law and theory of law, sociology of law, the state law, the fundamental rights, the philosophy of law and, definitely, from other legal perspectives as well. I chose to look for the answer to the question: legislation as the parliament's obligation, i.e., whether and to what extent the parliament has the right to delegate to other subjects of law the right to issue regulations that are binding upon a person. To conduct this research, I chose to focus attention on three questions: What is the law? What is the legislator? Does the parliament have the right to delegate the right to issue regulations binding upon a person – laws – to other subjects of power?

1 What is the Law?

Each society uses the law for its self-organisation. "Where there is society, there is the law," the ancient Romans said.[1] One might say that the law is the normative structure of the society [2] or the normative order of the society's life.[3] The law is a phenomenon of culture, which, alongside the rest of culture, is created by the society itself.[4] Therefore, different legal systems evolve in different cultures. Each of them is appropriate for the national identity and historical experience of the members of the particular society, which has influenced the legal culture.[5] Thus, the law is significant for the society as a whole, since it provides a normative frame for the life of the society as a whole and for the life of every person. Therefore, it should be sufficiently stable to harmonise the public life in the long-term, ensuring peace and justice. Here one might place **the first flag of precaution**: whether and how often the legislator has the right to change the stable legal order that has evolved in society and follows from the legal culture by creating new legal norms if it itself has been created and acts within the framework of this culture.

In the course of society's development, the understanding of the nature of law, justice, sources of law, etc., changes. While the society lives in faith or abides by the religious norms, the law is perceived as part of the world's divine order. For example, in ancient Egypt, Mesopotamia, Israel, etc., the law was perceived as eternal, unchanging canons of justice that guaranteed order on the earth and in the heaven.[6] The Old Testament clearly comprises the idea – the supreme

---

1 Раймон Леже Великие правовые системы современности. 3-е издание. Москва: Волтерс Клувер, 2011, с. 1.

2 Thomas Raiser Das lebende Recht. Rechtssoziologie in Deutschland. Baden-Baden: Nomos Verlagsgeselschaft, 1999, S.160.

3 Olaf Muthorst Grundlagen der Rechtswissenschaft. Methode -Begriff -System. München: C. H. Beck, 2011, S. 4,5.

4 "The law is a necessary rule for the cultural life of man and later – the law is a cultural factor," V. Sinaiskis wrote. Vasīlijs Sinaiskis Tiesības un ģimene. *Jurists*. Nr. 8., 01.11.1929, 225., 226. sl.

5 For example, about the differences in the separation between the public and the private law in various European states. See Edvīns Danovskis Publisko un privāto tiesību dalījuma nozīme un piemērošanas problēmas Latvijā. Rīga: Latvijas Vēstnesis, 2015, 20–31.

6 For example, Jan Assman (1938) underscores that in the ancient cultures the law was perceived as constant canons, the continuity of which was preserved also as the result of creating the law since this was ensured by the worldview of the members of society.

legislator is the God; therefore, the competence of the secular ruler is limited. In those times, deviations from the legal norms meant turning against the God. Although the understanding of law has notably evolved and currently it is not perceived as being eternal, unchangeable and divine norms; nevertheless, it still can be said that the law is a rather conservative phenomenon of culture, which changes slowly alongside transformations in the collective consciousness of the society. "*The organisation of a family, the state and society at large, sanctions applied and agreements concluded is simply the continuation of those ideas, which rule in the society over the society [itself], the state, the rule of law, etc. Therefore these and analogous phenomena cannot be viewed otherwise than ideas through ideas . . .,*" E. Durkheim wrote.[7] The ideas or perceptions, among others also the legal ones, form and develop in society in a logical succession. The sociologists of law (E. Durkheim, M. Weber, N. Luhmann, et.al.) express the opinion that certain purposefulness and collective rationality govern the organisation of the co-existence of each society.[8] Each legal norm is important for the effective functioning of the system even if *prima facie* it is not obvious. Therefore, amendments to each norm must be carefully considered, forecasting the possible consequences in the social reality.

Undoubtedly, the law is used in society as an effective social tool to provide regulatory protection of values.[9] Likewise, the law itself is perceived in society as a value.[10] Legal norms, alongside other social norms, for example, norms of ethics, religious norms, aesthetic norms, define the limits of an individual's discretion in society[11] and offer possible models of actions that the society expects of an individual in a particular society. The law is differentiated from other

---

JanAssmann Das kulturelle Gedächtnis: Schrift, Erinnerung und politische Identität in frühen Hochkulturen. München: C. H. Beck, 2002,S. 2.

7 Emile Durkheim Regeln der soziologischen Methode. Neuwied und Berlin: Luchterhand, 1965, S. 118.

8 See more extensively Sanita Osipova, Latviešu juridiskā kultūra un tiesiskā apziņa. No: Akadēmiskie raksti 4 sējumos „Latvieši un Latvija", III sējums „Atjaunotā Latvijas valsts". Rīga: Latvijas Zinātņu akadēmija, 2013. 151.–178. lpp

9 Густав Радбрух Философия права. Москва, Международные отношения, 2004, с. 41.

10 Vasīlijs Sinaiskis Tiesības un ģimene. Jurists Nr. 8., 01.11.1929, 225., 226. sl.

11 Thomas Raiser Das lebende Recht. Rechtssoziologie in Deutschland. Baden-Baden, Nomos Verlagsgeselschaft, 1999, S.171.

norms, firstly, by the nature of their application since only the legal norms can be legitimately enforced.[12]

Legal norms have a series of tasks in society; however, first and foremost, legal norms ensure justice. Although the understanding of justice is historically determined because it changes together with the society itself and the public consciousness, the law, on each level of society's development, guarantees the existence of justice.[13] Namely, exactly like the society and the culture created by it, including its self-understanding, also the law is constantly transforming.[14] With the development of society, also the understanding of the sources of law changes. Until the industrial society the customary law dominated, but the discretion of both the king and, later, of the parliament was limited.[15] In the European countries, the customary law (as the basic or auxiliary source of law) lost its legal force only in the course of the 19th and the 20th centuries. For example, in Germany the collection of medieval customary law "Mirror of the Saxons" lost its force in Prussia only in 1794 when the General State Laws for the Prussian States (*Allgemeines Landrecht für die Preußischen Staaten*) entered into force,[16] but in other German lands in 1900, with the coming into force of the German Civil Law (*Bürgerliches Gesetzbuch*).[17] In other countries, it occurred even later, during the course of the 20th century. Moreover, it is worth recalling that under the influence of the dominant historical school of law in the 19th century, the legislator, in adopting new laws, respected the legal norms that had taken root among the people, i.e., the traditional legal norms, which society had applied for generations.[18] The process of drafting the Latvian Civil Law in the inter-war period of the 20th century also confirmed that the commission that drafted the law was unwilling to break the legal order that existed among the people but rather wanted to compile and

---

12 Thomas Raiser Das lebende Recht. Rechtssoziologie in Deutschland. Baden-Baden, Nomos Verlagsgesellschaft, 1999, S.179.

13 Густав Радбрух Философия права. Москва, Международные отношения, 2004, c. 41–48.

14 Piemēram, Roger Cotterrell Sociological Jurisprudence. Juristic thought and social inquiry. London, New York, Routledge, 2018, pp. 223–229.

15 Uwe Wesel Geschihcte des Rechts. Von den Frühformen bis zur Gegenwart. 3. Auflage, München, C.H. Beck, 2006, S. 322–327.

16 Ibidem, S. 414, 415.

17 Sachsenspiegel. Rechtslexikon.Net. Retrieved from: http://www.rechtslexikon.net/d/sachsenspiegel/sachsenspiegel.htm [Accessed on 27.07.2018].

18 Jānis Lazdiņš Vēsturiskā tiesību skola un Latvija. No: *Latvijas Universitātes Raksti. Juridiskā Zinātne.*Rīga: Latvijas Universitāte, 2006, 703. sēj., 21.–43. lpp.

harmonise the law that had been traditionally applied by the people. Therefore, in drafting the Civil Law, a major problem was caused by the fact that in different regions the provisions of customary law differed significantly, for example, with respect to the property regime of married persons.[19] During the second half of the 19th century – the first half of the 20th century, the representatives of the school of legal positivism, who held that only the legal norms that had been duly issued by the state had to be recognised the law, provided the substantiation for the legislator's discretion in creating the law.[20] This finding gave the possibility to the parliaments to not only create modern judicial and legal systems but also to engage in social engineering. At the beginning of the 21st century, the Swedish Government officially admitted that, in order to create a healthy society, in a campaign organised by the state, from 1936 to 1976, enforced sterilisation of groups of certain persons had been performed.[21] Sterilisation and castration of "morally deficient" persons was part also of the Swiss social policy in the period from 1890 to 1970.[22] Similar experiments with humans, based on the scientific findings of the times that these were beneficial for the society as a whole, were conducted also in other countries of the world, *inter alia*, the democratic ones. And even more broadly interpreted findings of the legal positivism, during the first half of the 20th century, "allowed" the totalitarian regimes to apply the law extensively contrary to the meaning and the spirit of law, establishing such legal order that was unfair, anti-human, and did not permit personal freedom.[23] Exactly at the time when the legislator acquired the discretion to freely regulate the public life according to its views, Hans Kelsen substantiated the need for a constitutional

---

19 This is confirmed by Vladimiris Bukovskis' (1867–1937) report on the commission's work. For example, Vladimirs Bukovskis Jaunā civilkodeksa izstrādāšanas darbība. *Tieslietu Ministrijas Vēstnesis.* 1/3(1921)/3,32.-40. lpp.

20 Gabriel Nogueira Dias Rechtspositivismus und Rechtstheorie: das Verhältnis beider im Werke Hans Kelsens. Tübingen: Mohr Siebeck, 2005, S. 253.

21 [B.a.] Zviedrija lems par sterilizācijas upuriem. Available; http://www.diena.lv/lat/arhivs/arzemju-zinas/zviedrija-lems-par-sterilizacijas-upuriem [Accessed on 25.03.2018].

22 Huonker, T.Diagnose „Moralisch Defekt" Kastration, Sterilisation und „Rassenhygiene" im Dienst der Schweizer Sozialpolitik und Psychiatrie 1890–1970. Pieejamshttp://www.thata.net/thomashuonkerdiagnosemoralischdefektzuerich2003opt.pdf [Accessed on 25.03.2018].

23 For example, Christian Merkel has conducted a study on the way the ideas of legal positivism were used to legalise the programme "Euthanasia" in Germany. Christian Merkel "Tod den Idioten" – Eugenik und Euthanasie in juristischer Rezeption vom Kaiserreich zur Hitlerzeit. Berlin: Logos Verlag, 2006, S. 345, 346.

court, which would keep this legislator's discretion within the framework of the fundamental norms and the constitution, not permitting to disrupt society and deprive of human liberty

Thus, in the industrial society, the understanding of law as constant social norms that guaranteed eternally constant divine justice was gradually re-examined. In the second half of the 20th century, with the establishment of a post-industrial society, the currently dominant idea became consolidated. In other words, the law is a social compromise, which the representatives legitimised by the people – the members of the parliament, make generally binding by presenting it in the form of legal norms.[24] Here, **the second flag of precaution** could be set up: this understanding significantly influenced the constancy of law, thus also impacting the legal stability in society and caused inundation with norms.[25] Therefore a disclaimer is added to the aforementioned concept, namely, that although a legal norm is the outcome of a social compromise, to have stable law, to allow the society to develop long-term projects and to protect a person's legal expectations, in adopting it, the provisions for the legality of a norm that have been developed in the legal system must be met: the general principles of law, the constitution, a person's fundamental rights.[26] In various European countries, the safeguarding of the constitutional identity is proposed as a legal argument with increasing frequency. In the creation of law, the legislator should, primarily, respect the constitutional identity of each state. Moreover, fundamental values, fundamental norms, and fundamental rights exist in the society that must be respected by all – both the national legislator and the supranational organisations, for example, the European Union, adopting new legal norms, as a social compromise.[27]

---

24 Norbert Horn Einfürung in die Rechtswissenschaft und Rechtsphilosophie. 4., neu bearbeitete Auflage. Heidelberg: C. F. Müller, 2007, S. 76, 77.

25 Ernst Benda Die soziale Rechtsstaat. In: Handbuch des Verfassungsrechts der Bundesrepublik Deutschland. Hrsg. Ernst Benda, Werner Maihofer, Hans-Jochen Vogel, Berlin, New York: Walter de Gruyter, 2012, S. 752.

26 Daiga Rezevska Vispārējo tiesību principu nozīme un piemērošana. Rīga: Daiga Rezevska, 2015, 80., 81.lpp.

27 Christoph Degenhart Staatsrecht I. Staatsorganisationsrecht. Mit Bezügen zum Europarecht. 33. Auflage. Heidelberg: C.F. Müller, 2017, S. 5.

2 Who is the Legislator in a Democratic State Governed by the Rule of Law?

In a democratic state governed by the rule of law, the legislative procedure is based upon the democratic legitimisation of the legislator; i.e., the parliament is a representative elected by the people but the source of the state power as a whole and the bearer of the sovereign power is the people.[28] In Latvia's case, the constitution defines two legislators: the parliament and the people.[29]The legislative procedure, in turn, is a special procedural order, in accordance with which the *Saeima* or the people themselves achieve that a prepared draft law becomes a law, i.e., a regulatory enactment that occupies a certain place in the system of regulatory enactments.[30]

Everything seems to be simple; however, it turns out that at present it is not that easy at all to answer the question belonging to a lawyer's ABC: "Who is the legislator?" Examination of the transformation of the contemporary society allows concluding that, in the presence of interpersonal intensive supranational communication, the borders of the nation states are dismantled and the global society forms. The inhabitants of all contemporary states are creating ever more complex networks of relationships both domestically and, simultaneously, in cooperation with other societies. In contemporary Europe, the sovereign power of the state is exercised within the Western "open democracy", which is characterised by the free movement of persons, capital, and information. This, in the presence of the new opportunities offered by information technologies, makes the implementation of the national jurisdiction more complicated. Therefore, for the state to be able to control and to influence at least the conduct of its own citizens, it needs transnational legal authority.[31]

The cross-border contacts of national states and the members of their societies create the network of relationships, upon which the global society is based. In other words, the global society comprises a complex and complicated multidimensional system that is shaped by societies, which are relatively independent but in interact and which are mutually dependent.[32] This determines the

---

28 Ibidem, S. 63.

29 The Constitution of the Republic of Latvia. Available: https://likumi.lv/ta/en/en/id/57980 [Accessed on 27.08.2018.]

30 Satversmes tiesas 2009. gada 19. maija sprieduma lietā Nr. 2008-40-01 9. punkts.

31 Roger Cotterrell Sociological jurisprudence. Juristic thought and social inquiry. London, NewYork: Routledge, 2018, p. 123.

32 Ни́клас Луман Общесвто как социальная система. Москва: Логос, 2004, с. 160 - 162.

need to re-examine also the concept of the state's sovereignty and to develop new forms of cooperation between the states.[33] However, the establishment of a global society does not lead to the destruction of a nation state. Quite to the contrary, its significance grows because the nation state has to ensure the rule of law not only on the national level but also must participate in creating the supranational order and the rule of law. Thus, also the supranational or transnational level of legislation becomes more clearly outlined.[34]

The third precautionary flag: in examining the institute of legislator, it must be kept in mind that whoever the legislator might be: the national or the supranational parliament, the source of the sovereign power constantly is the people. Therefore, each legislator exercises the power of the people, not that of its own. Thus, both the national and the supranational binding norms must be created only in institutions particularly authorised by the people, and abiding by the limits of this authorisation. These limits of authorisation are clearly defined by the constitution of each state and interstate agreements.

Therefore, for the regulatory enactments adopted by the legislator to be legal, firstly, the legitimacy of the institution should be ensured, i.e., whether it has the appropriate authorisation by the people, and, secondly, the principle of separation of powers – the legislator is the parliament, which both institutionally and functionally is separated from the executive power.

Hence, only an appropriately authorised body of state power has the right to issue norms of conduct that are binding upon society. The legitimisation must be direct, and the people's authorisation cannot be transferred; however, in an exceptional case, in doing so, the limits set in the constitution and the law must be strictly observed. Moreover, this body authorised by the legislator has no right, without a special order by the legislator, to transfer the authorisation (to issue binding legal norms) to another body and to form a whole chain or cascade of "legislators", which, by becoming more and more distant from the sovereign and the parliament legitimised by it, arbitrarily restricts the persons' rights more than provided for in law. I do not know if the problem of authorisation and transfer of authorisation exists in Poland; however, it clearly exists in Latvia,

33 Cohen J. L. Sovereignty in the Context of Globalization: A Constitutional Pluralist Perspective. In: Besson S., Tasioulas J. *The Philosophy of International Law*. Oxford: Oxford University, 2010, p. 275.

34 However, I shall not include in this overview the supranational legislators or the interstate cooperation in legislator or the people as the legislator. My further study is limited to the parliament's discretion in performing the legislative function.

which is proven by the significant number of cases that have been heard by the Constitutional Court.

The remaining time will be dedicated to the following:

3 The Parliament's Discretion, in Authorising Other State Bodies to Issue Generally Binding Regulations?

The principle of a state governed by the rule of law first and foremost demands ensuring the supremacy of law over all decisions by the state – both the adopted regulatory enactments and the acts on applying legal norms (administrative acts, other individual decisions).[35] The legislative, the executive and the judicial power not only exercise the state power with the mediation of regulatory enactments and decisions but also are themselves linked to them, *inter alia*, to the constitution.[36] The institutional and functional separation of the respective powers also is constitutional.

I would like to emphasise that the authorisation to legislate, granted by the sovereign, is both the right that the parliament is entrusted with and also its main duty and the purpose, for which it has been created. John Locke, upon initiating the principle of separation of powers, considered separation of the legislation from the executive power as being of primary importance.[37] Since only those authorised by the people – the parliament – may decide on generally binding rules of co-existence. The parliament, in turn, may not be dependent from or subject to the executive power, not even in organisational matters.[38] Therefore, since the principle of separation of powers has been laid in the foundations of a contemporary democratic state governed by the rule of law,[39] only a regulatory enactment that has been adopted by the parliament in a procedure that complies

35 Valsts prezidenta Konstitucionālo tiesību komisijas 17.09.2012. viedoklis par Latvijas valsts konstitucionālajiem pamatiem un neaizskaramo Satversmes kodolu, [231]. Available: http://tzpi.lu.lv/files/2017/03/17092012_Viedoklis_2.pdf.

36 Martin Krygier Rule of Law. In: The Oxford Handbook of Comparative Constitutional Law. Edited by Mischel Rosenfeld and Andras Sajo. Oxford: Oxford University Press, 2012, p. 237.

37 Uwe Wesel Geschihcte des Rechts. Von den Frühformen bis zur Gegenwart. 3. Auflage, München: C.H. Beck, 2006, S. 417.

38 John Locke Second Treatise of Government. Barnes&NoblePublishing, 2004, p. 100, 101.

39 Эбенхард Шмидт-Асман Правовое государство. В: Государственное право Германии. Том. 1. Москва: РАН Институт государства и права, 1994, с. 57.

with the constitution is recognised as being a law.[40] The Constitutional Court also has underscored: "The *Satversme* sets definite procedural requirements for every decision that pertains to a matter of importance in the life of the state and society that ensure that decisions are adopted in compliance with the requirements of a democratic state governed by the rule of law. Abiding by the pre-requisites and requirements that are regulated in the *Satversme* and the *Saeima* Rules of Procedure is an important condition to be met so that the legislator would have abided by the limits of discretion, i.e., so that the adopted acts would be legal."[41]

However, although in terms of the state law, when discussing the legislator we mention one constitutional body – the parliament, with the contemporary society becoming more complex and multi-cultural, the need for new regulatory solutions is growing rapidly. The state must prepare and adopt such decisions without delay. Moreover, it should be taken into consideration that the larger in size and more complicated the society becomes the more significant the role of law becomes in it. Part of society members no longer looks for a solution to complications in their mutual relationships individually but relies upon legal norms and involves state institutions in conflict solution.[42] This causes overloading of the institutions of the state power, including the legislator. Only one "player", the body that represents the people – the parliament can no longer cope with this "work of producing legal norms"[43]. In the case of Latvia, these would be one hundred members of the parliament,[44] with each of them having no more than two assistants.[45] Therefore, a number of specialists and state institutions are involved in the process of legislation.[46] The legal system and legal institutions are analysed, laws are drafted, regulatory enactments are issued on

40 Christoph Degenhart Staatsrecht I. Staatsorganisationsrecht. Mit Bezügen zum Europarecht. 33. Auflage. Heidelberg: C.F. Müller, 2017, S. 62.

41 Satversmes tiesas 2012. gada 3. februāra sprieduma lietā Nr. 2011-11-01 11.2. punkts.

42 Niklas Luhmann Legitimation durch Verfahren. Neuwied und Berlin: Luchterhand, 1969, S. 101.

43 Formally, the process of legislation consists of: the legislative initiative, discussions of the draft law, adoption of the law, publishing of the law. However, actually, the scope is even larger, because prior to the legislative initiative there should be public pressure regarding the need for a new legal solution, lobbyists are involved, etc.

44 The constitution of the Republic of Latvia. 5. paragraph. Available: https://likumi.lv/ta/en/en/id/57980 [Accessed on 28.08.2018].

45 Saeimas kārtības rullis. 195.p.1.d. Available: https://likumi.lv/doc.php?id=57517 [Accessed on 28.08.2018].

46 Sussane Baer Rechtssoziologie. Eine Einfürung in die interdisziplinäre Rechtsforschung. 2. Auflage. Baden-Baden: Nomos, 2015, S. 175.

the basis of the law, which help to implement the law, training is organised on applying the reform laws, etc.

Here we encounter reality. On the one hand, only the parliament is legitimised to adopt regulations that are binding upon society. On the other hand, the parliament lacks the capacity to regulate all social relationships, with respect to which members of society expect a state established regulation. Thus, we have to admit that the parliament needs the right to delegate a part of its functions to other state bodies. It is done to adjust the law to the changing life of society more effectively. Moreover, most often, the government and other authorised state institutions are more competent in drafting the technical norms than the legislator, and the procedure of decision taking in these institutions is less complicated.[47] Traditionally these subjects are the government and the local governments, and in many countries, it is stipulated already in the constitution. The Latvian *Satversme* also had Article 81, which defined the government's rights, in the case of necessity, to adopt regulatory enactments with the force of law in-between the sessions of the *Saeima*.[48] However, this kind of delegation, although regulated constitutionally, is an extraordinary procedure. The Constitutional Court of the Republic of Latvia had to remind the government: "Article 64 of the *Satversme* must be taken into account, which provides that "the *Saeima*, and also the people, have the right to legislate, in accordance with the procedures, and to the extent, provided for by this *Satversme*" and that Article 81 of the *Satversme* delegated the right to legislate to the Cabinet only in especially envisaged cases. Hence, the Cabinet, on the basis of Para 3 of Section 14 of the law "On the Structure of the Cabinet of Ministers" may not issue regulations on matters that fall within the legislator's competence."[49]In other words, the procedure that the government and not the parliament decides on generally binding norms is a deviation from the principle of separation of powers and must be used very cautiously, in accordance with the requirements of a state governed by the rule of law because "the executive power – the Cabinet – has the right to issue regulations, in cases provided for in law, in the framework of law, and these cannot be contrary to the *Satversme* and other laws. This follows from the principles of the people's sovereignty and of separation of powers, which are the basis for the existence of any state governed

47 Satversmes tiesas 2005. gada 21. novembra spriedums lietā Nr. 2005-03-0306.

48 Latvijas Republikas Satversme 81. p. "Between the sessions of the *Saeima*, the Cabinet has the right, if there is an urgent need, to issue regulations with the force of law. . ." Available: https://likumi.lv/ta/id/57980-latvijas-republikas-satversme#p81 [Accessed on 28.08.2018].

49 Satversmes tiesas 2001. gada 3. aprīļa spriedums lietā Nr. 2000-07-0409, #22D.

by the rule of law."[50] On 17 May 2007, the Latvian parliamentarians decided to exclude from the constitution Article 81, i.e., the provision that delegated to the government the right to issue generally binding regulatory enactments[51] because they considered that the government was exercising this right too actively, waiting especially for the recess of the parliament to introduce significant amendments to laws. The President Vaira Vīķe-Freiberga, in supporting the need for this amendment to the *Satversme*, said: "I do not see the reason why the *Saeima*, in a situation of crisis, could not express its will in an electronic form," noting, in addition, that she considered a situation that in such cases the adoption of laws would be delegated to the government as inadequate.[52]

However, the delegated legislation should not be considered as being generally inadmissible or anti-constitutional. The Constitutional Court has recognised: "To ensure more effective exercise of the state power, exemptions from the principle of the legislator's supremacy are admissible. These exemptions follow from the *Satversme*. The aim thereof is to make the legislative process more efficient and also respond faster and more adequately to the need for amending the legal regulation."[53] Thus, in the case of necessity, the legislator has the right to delegate to the government or a local government the issuing of generally binding regulatory enactments; however, there are a number of rules that restrict the government and the local government in the performance of this obligation. The government and the local government may issue only regulatory enactments that are subordinated to the law, that comply with the law, to facilitate the actual enforcement of laws. This is achieved by specifying those provisions of the law the implementation of which requires a more detailed regulation. In issuing regulations, the Cabinet may not include in them such norms that cannot be considered as being auxiliary measures for enforcing a legal provision.[54]Thus, all subjects who are not the parliament are strictly legally restricted in issuing generally binding norms. First of all, the legislator's delegation to issue such norms is required, and,

---

50 Satversmes tiesas 1998. gada 10. jūnija spriedums lietā Nr. 04–03, #6D.

51 2007. gada 17. maija likums Grozījumi Latvijas Republikas Satversmē. Available: https://likumi.lv/ta/id/157308-grozijumi-latvijas-republikas-satversme[Accessed on 28.08.2018].

52 14. marts 2007. Koalīcija vienojas svītrot Satversmes 81. pantu. Available: http://www.delfi.lv/news/national/politics/koalicija-vienojas-svitrot-satversmes-81pantu.d?id=17170056 [Accessed on 28.08.2018].

53 Satversmes tiesas 2016. gada 2. marta sprieduma lietā Nr. 2015-11-03 21.1. punkts.

54 Satversmes tiesas 2001. gada 3. aprīļa sprieduma lietā Nr. 2000-07-0409 secinājumu daļas 5. punkts.

in exercising it, the limits of the delegation must be precisely adhered to, as well as the principles of the separation of powers and legality. Likewise, the Latvian case law and the legal doctrine have clearly defined the prohibition to transfer the delegation granted by the legislator to another subject of law.[55]

However, also the legislator, in delegating to other state bodies the right to issue generally binding regulatory enactments, enjoys rather limited discretion. The Constitutional Court in its case law has underscored a number of criteria that the legislator must take into consideration when granting such authorisation.

First, the legislator does not have the right to transfer any matter to the executive power to decide on. There are matters, on which only the parliament itself may decide, for example:

1. The *Saeima*, acting as the legislator, does not have the right to transfer to the executive power for deciding matters, which, pursuant to the *Satversme*, are within the exclusive competence of the *Saeima* itself.[56]
2. The fundamental rights may be restricted only by law or on the basis of a law, which clearly defines the scope of the restriction on fundamental rights. Restriction of fundamental rights without clear authorisation by the legislator is inadmissible. When exercising the authorisation, in turn, a restriction on a person's fundamental rights must be avoided if the authorising norm does not directly point to the need for a restriction.[57]
3. The legislator itself must decide on the regulation on all matters that are important in the life of the state and the society, which require a conceptual choice and a political discussion.[58]

Secondly, the parliament must abide by the formal requirements regarding granting the authorisation:

1. The legislator, in authorising the executive power to draft regulation on a certain matter, may not cause the risk that the balance between the legislative

---

55 "The Cabinet had the right and the obligation to establish the respective procedure; however, it did not have the right to delegate the establishing of this order to someone else since the law did not provide for such right of the Cabinet. It has been emphasized also in the Latvian legal science that only that administrative body, to whom this right has been granted or delegated by law, can issue regulations; however, it may not transfer this right to another body." Satversmes tiesas 1998. gada 23. februāra spriedums lietā Nr. 04–04, 3. punkts.

56 Satversmes tiesas 2015. gada 14. oktobra sprieduma lietā Nr. 2015-05-03 10. punkts.

57 Satversmes tiesas 2016. gada 2. marta sprieduma lietā Nr. 2015-11-03 23.4. punkts.

58 Satversmes tiesas 2011. gada 11. janvāra sprieduma lietā Nr. 2010-40-03 10.1. punkts.

and the executive power would weigh towards the executive power to the extent that the principle of separation of powers and, thus, also the essence of a democratic state order, would be jeopardised.[59]
2. The authorisation should be concrete, i.e., clearly defined.[60] The parliament has the obligation to define clearly in the authorising norm "the scope of authorisation granted to the authorities and the way of implementing it, taking into consideration the legitimate aim of the particular measure to provide adequate protection to an individual against arbitrary interference."[61]
3. The authorisation must be legal. First and foremost, the legislator is responsible for compliance of the authorisation with norms of higher legal force.[62]

Thirdly, the parliament is co-responsible for the implementation of the authorisation that has been granted. The legislator must ensure, through the parliamentary control or other legal remedies at its disposal, that the authorisation would be implemented in accordance with the *Satversme*and also considerations of expedience and reasonableness.[63]

Conclusions

1. Over time, the understanding of what law is has changed; however, the objectives of law in society have not changed – to ensure justice, peace and social stability.
2. With the changes in the understanding of the sources of law and the legislator's discretion, the contemporary democratic state governed by the rule of law formed, in which constitutional justice was created to ensure that the legislator would act within the limits of law, i.e., by complying with the general legal principles, the constitution, a person's fundamental rights, international commitments, which limit the legislator's discretion.
3. The legislator authorised by the people – the parliament – must primarily adopt the legal regulation itself in all matters important for society, in particular, regarding such that pertain to restrictions on a person's fundamental rights and matters of national importance. However, it follows from the nature of the contemporary state and society that the legislator alone is

---

59 Satversmes tiesas 2011. gada 11. janvāra sprieduma lietā Nr. 2010-40-03 10.2. punkts.
60 Satversmes tiesas 2016. gada 2. marta sprieduma lietā Nr. 2015-11-03 23. 4. punkts.
61 Satversmes tiesas 2002. gada 20. maija spriedums lietā Nr. 2002-01-03.
62 Satversmes tiesas 2011. gada 11. janvāra spriedums lietā Nr. 2010-40-03: 10.
63 Satversmes tiesas 2011. gada 11. janvāra spriedums lietā Nr. 2010-40-03: 12.

unable to adopt all legal regulation that a society needs. Therefore, the legislator has the right to authorise other state bodies to issue generally binding regulatory enactments.

4. In authorising other state bodies to issue generally binding regulatory enactments, the legislator, both as an authorising body and the authorised body, is closely linked to the principles of the people's sovereignty, the separation of powers and legality. If deviations from the principle of people's sovereignty, separation of powers or legality have occurred in the legislator's authorisation or in the implementation thereof then the act has been adopted *ultra vires* and is void since its adoption.

References

1. Assman, Jan, Das kulturelle Gedächtnis: Schrift, Erinnerung und politische Identität in frühen Hochkulturen. München: C. H. Beck, 2002.
2. Baer, Sussane, Rechtssoziologie. Eine Einfürung in die interdisziplinäre Rechtsforschung. 2. Auflage. Baden-Baden: Nomos, 2015.
3. Benda, Ernst, Die soziale Rechtsstaat. In: HandbuchdesVerfassungsrechts der Bundesrepublik Deutschland. Hrsg. Ernst Benda, Werner Maihofer, Hans-Jochen Vogel. Berlin, New York: Walter de Gruyter, 2012. S. 719–798.
4. Bukovskis, Vladimirs, Jaunā civilkodeksa izstrādāšanas darbība. Tieslietu Ministrijas Vēstnesis. 1/3 (1921)/3, 32.-40. lpp.
5. Cohen, Jean L., Sovereignty in the Context of Globalization: A Constitutional Pluralist Perspective. In: The Philosophy of International Law. Hrsg. Samantha Besson, John Tasioulas.Oxford: Oxford University, 2010.
6. Cotterrell, Roger, Sociological Jurisprudence. Juristic thought and social inquiry. London, New York: Routledge, 2018.
7. Danovskis, Edvīns, Publisko un privāto tiesību dalījuma nozīme un piemērošanas problēmas Latvijā. Rīga: Latvijas Vēstnesis, 2015.
8. Degenhart, Christoph, Staatsrecht I. Staatsorganisationsrecht. Mit Bezügen zum Europarecht. 33. Auflage. Heidelberg: C.F. Müller, 2017.
9. Dias, Gabriel Nogueira, Rechtspositivismus und Rechtstheorie: das Verhältnis bei der im Werke Hans Kelsens. Tübingen: Mohr Siebeck, 2005.

10. Durkheim, Emile, Regeln der soziologischen Methode. Neuwied und Berlin: Luchterhand, 1965.
11. Horn, Norbert, Einführung in die Rechtswissenschaft und Rechtsphilosophie. 4. neubearbeitete Auflage. Heidelberg: C. F. Müller, 2007, S. 76, 77.
12. Huonker, Thomas, Diagnose „Moralisch Defekt" Kastration, Sterilisation und „Rassenhygiene" im Dienst der Schweizer Sozialpolitik und Psychiatrie 1890–1970. Zürich: Orell Füssli Verlag, 2003.
13. Krygier, Martin, Rule of Law. In: The Oxford Handbook of Comparative Constitutional Law. Hrsg. Mischel Rosenfeldand, Andras Sajo. Oxford: Oxford University Press, 2012.
14. Lazdiņš, Jānis, Vēsturiskā tiesību skola un Latvija. No: Latvijas Universitātes Raksti. Juridiskā Zinātne. Rīga: Latvijas Universitāte, 2006, 703. sēj., 21.–43. lpp.
15. Locke, John, Second Treatise of Government. New York: Barnes & Noble Publishing, 2004.
16. Luhmann, Niklas, Legitimation durch Verfahren. Neuwied und Berlin: Luchterhand, 1969, S. 101.
17. Merkel, Christian, "Tod den Idioten" – Eugenik und Euthanasie in juristischer Rezeption vom Kaiserreich zur Hitlerzeit. Berlin: Logos Verlag, 2006.
18. Muthorst, Olaf, Grundlagen der Rechtswissenschaft. Methode -Begriff -System. München: C. H. Beck, 2011.
19. Osipova,Sanita, Latviešu juridiskā kultūra un tiesiskā apziņa. No: Akadēmiskie raksti 4 sējumos „Latvieši un Latvija", III sējums „Atjaunotā Latvijas valsts". Rīga: Latvijas Zinātņu akadēmija, 2013,151.-178. lpp.
20. Raiser, Thomas, Das lebende Recht. Rechtssoziologie in Deutschland. Baden-Baden: Nomos Verlagsgeselschaft, 1999.
21. Rezevska, Daiga, Vispārējo tiesību principu nozīme un piemērošana. Rīga: Daiga Rezevska, 2015.
22. Sachsenspiegel. Rechtslexikon.Net. Retrievedfrom: http://www.rechtslexikon.net/d/sachsenspiegel/sachsenspiegel.htm [Accessedon 27.07.2018].
23. Sinaiskis,Vasīlijs, Tiesības un ģimene. Jurists. Nr. 8., 01.11.1929, 225., 226. sl.
24. Valsts prezidenta Konstitucionālo tiesību komisijas 17.09.2012. viedoklis par Latvijas valsts konstitucionālajiem pamatiem un

neaizskaramo Satversmes kodolu, [231]. Available: http://tzpi.lu.lv/files/2017/03/17092012_Viedoklis_2.pdf [Accessedon 28.08.2018].

25. Wesel, Uwe, Geschichte des, Rechts. Von den Frühformen bis zur Gegenwart. 3. Auflage. München: C.H. Beck, 2006.
26. Леже, Раймон, Великие правовые системы современности. 3-еиздание. Москва: Волтерс Клувер, 2011.
27. Луман, Ни́клас,Общесвто как социальная система. Москва: Логос, 2004.
28. Радбрух, Густав,Философия права. Москва: Международныеотношения, 2004.
29. Шмидт-Асман, Еберхард Правовое государство. В: Государственное право Германии. Том. 1.Москва: РАН Институт государства и права, 1994.

Legislations

1. The Constitutionof the Republic of Latvia. Available: https://likumi.lv/ta/en/en/id/57980 [Accessed on 27.08.2018].
2. 2007. gada17. maija likums Grozījumi Latvijas Republikas Satversmē. Available: https://likumi.lv/ta/id/157308-grozijumi-latvijas-republikas-satversme [Accessed on 28.08.2018].
3. 1994. gada28. jūlija. Likums Saeimas kārtības rullis. Available: https://likumi.lv/doc.php?id=57517 [Accessed on 28.08.2018].

Latvian Constitutional Court Cases

1. Satversmes tiesas 1998. gada 10. jūnija spriedums lietā Nr. 04-03.
2. Satversmes tiesas 2001. gada 3. aprīļa sprieduma lietā Nr. 2000-07-0409.
3. Satversmes tiesas 2002. gada 20. maija spriedums lietā Nr. 2002-01-03.
4. Satversmes tiesas 2005. gada 21. novembra spriedums lietā Nr. 2005-03-0306.
5. Satversmes tiesas 2009. gada 19. maija sprieduma lietā Nr. 2008-40-01.
6. Satversmes tiesas 2011. gada 11. janvāra sprieduma lietā Nr. 2010-40-03.
7. Satversmes tiesas 2012. gada 3. februāra sprieduma lietā Nr. 2011-11-01.
8. Satversmes tiesas 2015. gada 14. oktobra sprieduma lietā Nr. 2015-05-03.
9. Satversmes tiesas 2016. gada 2. marta sprieduma lietā Nr. 2015-11-03.

Dobrochna Minich

8 Constitutional Court –a Controller or Co-Legislator?

Abstract: From the legal and dogmatic perspective Constitutional Tribunal of the Republic of Poland does not have explicitly expressed legislative competences. It is not a body of statutory authority. There is no competence norm that grants Tribunal the power to create the law. Does the examination of compliance of statutory law and other acts with the Constitution cannot be treated as a form of law-making?Legal discourse has a complex character. Polish doctrine presupposes a two-layer nature of law. It consists of:"Law understood as text", defined as positive law (statutory law), in civil law countries identified with provisions created by the legislator which must be consistent with the Constitution (Constitutional Court or Tribunal have a special role as a judicial body established to supervise the compliance of statutory law with the Constitution); application of law – resolution of specific court cases (judgment), individual decisions (administrative decisions) and behavior of legal life actors.If the law is applied then it must exist before the acts of application. This existence is determined by proper law-making and its compliance with the Constitution. This situation leads to a continuous dialogue between the law-making bodies, Constitutional courts/Tribunals and entities applying the law.The aim of the article is to prove that the Constitutional Court/Tribunal is departing from its classic role as a "negative legislator" by becoming also a positive one.

Keywords: Constitutional Tribunal, Constitution, legal discourse, legislator

From the legal and dogmatic point of view, the Constitutional Court does not have explicitly expressed legislative powers. First of all, it is not an organ of legislative power. Chapter VIII of the Constitution: *Courts and Tribunals* is devoted to it. It is also emphasized that "Courts are separate authorities and they are independent of other authorities" (Article 173)[1]. There is no competent standard that grants the Constitutional Court the power to create law. Yet, can't the examination of the compliance of laws and other acts with the Constitution be treated as a form of law-making or participation in the creation of law?

Polish Constitutional Court has been included in the judiciary, but it does not exercise the judiciary. In Polish literature, the distinction between the concept of

1 Constitution of the Republic of Poland of April 2, 1997 (Journal of Laws 1997, No. 78, item 483).

the creation and application of law is strongly emphasized. Legislative activity consists in creating the law – establishing by authorized entities abstract and general norms by virtue of these entities' legislative powers. The administration of justice consists in the application of the law, which results in the issuing of acts "establishing individual and specific norms"[2]. In the process of applying the law, an important role is played by the interpretation of legal regulations defining the "pattern" (norm) with which the actual state is confronted. In case of subsumption, the entity using the law decides about the legal consequences for the entity whose behavior does not correspond to the "model".

However, when The Constitutional Court is examining the compliance of an abstract and general norm, constituting the object of control, with a constitutional norm, it does not simply subsume. This activity does not fall within the traditional understanding of the application of law. The act of control consists in examining the compliance of laws and other normative acts with the constitution. It is made taking into account three criteria: material, competence and procedural. The examination of constitutionality is only to some extent an act of applying the law within the meaning of the practice of law enforcement bodies (e.g., by common courts). It refers only to the examination of the formal (competence and procedural) aspect of the object of control (act and other laws). In this respect, they are individual and specific, like all acts of law. A different nature is the examination of the conformity of acts constituting the object of control in the material aspect. This control is of an abstract nature, and this is the source of controversy regarding the nature of the Constitutional Court's control. Does it have the character of law-making, or is it a specifically understood application of law?[3]

Traditional understanding of the term 'application of law' (the process of individualization and concretization of an abstract and general norm) to the analysis of the structure of examination of the conformity of laws and other acts with the Constitution does not cover all the activities performed by the Constitutional Court. The construction of the application of law by Zygmunt Ziembiński can be adopted here. He understands the application of law as the decision-making process consisting in the performance of a conventional action that is legally significant when it is implemented under the authorization granted to a given

2 See L. Leszczyński, *Zagadnienia teorii stosowania prawa. Doktryna i tezy orzecznictwa*, Cracow 2001, p. 15 and n.

3 See S. Oliwniak, *Wpływ orzecznictwa Trybunału Konstytucyjnego na system prawa w latach 1985–1997*, Białystok 2001, p. 212.

entity by a competence norm. These are the activities of the entity, which consist in making use of the competence conferred upon it to perform a specific, legally significant act[4]. In that sense, the Court's audit acts fall within the scope of the law. This concept is referred to by Sławomira Wronkowska for whom a control act carried out by the Constitutional Court is an act of the application of the law so understood. "On the basis of the hierarchically higher norm (control pattern) reconstructed by the constitutional court in the process of the interpretation and the comparison of this norm with a hierarchically lower norm (object of control) the court makes use of the competence granted to it, declaring that the latter is or does not comply with the norm which is the control pattern"[5].

One may also to adopt a construction which assumes that in addition to the creation and application of law, we are dealing here with the third type of the activity of the state – one in which the Constitutional Court also controls the legality of establishing and applying the law[6].

Regardless of how the activities carried out by the Court in the process of examining the compliance of the subject of control with the constitutional model are understood, this authority must perform two operations: interpretation of the provisions being the subject of control and interpretation of regulations constituting the control pattern[7]. The Constitutional Court analyzes whether the subject of control (e.g., an Act) is consistent with the pattern (constitution), it compares legal norms of a different level by assessing their hierarchical compatibility[8], which is then expressed by the Court in the form of a statement qualifying a lower standard as compliant or inconsistent with a constitutional norm[9]. It is an expression of the so-called double-layered properties of law. According to this

---

4 Z. Ziembiński, *Problemy podstawowe prawoznawstwa*, Warsaw 1980, p. 418 and n.; idem, *O stanowieniu i obowiązywaniu prawa. Zagadnienia podstawowe*, Warsaw 1995, pp. 41 and n.

5 S. Wronkowska, *O niektórych osobliwościach konstytucji i jej interpretacji* [in:] *Wykładnia konstytucji. Aktualne problemy i tendencje*, ed. M. Smolak, Warsaw 2016, pp. 20–21.

6 See J. Trzciński, *Charakter podstawowej działalności Trybunału Konstytucyjnego*, [in:] *Trybunał Konstytucyjny*, ed. idem, Wrocław 1987, pp. 83–85.

7 P. Tuleja, *Podstawowe problemy związane z interpretacją Konstytucji Rzeczypospolitej Polskiej w orzecznictwie Trybunału Konstytucyjnego*, [in:] *Księga XX-lecia orzecznictwa Trybunału Konstytucyjnego*, ed. M. Zubik, Warsaw 2006, p. 209.

8 R. Guastini, *Lezioni di teoria del diritto e dello stato*, Torino 2006, pp. 33–52.

9 About qualifying statements see J. Wróblewski, *Zwroty stosunkowe – wypowiedzi o zgodności z normą*, [in:] idem, *Pisma wybrane*, selection and introduction M. Zirk-Sadowski, Warsaw 2015, pp. 100–114.

approach, law is the text and its use. "Since the law is applied, it exists in some sense of this word, it «exists» before the acts of its application"[10]. This "existence" is determined by the proper establishment of the law and its conformity to the constitution. This means that between the legislature, the Constitutional Court and the entities applying the law there tends to be co-operation and rivalry.

In the process of examining the hierarchical compliance of laws and other acts with the constitution, the method(s) of interpretation of the regulations that constitute its subject do not raise any major controversies. Commonly accepted typical interpretation methods (linguistic, system, functional) are applied by the Constitutional Court, but a problem arises in case of an interpretation of the control pattern, i.e., the study of the constitution. According to Gero Kellermann, the discussion on the correct methods of constitutional interpretation is the "Archimedes point" of constitutional law[11]. Polish Constitutional Court adopted interpretative techniques of other constitutional courts. It sought the sources in American practice of constitutional jurisprudence – in harmony with the Constitution[12]and the German concept of *fervassungskonforme Auslegung von Gesetzen*[13].

The views of the subject in the literature are not homogeneous. Some include this interpretation technique to system interpretation[14]; others include it to functional interpretation. The interpretation that takes into account the axiology of the constitution is of particular importance. Axiological arguments are closely related to functional and teleological interpretation[15]. Attempts are also made to locate interpretation directives in accordance with the constitution

---

10 J. Mikołajewicz, *Orzeczenia zakresowe i interpretacyjne Trybunału Konstytucyjnego jako przejaw kryzysu legitymacji legalnej*, [in:] *Normalność i kryzys. Jedność czy różnorodność*, ed. J. Oniszczuk, Warsaw 2010, p. 225.

11 G. Kellermann, *Verfassungsinterpretation. Das Grundgesetz als normative Ressource im gesellschaftlichen Wandel*, Schwalbach 2011, p. 25.

12 See A. Scalia, B. A. Garner, *Reading Law: The Interpretation of Legal Text*, St. Paul 2012, p. 53; Z. Czeszejko-Sochacki, *Orzeczenia Trybunału Konstytucyjnego: pojęcie, klasyfikacja, skutki*, „Państwo i Prawo" 2000, no. 12, p. 22.

13 R. Wahl, *Verfassungsänderung – Verfassungswandel – Verfassungsinterpretation*, [in:] *Verfassungsänderung, Verfassungswandel, Verfassungsinterpretation: Vorträge bei deutsch – japanischen Sympozien in Tokyo 2004 und Freiburg 2005*, Berlin 2008, p. 29.

14 See L. Morawski, *Wykładnia w orzecznictwie sądów. Komentarz*, Toruń 2002, p. 168 and n.

15 P. Tuleja, *Stosowanie Konstytucji RP w świetle zasady jej nadrzędności (wybrane problemy)*, Cracow 2003, p. 308.

between the first- and second-degree interpretative directives[16]. An interpretation in accordance with the constitution is also presented as a kind of operative interpretation[17].

The difference between the Constitutional Court and other courts, or law enforcement bodies lies in the fact that the process of its operationalization of the interpretation of law is abstract[18]. Piotr Tuleja rightly observed that it is primarily about defining by the Court such a meaning of a regulation of an Act on the general-abstract level that is binding for other authorities, and in the case of bodies applying the law, it is about determining the normative content of an act being the basis for a specific-individual norm[19]. Thus, the interpretation of law made by courts and bodies applying the law constitutes an interpretive activity carried out in concreto. However, this distinction is an expression of some idealization since, after all, courts, such as the Supreme Court or the Supreme Administrative Court, not only determine the legal consequences limited to a specific case, but they also make an abstract interpretation. The Constitutional Court must take into account an interpretation of the legal regulations set out in the case-law or its application, and it can apply in this matter to all judicial authorities for information (Art. 70)[20]. In certain aspects, the Court itself also applies the interpretation in concreto. This applies above all to the aspect of a formal examination of the compliance of law with the Constitution. It consists, as previously stated, in the examination whether the relevant formal requirements, such as the competence to issue a normative act and the manner of its issuance (Article 68)[21], were observed, as well as in the examination of the objections that are formulated in the legal question or in a constitutional complaint, which the Constitutional Tribunal is bound by (Article 67)[22]. This formal aspect of an operative interpretation legitimizes the result of the interpretation in every decision-making process, both in concreto and in abstracto.

---

16 See A. Bator, A. Kozak, *Wykładnia prawa w zgodzie z konstytucją*, [in:] *Polska kultura prawna a proces integracji europejskiej*, ed. S. Wronkowska, Cracow 2005, p. 44–45.

17 See T. Stawecki, *Operatywna wykładnia konstytucji w świetle badań empirycznych*, [in:] *Wykładnia operatywna prawa – perspektywa teoretyczna i dogmatyczna*, ed. L. Leszczyński, A. Szot, Toruń 2017, p. 49–73.

18 A. Bator, A. Kozak, *Wykładnia prawa...*, p. 57.

19 P. Tuleja, *Stosowanie Konstytucji...*, p. 307.

20 Organizacja i tryb postępowania przed Trybunałem Konstytucyjnym (Journal of Laws of 2016, item 2072).

21 *Ibidem*.

22 *Ibidem*.

The competence of the Constitutional Court focuses primarily on the hierarchical control of norms. The very notion of norm controls in the aspect of testing their conformity with the constitution presupposes their hierarchy[23]. "The idea of a hierarchical ordering of the legal system is universally accepted in jurisprudence"[24]. Each legal system is in its essence a complete, consistent and hierarchically ordered set of norms. By referring in this respect to the classic models of static and dynamic law systems of Hans Kelsen, the concept of gradual construction of a legal order of Adolf Merkel, and models constructed by Jerzy Wróblewski, Krzysztof Płeszka demonstrated that the legal system can be ordered hierarchically in two aspects: validity and derogation[25]. These hierarchies are not identical. The hierarchy in terms of validity means a competence link between legal norms. The norm constituting the basis of the validity of another norm takes a higher position in the hierarchy. This relationship is often connected with the concept of legal status. This, in turn, is a derivative of the hierarchical structure of state organs[26]. The author showed that a lawyer "wishing to determine the validity of an element of the legal system (e.g., the Regulation of the Council of Ministers) directs his attention to the so-called legal basis – that is, he or she examines whether there is an appropriate norm of legislative competence authorizing the establishment of the regulation mentioned above"[27]. According to Anna Michalska and Sławomira Wronkowska, this legal power is "the most important feature determining the position of an act in the system of law-making acts". Thus, "the basis for legality of a law-making act with a lower legal force is a legally binding act of a higher force"[28].

K. Płeszka disagrees with the above statement. After all, "a given act of the creation of law is an act of a higher legal force precisely because it forms the basis

---

23 See L. Garlicki, Constitution of the Republic of Poland – Commentary on Chapter VIII "Courts and Tribunals", art. 188, p. 7; R. Guastini, *Lezioni di teoria. . .*, pp. 33–52; idem, *Lex superior. Pour une theorie des hierarchie normatives*, „Revus. Journal for Constitutional Theory and Philosophy of Law" 2013, no. 21, pp. 47–55.

24 K. Płeszka, *Hierarchia w systemie prawa*, „Zeszyty Naukowe UJ – Prace z nauk politycznych" 1988, no. 33, p. 53.

25 See *Ibidem*, pp. 53–162.

26 See K. Działocha, *Konstytucyjna determinacja formy prawa* [in:] *Konstytucyjny model tworzenia prawa w PRL*, ed. idem, Wrocław 1981, p. 126; A. Michalska, S. Wronkowska, *Zasady tworzenia prawa*, Poznań 1983, p. 72.

27 K. Płeszka, *Moc prawna a hierarchia w systemie prawa*, [in:] *Prawo i Polityka*, ed. A. Bodnar, J. J. Wiatr, J. Wróblewski, Warsaw1988, p. 61.

28 A. Michalska, S. Wronkowska, *Zasady tworzenia prawa*, Poznań 1983, p. 72.

of the validity for another law-making act. What is more, it is an act of a higher legal force only against that act (or acts) for which it is the basis of validity"[29]. In the light of the above remarks, one can conclude that it is only as a result of establishing a hierarchical competence profile that we can determine the legal force of the elements of a given legal system. However, the legal force determined by such a competence profile is an insufficient basis for eliminating collisions or incompatibilities between the elements of the system.

The ordering in the aspect of derogation depends on the repealing force of acts, which consists in the fact that "one element of a legal system has the ability to derogate another element of the system"[30]. This power depends on the scope of normative acts, which must be compatible with the act concerned[31]. According to Kazimierz Działocha, "the legal force of an act consists in the inability of derogation of the act by acts of the lower force . . . and the possibility of repealing these acts by an act of law". Although the author expressed this view in a totally different sociocultural reality, he stated already at that time that "in terms of its legal force each act of law gives way to the constitution. This imposes an obligation on each act of law to implement the constitution and prohibit its violation"[32]. Nowadays, it is indicated that the act which constitutes a model in the scope of content compliance for another normative act should have a superior force in terms of derogation, and thus it should occupy a higher position in the hierarchy of legal sources[33].

K. Płeszka showed that these two types of hierarchy are not identical, but the ordering in the aspect of derogations is significantly stronger. "Even if there is an order in terms of validity, we are still unable to resolve [. . .] the problems associated with derogation. However, it can be noticed that ordering in the aspect of derogation means, in a sense, ordering in the aspect of being valid"[34]. The place of a normative act in one and the other hierarchy does not always coincide. It should also be borne in mind that in the situation of multi-centrality of law within the territory of a given state, different legal systems may be used, and, although they are separate, they interact with each other[35]. It is also important

29 K. Płeszka, *Moc prawna*. . ., p. 61; see R. Guastini, *Lezioni di teoria*. . ., pp. 41–46.

30 *Ibidem*, p. 58.

31 K. Płeszka, *Hierarchia w systemie*. . ., pp. 53–63, 65–111, 119–130.

32 K. Działocha, *Konstytucyjna determinacja*. . ., p. 127.

33 K. Wojtyczek, *Sądownictwo konstytucyjne w Polsce. Wybrane zagadnienia*, Warsaw 2013, p. 37; R. Guastini, *Lezioni di teoria*. . ., pp. 50–52.

34 K. Płeszka, *Hierarchia w systemie*. . ., p. 130.

35 K. Wojtyczek, *Sądownictwo konstytucyjne*. . ., p. 40.

that some control systems of norms rely on the concept of a multi-level nature of this control. The Polish control model is just such a case. Thus, it is possible to distinguish protection of the supremacy of norms at the constitutional level, at the level of ratified international agreements and at the statutory level. The Court is competent to test the conformity of lower government standards on each of these levels, and the character and role of this body are different at different levels of this protection[36].

The derogative type of a system of law is applicable when "there is a collision between the elements of the system (incompatibility)"[37]. The collision rule, *lex inferior non derogat legi superiori / lex superior derogat legi inferiori*, has to eliminate such inconsistency. However, both "derogation linking and competence linking have to (though in a different way) determine the validity of a given element of the legal system, so they are useful if we want to estimate systemic validity"[38].

It can be noticed that in a hierarchically ordered legal system, normative acts occupy different places and are linked with each other by two types of ties: dynamic and static. Dynamic ties correspond to the order of validity, where higher-level normative acts give competence to make normative acts of the lower order. Norms of legislative competence indicate a competent authority to establish a legal act, its scope and the procedure for its establishment[39]. Static bonds, in turn, refer to the content conformity of lower-level norms in reference to higher-level norms[40]. Normative acts with a higher derogation force determine "the limits of the permissible content of normative acts with a lower derogation force. Normative acts of a lower level on the one hand cannot contain any content contrary to higher-level normative acts, and, on the other hand, they should implement and specify provisions of higher-level normative acts"[41].

It should be borne in mind that derogation may refer to three different elements:

---

36 See. L. Garlicki, Komentarz do Rozdziału VIII „Sądy i Trybunały", art. 188, p. 8.

37 K. Płeszka, T. Gizbert-Studnicki, *Obraz systemu prawa w dogmatyce prawniczej*, [in:] *Szkice z teorii prawa i szczegółowych nauk prawnych*, ed. S. Wronkowska, M. Zieliński, Poznań 1990, p. 168.

38 K. Płeszka, *Moc prawna...*, p. 58.

39 A. Ross, *Directives and Norms*, London 1968, p. 130.

40 *Z teorii i filozofii prawa Zygmunta Ziembińskiego*, ed. S. Wronkowska, Warsaw 2007, pp. 127–158.

41 K. Wojtyczek, *Sądownictwo konstytucyjne...*, p. 37.

- legal acts (understood as a set of legal provisions) that may be present at various levels of the hierarchy of a legal system;
- regulations;
- legal norms[42].

This makes us consider the problem, which was pointed out by K. Płeszka: is it possible to talk about the hierarchy of legal norms in such a situation? He concluded that this question cannot be answered in an affirmative way. In the light of the concepts of legal interpretation adopted in Poland (clarification and derivation), it is emphasized that the interpretation is a reconstruction of norms from legal regulations that are included in various legal acts (sources), characterized by "different hierarchical level". As a result of such an interpretation, we obtain a set of unambiguous legal norms, equivalent in terms of hierarchy[43].The concept of a norm understood as the result of an interpretation of law (reconstruction of acts of different hierarchical level), does not allow us to talk about the hierarchical ordering of norms. Yet, it does not mean that the problems of this arrangement can be omitted. It turns out that the hierarchy of normative acts resolves the issues of inside-the-system validity. The derivative interpretation of law assumes legal regulations from which legal norms, which underlie the above-mentioned hierarchy, are reconstructed. The clarification approach requires a hierarchy of norms which is necessary to consider the issue of derogation by the *lex superior/lex inferior* rule[44]. In what way, when norms are homogeneous in their hierarchical nature, can one resolve their incompatibility in the light of the *lex superior / lex inferior* rules? In such a case, it is necessary to refer to the provisions on the basis of which the norms of the reconstruction were made. On the other hand, it is difficult to determine the contradiction of legal texts (acts, legal regulations) without reference to non-compliance of standards[45].

I have adopted, in this work, a concept developed on the basis of our legal culture referred to as an integrated concept of interpretation (Leszek Leszczyński's validation and reconstruction concept). It has a universal character so it can be used to interpret all legal texts, including the constitution[46]. The specificity of

---

42 K. Płeszka, *Hierarchia w systemie...*, p. 127.

43 *Ibidem*, p. 42.

44 *Ibidem*, s. 46.

45 *Ibidem*.

46 See. M. Romanowicz, *Pomiędzy uniwersalnym a partykularnym wymiarem wykładni prawa. Wpływ teorii prawa i nauki prawa konstytucyjnego na wzorce wykładni konstytucji*, [in:] *Wykładnia konstytucji. Inspiracje, teorie, argumenty*, ed. T. Stawecki, J. Winczorek, Warszawa 2014, pp. 212–241.

the interpretation of the constitution is not determined by other methods of this kind of interpretation, but by the way of using the instruments as provided by the validation and reconstruction interpretation. There are three phases of this interpretation:

- validation – it aims to establish the source of the legal basis,
- derivative – it reconstructs the content of the decision base (legal norm),
- clarification – it is based on determining the meanings of normative expressions.

In each of these phases, all methods (rules) of interpretation are used. The diversity of their roles is recognized within the framework of individual interpretive activities. The same rules implemented at various stages of interpretation have different functions. They are often used in a different order and affect the final result of each interpretation in a different way. This approach allows for interpretation in every decision-making process regardless of the nature of the source of reconstruction and the context of interpretation. Adopting a complete catalogue of interpretation rules and applying them in any order makes the scope of interpretative freedom much wider. It is implemented in every law application process, including the activities carried out by the Constitutional Court as part of the hierarchical examination of the conformity of normative acts with the Constitution.

The constitution is not only an act regulating the normative model of the political sphere, but it has been made a superior act in the entire legal order (system)[47]. Recognition of this act as primary and placing it above other elements of the legal order means that it is considered the basis of the principle of constitutionalism[48]. The assumption of constitution's superior role, not only in the formal but also in the material aspect is the key concept behind this principle[49]. Each act functioning in the legal circulation is subordinated to it. This makes it possible to derogate any act standing below in a given legal order (system).

Taking into account the linguistic features of the text of the constitution, its thematic richness, the so-called autonomic concepts, assessments and values,

---

47 More on the subject cf. D. Minich, *Światopogląd konstytucyjny jako granica prawa i jego wykładni (aspekt filozoficzno-metodologiczny)*, Studia Politologiczne 2012, vol. 23, pp. 121–141; eadem, *Filozoficzne konteksty prawa i konstytucjonalizmu – poszukiwanie podstawności prawa*, Rzeszów 2012, *passim*.

48 See E.-W. Böckenförde, *Constitutional and Political Theory. Selected Writings*,Oxford 2017, pp. 141–151.

49 See P. Tuleja, *Stosowanie Konstytucji...*, *passim*.

as well as its socio-political context, it can be said that in this aspect, interpretation in accordance with the constitution is extremely complex in its nature[50]. It is based on a formal (structural) hierarchy that exists between the norms governing the creation of law and the application of law. At the same time, it is based on the material (content) hierarchy between the constitutional norm and the subordinate norm, which should be consistent with the constitution. One can also speak of the logical (linguistic) hierarchy taking place between norms due to the language structure of the sources of law (the collisional rules which help to eliminate contradictions play a significant role here). The fourth type of hierarchy related to interpretation in accordance with the constitution is the axiological hierarchy. It is an expression of the superiority of constitutional norms and the values expressed in them in relation to sub-constitutional norms. Structural and logical hierarchies depend on the structure of the language of sources of law. The material hierarchy depends on the norm which establishes the conformity of legal norms with the constitution. Each axiological hierarchy is conditioned by principles and values expressed in the constitution, and their reconstruction is entrusted to the Constitutional Court. It is the Constitutional Court that by means of interpretation determines the meaning of the principles and values expressed in the Constitution.

Summarizing the analysis, it can be claimed that by making interpretations in accordance with the constitution, the Constitutional Court is not only a controller of constitutional compliance, but it is also a co-legislator. It is this court which defines through the interpretation in accordance with the constitution, which values a constitutional norm expresses and in what sense the norm is legal (complies with the Constitution).

References

Bator A., Kozak A., *Wykładnia prawa w zgodzie z konstytucją*, in S. Wronkowska (ed.) *Polska kultura prawna a proces integracji europejskiej* [Polish legal culture and the process of european integration], (Cracow: Zakamycze, 2005).

Constitution of the Republic of Poland of April 2, 1997 (Journal of Laws 1997, No. 78, item 483).

Czeszejko-Sochacki Z., *Orzeczenia Trybunału Konstytucyjnego: pojęcie, klasyfikacja, skutki* [Decisions of the Constitutional Tribunal: concept, classification, effects], (2000) 12 Państwo i Prawo.

50 More on the subject of cf. R. Guastini, *Lex superior...*, pp. 47–55.

Działocha K., *Konstytucyjna determinacja formy prawa* in K. Działocha (ed.) *Konstytucyjny model tworzenia prawa w PRL* [Constitutional model of law making in the PRL], (Wrocław: 1981).

Garlicki L., Constitution of the Republic of Poland – Commentary on Chapter VIII "Courts and Tribunals", (Warszawa: Wydawnictwo Sejmowe, 2005).

Guastini R., *Lezioni di teoria del diritto e dello stato*, (Torino: Giappichelli, 2006).

Guastini R., *Lex superior. Pour une theorie des hierarchie normatives*, (2013) 21 Revus. Journal for Constitutional Theory and Philosophy of Law.

Kellermann G., *Verfassungsinterpretation. Das Grundgesetz als normative Ressource im gesellschaftlichen Wandel*, (Schwalbach: Wochenschau Verlag, 2011).

Leszczyński L., *Zagadnienia teorii stosowania prawa. Doktryna i tezy orzecznictwa* [Issues of the theory of law application. Doctrine and case law], (Cracow: Wolters Kluwer, 2001).

Michalska A., Wronkowska S., *Zasady tworzenia prawa* [Rules for creating law], (Poznań: Wydawnictwo Naukowe Uniwersytetu im. Adama Mickiewicza, 1983).

Mikołajewicz J., *Orzeczenia zakresowe i interpretacyjne Trybunału Konstytucyjnego jako przejaw kryzysu legitymacji legalnej*, in J. Oniszczuk (ed.) *Normalność i kryzys. Jedność czy różnorodność* [Normality and crisis. Unity or diversity], Warsaw: Oficyna Wydawnicza SGH, 2010).

Minich D., *Filozoficzne konteksty prawa i konstytucjonalizmu – poszukiwanie podstawności prawa* [Philosophical contexts of law and constitutionalism – the search for the fundamentality of law], (Rzeszów: Wydawnictwo Mitel, 2012).

Minich D., *Światopogląd konstytucyjny jako granica prawa i jego wykładni (aspekt filozoficzno-metodologiczny)* [Constitutionalism as the limit of law and its interpretation (philosophical and methodological aspects)] (2012) 23, Studia Politologiczne.

Morawski L., *Wykładnia w orzecznictwie sądów. Komentarz [Interpretation in the jurisprudence of the courts. Commentary*], (Toruń: TNOiK Dom Organizatora, 2002).

Oliwniak S., *Wpływ orzecznictwa Trybunału Konstytucyjnego na system prawa w latach 1985–1997* [Impact of the jurisprudence of the Constitutional Tribunal on the legal system in the years 1985–1997], (Białystok: Temida 2, 2001).

Organizacja i tryb postępowania przed Trybunałem Konstytucyjnym (Journal of Laws of 2016, item 2072).

Płeszka K., *Hierarchia w systemie prawa* [Hierarchy in the legal system] Zeszyty Naukowe UJ – Prace z nauk politycznych" no. 33 (Kraków: Wydawnictwo UJ, 1988).

Płeszka K., *Moc prawna a hierarchia w systemie prawa*, in A. Bodnar, J. J. Wiatr, J. Wróblewski (eds.) *Prawo i Polityka* [Law and Politics], (Warsaw: PWN, 1988).

Płeszka K., Gizbert-Studnicki T., *Obraz systemu prawa w dogmatyce prawniczej*, in S. Wronkowska, M. Zieliński (eds.) *Szkice z teorii prawa i szczegółowych nauk prawnych* [Sketches from the theory of law and specific legal science], (Poznań: Wydawnictwo Naukowe im. Adama Mickiewicza, 1990).

Romanowicz M., *Pomiędzy uniwersalnym a partykularnym wymiarem wykładni prawa. Wpływ teorii prawa i nauki prawa konstytucyjnego na wzorce wykładni konstytucji*, in T. Stawecki, J. Winczorek (eds.) *Wykładnia konstytucji. Inspiracje, teorie, argumenty* [Interpretation of the constitution. Inspirations, theories, arguments], (Warszawa: Wolters Kluwer, 2014).

Ross A., *Directives and Norms*, (London: Routledge and Kegan Paul, 1968).

Scalia A., Garner B. A., *Reading Law: The Interpretation of Legal Text*, (St. Paul: West, 2012).

Stawecki T., *Operatywna wykładnia konstytucji w świetle badań empirycznych*, in L. Leszczyński, A. Szot (eds.) *Wykładnia operatywna prawa – perspektywa teoretyczna i dogmatyczna* [Operative interpretation of law – theoretical and dogmatic perspective], (Toruń: Wydawnictwo Adam Marszałek, 2017)

Trzciński J., *Charakter podstawowej działalności Trybunału Konstytucyjnego*, in J. Trzciński *Trybunał Konstytucyjny* [Constitutional Tribunal], (Wrocław: Wydawnictwo UWr, 1987).

Tuleja P., *Podstawowe problemy związane z interpretacją Konstytucji Rzeczypospolitej Polskiej w orzecznictwie Trybunału Konstytucyjnego*, in M. Zubik (ed.) *Księga XX-lecia orzecznictwa Trybunału Konstytucyjnego*, [Book of the 20th anniversary of the Constitutional Court's jurisdiction] (Warsaw: Biuro Trybunału Konstytucyjnego, 2006).

Tuleja P., *Stosowanie Konstytucji RP w świetle zasady jej nadrzędności (wybrane problemy)*, [Application of the Polish Constitution in the light of the principle of its supremacy (selected problems)], (Cracow: Zakamycze, 2003).

Wahl R., *Verfassungsänderung – Verfassungswandel – Verfassungsinterpretation*, in *Verfassungsänderung, Verfassungswandel, Verfassungsinterpretation: Vorträge bei deutsch – japanischen Sympozien in Tokyo 2004 und Freiburg 2005*, (Berlin: Duncker & Humblot, 2008).

Wojtyczek K., *Sądownictwo konstytucyjne w Polsce. Wybrane zagadnienia* [Constitutional court in Poland. Selected issues], (Warsaw: Biuro Trybunału Konstytucyjnego, 2013).

Wronkowska S., *O niektórych osobliwościach konstytucji i jej interpretacji* in M. Smolak (ed.) *Wykładnia konstytucji. Aktualne problemy i tendencje* [Interpretation of the constitution. Current problems and trends], (Warsaw: Wolters Kluwer, 2016).

Wronkowska S. (ed.), *Z teorii i filozofii prawa Zygmunta Ziembińskiego* [From the theory and philosophy of law of Zygmunt Ziembiński], (Warsaw: Wolters Kluwer, 2007).

Wróblewski J., *Zwroty stosunkowe – wypowiedzi o zgodności z normą*, in J. Wróblewski (selection and introduction M. Zirk-Sadowski), *Pisma wybrane* [Selected writings], (Warsaw: Wolters Kluwer, 2015),

Ziembiński Z., *O stanowieniu i obowiązywaniu prawa. Zagadnienia podstawowe* [On law making and validity. Basic issues], Warsaw: Wydawnictwo Sejmowe, 1995).

Ziembiński Z., *Problemy podstawowe prawoznawstwa* [Basic problems of jurisprudence], (Warsaw: PWN, 1980).

Martin Škop

9 Sociological Context of Legislation[1]

Abstract: This chapter deals with some methodological aspects of empirical (qualitative) research in the area of legislation. It is devoted to the so-called bureaucratic stages of legislative process, in particular on the so-called statutory drafting. The chapter first focuses on the reasons why it is relevant to examine this part of the legislation process, especially with regard to the much more explored area of the parliamentary stages of the legislative process. It will also focus on the nature of drafting statutes - the statutory drafting is rather to be an art rather than a science or other strictly formalized activity. However, rational elements are essential for drafting a statute. Finally, the chapter applies theoretical knowledge to data obtained from in-depth interviews with legislative experts and points out possible differences between what the legislative experts themselves say and how the writing process is theoretically conceptualized.

Keywords: legislation, law-making, sociology of law, statutory drafting, methodology of legal research

When examining how statutes are written, it is very often possible to discern a lamentation over the abilities of those who write them. For instance, German historian Friedrich Carl von Savigny warned of the incompetence of legislators in 1814. He complained that the force and vigor of the language used by legislators could not be compared to that used in the *Constitutio Criminalis Carolina*.[2] More than a hundred years later, in 1917, French professor Henri Capitant complained that a work such as the Code civil des Françaiscould no longer to be created because legislators have completely lost the art of making laws and the legislative capacity is very low.[3] Around another eighty years later, in 1993, another

---

1 This chapter is a result of research funded by the Czech Science Foundation (GAČR), grant NoGA17-14903S – "Methodology of Empirical Research on the Usage of Interpretative Methods in Law-making". The text is based on the article "*Being a Legislator: Empirical Investigations in Administrative Legislation*" submitted for review in the *Časopis pro právní vědu a praxi* (https://journals.muni.cz/cpvp/).

2 CF von Savigny, *VomBerufunsererZeitfür Gesetzgebung undRechtswissenschaft* (MohrundZimmer 1814) 52.

3 H Capitant, "Comment on fait les lois aujourd'hui" (1917) 91 Revue Politique & Parlementaire 305–317 305 – 307.

French lawyer, Guy Braibant, uttered a similar lamentation that the art of writing laws had deteriorated.[4] In his opinion, too many civil servants write laws that express something different to what they intend. Their creators do not know anything about used steady concepts or legislative techniques, or they have no idea that what they congratulate themselves on creating actually already exists. For Braibant, this is one reason why the nonprofessional has no chance to know the law, which is only accessible to a specialist: and even so only within his specialization. A holistic view of the law has been lost and the legitimation of law as a rationally structured system disturbed. While this opens up space for greater interpretative freedom,[5] certainty has decreased and the possibility of ideology and hegemony increased.

On one side, there are critics of the quality of legislation, while on the other *creators*, i.e., the legal experts who actually write the draft legislation. Their view, which often expresses similar skepticism and a reflection of their own work, is enriched by the necessity of introducing "*a sly addressee*" who will try to circumvent the law. Alternatively, it is enriched by the pressure the public or the audience exerts on them – for *everyone* understands how to draft a statute and, in particular, how the statute should look at the end of the process so that it is clear and comprehensible. Legislative experts are thus in a *juridical field*[6] whose boundaries, in our case, are created by the public through their comments and the expectations placed on the final product (legal regulation) and by the legal academics who prescribe the precise form of the legislation.

Why Examine the Bureaucratic Parts of the Legislative Process?

This chapter seeks to ascertain whether the drafting of a legislative proposal is more an art or a formalized activity. The reason is that theoretical literature, as we will see below, suggests it is a creative activity. In-depth interviews with legislative experts, on the other hand, indicate that they consider their activity to be strictly formalized. The text will therefore focus on whether the creation of the *law* is a formal, rationalized activity with a routine nature, or art (l'art), and thus a creative activity. It is highly probable that the drafting of legislative proposals

---

4 G Braibant, "Qui fait la loi?" (1993) 64 Pouvoirs: Revue française d'études constitutionnelles et politiques 43–46 45.

5 See e.g., R Mańko, *W stronę krytycznej filozofii orzekania.: Polityczność, etyka, legitymizacja.*(Wydawnictwo Uniwersytetu Łódzkiego 2018) 95–96.

6 P Bourdieu, "The Force of Law: Toward A Sociology of Juridical Field" (1987) 38 The Hastings Law Journal 814–853.

is both creative and formalized – in this case, it is also necessary to look for their mutual relationships. What is the nature of the specific actions, or does the predominance of one or the other characteristic have fixed causes? It implies that the process of statutory drafting can be perceived on the one hand as art,[7] and on the other as a strictly formalized, rational activity.[8]

This text focuses on analyzing the testimony of legislative experts, especially officials working at ministries in legislation departments, and on placing them in context with theoretical approaches to law-making – particularly with an emphasis on the understanding of law-making as so-called *anticipated interpretation*[9] based on the expected identical forms of law creation and interpretation. The text is therefore based on data from in-depth interviews (a qualitative inquiry) with employees at the legislative departments of some ministries in the Czech Republic. The focus is not on denying other influences in law-making, but on concentrating on this part of the legislative process. It is also important for the selection of this part that its bureaucratic stages are not only creative as such, but also include policy-making, i.e., the introduction of topics to be dealt with through legislation, possibly including statements and comments on other suggestions. Therefore, legislative experts have a significant impact on law-making[10]that needs to be explored. Knowledge of the administrative stages of law-making, i.e., how authors create a normative text, can also contribute towards mutual reflection in practice, i.e., the *interpretative dialogue* between law-makers and application entities. Knowledge of these stages of the legislative process will help improve legislative outputs and the overall functioning of the law, and will assist the legitimate evolution of the law.[11]

In the Czech Republic – and, according to relevant findings across Central and Eastern Europe – the number of legal regulations (legal norms) has

---

7 See e.g. J Bentham, "Nomography", *The Works of Jeremy Bentham: Volume III.*(William Tait 1843) 233.

8 J Wróblewski, *TeoriaRacjonalnegoTworzeniaPrawa* (ZakładNarodowyim. Ossolińskich 1985) 8.

9 J Kysela in R Boháč, *Legislativní proces: (teorie a praxe)* (Tiskárna Ministerstva vnitra 2011) 45.

10 CA Robinson, *The Bureaucracy and the Legislative Process: A Case Study of the Health Care Financing Administration* (University Press of America 1991) 1.

11 MR Chritiansen and WN Eskridge Jr., "Congressional Overrides of Supreme Court Statutory Interpretation Decisions, 1967–2011" (2014) 92 Texas Law Review 1317–1541 1322.

steadily increased.[12] This has been linked to the potential destabilization of the rule of law. Luc Wintgens assumes that one cause of this increase may be the declining quality of preparation of legislative proposals.[13] Norms that result from procedures that do not follow all desirable practices can actually cause more problems than they solve. Of course, this also applies to a normative text whose deficiencies can literally paralyze legal practice. Chester A. Robinson considers it necessary to understand the bureaucratic stages of the law-making process, because in a democratic society it is important to know how the administration works, how it makes decisions, how it is influenced, and how it formulates its outputs.[14] The study of the administrative aspects of the law-making process is therefore of scientific (knowledge of the process of production itself), communication (communication of extra-legal content) and economic (costs of the process of creation and subsequent application of the legal regulation) significance. Another reason for research in this area of legislation is its importance for legal interpretation. The objectified form of legislative work, legislative history (or *travaux préparatoires*)[15]is used as one of the sources of intentionalist-based theories[16] of interpretation, the use of which can, for example, result in the achievement of the intended economic, political or social goals that cannot be expressed in the legal text.[17] Considering the number of actors involved in the preparation of proposals or the composition of a normative text, it is possible to say that statutory drafting is performed by a set of actors, which – paradoxically – can lead to increasing uncertainty in the text.[18]An analysis of these processes can help subsequent interpretation by providing an understanding of the rules and conventions used in the drafting of the normative text.

---

12 F Cvrček and F Novák, *Legislativa: Teoretická východiska a problémy* (Vydavatelství a nakladatelství Aleš Čeněk 2017).

13 LJ Wintgens, "The Rational Legislator Revisited. Bounded Rationality and Legisprudence", *The Rationality and Justification of Legislation: essays in legisprudence* (Springer 2013) 4.

14 Robinson (n 10) 15.

15 See e.g., P Jestaz, "Les sources du droit: Le déplacement d'un pôle à un autre" (1996) 27 Revue générale de droit 5–19. 15.

16 LD Jellum, *MasteringStatutoryInterpretation* (Carolina AcademicPress 2008) 21.

17 T Sobek, *Právní myšlení: Kritika moralismu* (Ústav státu a práva AV ČR ve spolupráci s Vydavatelstvím a nakladatelstvím Aleš Čeněk, Plzeň 2011) 242.

18 Braibant (n 4) 44.

The Nature of Statutory Drafting

Statutory drafting can be considered as both a rational activity and a creative activity. Most often, these two aspects of legislation are interconnected. The rationality of the creator lies above all in his intentions and the normative concepts, while the activity through which he essentially works with words and therefore expresses legal norms in the form of a general (or legal) language is rather creative. The relationship between the purpose of the regulation and the legislative means chosen is, without any doubt, rational. The discourse is also rational, as is, in particular, the socio-political context in which the legislator operates.[19] John Stuart Mill considered that art serves to find the goals that science provides – but that art is also capable of forming a rule or prescription from scientific knowledge.[20] Jeremy Bentham, in *Nomography* –the form of discourse superiors use to communicate to subordinates to determine the manner of their behavior – expressed that the process of creating legislation is tied to *science and art*.[21]It is an activity that necessarily requires knowledge of methods (writing procedures) and knowledge of the subject of regulation, but also requires a creative approach in the formation of a normative text. This, after all, stems from a single statement of legislation in the pilot survey: "*Legislation is a social competence that cannot be learned. It is an experience that is based on the building of social ties.* "This is a basic element of law-making – it is a social concept requiring the coordination of several subjects whose intentions do not necessarily have to be identical, and whose approaches and procedures can differ. However, a product that passes through parliamentary institutions can be considered a *patchwork* whose integrity can be greatly disturbed.[22]

The necessity of legitimizing the outcome of the legislative process is given by the necessity of a rational element in the creation of law. The rational process must lead to a rational result. This corresponds to the concept of Max Weber, in which the system of deliberately created rational rules is both a source of legitimacy and a basis for the obligatory character.[23] However, the emphasis placed on

19 Wróblewski (n 8)11.

20 JS Mill, *System of Logic Ratiocinative, and Inductive: Being a Connected View of the Principles of Evidence and the Methods of Scientific Investigation* (JM Robson ed. University of Toronto Press 1974) 944 – 945.

21 Bentham (n 7)233.

22 D Kyritsis, *Shared Authority: Courts and Legislatures in Legal Theory* (Hart Publishing 2015) 101.

23 M Weber, *Economy and Society: An Outline of Interpretive Sociology* (G Roth and C Wittich eds, University of California Press 1978) 954.

the rational aspect of legislative activity and on how important and how limited the creative component of this activity can be, varies.

Dominique Rémy considers the fashioning of a normative text to be as creative as urban practice.[24] In this case, the creative activity lies in the combination of possible (real and rational) procedures in individualized cases and the creation of a whole that is determined, yet whose resulting form is not causally dependent only on these determinants. In addition, Rémy argues, it is necessary to restrict the excessive tendency of the courts (or other entities applying authority) to project their own ideas onto the normative text and create their own laws, or the general tendency of lawyers to negotiate the content of laws.[25] A possible understanding of legislation as a creative activity may also mean it is easier to achieve clarity even for different interest groups. In fact, the creator (real writer) should avoid a mechanical activity that fully remains in one specialized sector, and should look for solutions acceptable to the various actors or solutions that have meaning not only at the legal but also at the pragmatic and/or moral levels.[26] Rémy compares the creation of law to urbanism. He refers to the work of the Austrian town planner Camillo Sitte *Der Städtebau nach seinen künstlerischen Grundsätzen*.[27] In spite of many technical constraints and the necessity of functionality, there is room for creative activity in both urban and law-making – at least to the extent it complies with all the limitations and requirements. From this point of view, the creation of law is close to the notion of *Gesamtkunstwerk*, as elaborated by German composer Richard Wagner, which he understood as the union of several individual arts in one piece.[28] Even in the case of legislation, there is no doubt that multiple activities must be linked to it to provide a functional result.

This does not mean, however, that we exclude a rational concept of law-making or even statutory drafting. None of the authors denies the presence of a rational element in statutory drafting. For example, Jerzy Wróblewski considered that law-making should be a rational activity,[29] which does not exclude the

---

24 D Rémy, *Légistique: L'art de faire les lois* (Romillat 2004) 15.

25 Ibid.

26 W Cyrul, "Lawmaking: Between Discourse and Legal Text", *Legislation in Context: Essays in Legisprudence* (Routledge 2016)51.

27 C Sitte, *Der Städtebaunach seinen künstlerischen Grundsätzen: Ein Beitrag zur Lösung modernster Fragen der Architektur und monumentalen Plastik unter besonderer Beziehung auf Wien* (Carl Graeser 1889).

28 R Wagner, *Das Kunstwer kder Zukunft* (Otto Wigand 1850) 32.

29 Wróblewski (n 8) 8.

fact that, in addition to the rational element, there is also a distinctive element of skill. The presence of rationality is also caused by the fact that the author of the normative text is responsible for the rationality of the legislation (the draft law) and must act in accordance with the social context,[30]moreover with the limitation that the legislative activity outcome must be comprehensible, since the interpreter assumes the rational creation of the law.[31]

Empirical Findings

There is no generally binding regulation for how legislative proposals are drafted in the Czech Republic. However, in the administrative stages we see codified rules issued by the government of the Czech Republic for all administrative authorities: Legislative Rules of the Government (LRG). LRG derive their legal authority from the form of government resolutions, and therefore are binding on all entities in a subordinate position to the government. They are not binding outside the governmental structure and are therefore not binding on members of the Czech parliament in their legislative activity. The government's rules of procedure determine that a government resolution, which is a form of its decision, obliges all members of the government, ministries, other central state administration bodies, other administrative authorities, and other entities appointed under general law. LRG are considered to be internal rules that oblige agencies controlled by the government to unify legislative procedures for the preparation of legislation and to contribute to improving legislation quality.[32] However, given their potentially rational core, it would be appropriate for them to be respected by "external" entities as well (e.g., courts). LRG, for example, are not binding on the Constitutional court of the Czech Republic. However, they are the most appropriate source of knowledge of legislative technique,[33] so even those entities should use them. The reason is again legal certainty and clarity of the legal provisions, as it may be confusing for an interpreter if the creators (and interpreters) use different sets of legislative rules.

---

30 Wintgens (n 13) 8.

31 Ibid 9.

32 Z Šín, *Tvorba práva: Pravidla, metodika, technika* (2ndC.H. Beck 2009) 65.

33 J Filip, "Ústavní soud a problémy legislativy v ČR", *Otázky tvorby práva v České republice, Polské republice a Slovenské republice: Sborník příspěvků z mezinárodního vědeckého sympozia "Aktuální otázky tvorby práva v České republice, Polské republice a Slovenské republice", Praha, 29.-30. 11. 2004* (Vydavatelství a nakladatelství Aleš Čeněk 2005) 109.

Despite the existence of these codified rules governing how legislative work should be governed (LRG), our focus is not the description and critical examination of these rules. On the contrary, it is aimed at proposing a method for investigating how these rules are reflected in the creation process, and how the resulting text is affected by other external factors. In other words, our goal is to explore social practice. It is an initial insight into the complex field (the juridical field) in which legal texts are written so that we can suggest ways for their further exploration. To do this, a qualitative survey method seemed most appropriate. In qualitative research, the researcher searches for answers to his questions from the social actors themselves. He assumes that while he does not understand the world, the participants (respondents) are experts, while this expertise may be *unconscious*. The researchers in this type of research assume that if anyone understands the world they are interested in, it is the participants, since they live in it and shape it. Researchers are only *outsiders* in these worlds, mediated by the experience and meanings of the individual actors involved in them.[34] The role of researchers is to best translate their findings into the language of science to enrich knowledge.

In the pilot study, we asked, among other things, how legislators understand their work, what it represents and what meanings they ascribe to it. In the pilot data collection, which is preparation for further possible empirical investigations, the so-called in-depth interview method was employed. The advantage of an in-depth interview is that while researchers raise their themes, there is still room for sensible leadership to ask enthusiastic participants to suggest their own themes, and sometimes encourage them to talk.[35] And it can be the opposite, such as when the activity is taken over by a participant. The in-depth interviews consisted of two parts, the first one focused on the writing process itself, the other on the possibilities for interpreting the legal text. The following lines are based on a section where researchers talked to research participants about their work and its course. The interview consisted of five thematic parts in which we asked about the whole process of writing and its main moments, the actors influencing the writing, the addressees of the text, the purely practical pages of writing (e.g., working conditions) and the relation to their own work. It should be said that this text is based primarily on an analysis of the six entry interviews,

---

34 M Hammersley and P Atkinson, *Ethnography: Principles In practice* (3rd ed. Routledge 2007).

35 See J-C Kaufmann, *L'entretien compréhensif: L'enquête et ses méthodes* (3e Armand Colin 2011).

the collection of which then continued and was continuously modified considering the ongoing results.

Analytical Part

In the following text, we will deal primarily with how legislative experts describe their work. We emphasize in particular the phenomena, which according to a *prima facie* analysis, seem to be decisive for the resulting legal text. We therefore focus on elements relevant to further deeper research. The basic areas of interest are characterized by two questions: "*What is the nature of the drafting of a legal text?*" and "*What is the nature of the work of the legal experts?*" These two questions, and the answers to them, are interrelated. However, they also describe two different things. The first question focuses on understanding the nature of writing (drafting), for example, to identify important phases of writing or its symbolic meaning. The answers to the second question give an insight into how the legislators understand their work not as a "simple writing" but as a position and activity that is part of a larger body of law-making, or a social field with different actors. In other words, we are seeking to understand writing not only as a specific professional activity but also as a specifically experienced working position.

To Draft a Statute

This text focuses exclusively on the writing of normative text. Part of the work of the legislative expert is, of course, the writing of many other texts – reason reports, letters, explanations, opinions, comments, etc. Nevertheless, our goal is to describe what, in simple terms, writing the text of an act (statute) actually entails. From the point of view of the needs of future research, we have tried to define the important moments of the whole writing process and related important actors. We were also interested in the idea of "ideally" performed work. At all these points, we surprisingly found a wide range of answers. We will first focus on the nature of writing as such, and on the question of important moments in the drafting process.

In the in-depth interviews, there is a certain tension between whether the writing of the legislative text is a creative activity, or whether it is an activity strictly determined by precise rules that eliminate the possibility of individual creativity. In other words, whether it is an activity in which the writer is nothing but an essentially "invisible" creator, who *merely* communicates the text of the will of the contracting authority. Social reality is not usually strictly formed through such ideal situations (creative activity/formal mediation). If both these poles appear in the testimony, they do not necessarily appear as two ends of one scale. We do not see a freethinking creative on the one hand and a "writing machine" subordinated to rigid rules on the other. Conversely, we can identify characters that more or less correspond to one or the other approach, with one or more participants, but with different emphasis, or in different contextual situations. First of all, we are faced with the fact that the legal experts deal with formal questions related to the nature of the content. For example, one testimony pointed out the need to violate the formal rules on the labeling of individual pieces of legislation so that the content could be better understood by the addressees. Just *being understood* is a very important requirement for text quality. It turns out that its preservation (or development) requires that the creator imagines, at least in that respect, who the addressee of the text will be.

LRG are the guidelines for writing every legal text proposed by the government of the Czech Republic as an authority appointed to propose a bill to the parliament of the Czech Republic. LRG are documents that all communication partners refer to. The phrase "*Legislative rules are silent about it*" is an important note referring to the unwritten rules of writing texts being observed. The experience of legislative experts, which is an essential part of their expertise (yes, not vice versa), tells them which wording and formal adjustments may be accepted or, on the other hand, returned by the government advisory body in the area of legislative work, the Government Legislative Council, the highest authority evaluating the quality of legislation under preparation. By the way, the Government Legislative Council is sometimes considered the direct *addressee* of the legislation – the lawmakers write the regulations directly for it and not for the "common" addressees for which the regulation is actually intended.

Furthermore, it turns out that legislators do not have a concrete and unified idea of what the requirement of clarity means. The range of responses ranges from the idea that everyone should really understand the text, to the notion that general clarity ultimately concerns only the primary actors in the legal field. Therefore, the ability to understand legal text is not self-evident but something to be learned. In addition, legislators' expectations from the text are associated with clarity. An interesting moment can be seen in the response of a relatively experienced legal expert with long practice: "*If she* (the legal expert) *writes clearly and without errors, her work is completely the same as the work of her colleagues who can write in a clear and error-free manner.*" In this response, the legal expert excluded the possibility to write *better than good* legal text. This answer seems to be a move towards mechanical compliance with formal standards as the highest perfection.

As far as the individual stages of the writing process are concerned, deeper inquiries show that legislators differ in the importance they attach to the individually prescribed stages of the process. They even differ as regards when they consider their work completed. While some see it as finished when the text goes into the approval process, others only see its factual conclusion when the text is approved by parliament. For example, one participant reported the last check before official publication as a specific ritual.

To Be a Legislator

Now we are moving on to how legislators see themselves. In our communication partners' narratives, several labels have emerged expressing the nature of the work of legislators and describing the fact we mentioned above. *Writing laws* is much more negotiation than simple text creation. Therefore, legislators assume different roles during this process. We have highlighted these in our participants' testimonies:

In the first phase of work, the legislator is primarily an *analyst*. She must assess exactly what the proposal is intended to do, who the concerned actors are, and what areas will be affected, whether deliberately or unintentionally. The legislative expert must divide the intent into individual parts, and then convert them into legal practice. After this method of designing the proposal, another role mentioned is the *guard's* role. It must be assessed whether the proposals and requirements submitted in the substantive intention are justified and even whether they are (un)lawful. When it is established that it is possible to start such proposal, the legislative expert becomes the *guarantor* of the quality of the text – especially in the sense of whether it corresponds to its surroundings, i.e., whether it will comply with other laws – and at the same time must keep an eye on where the law manifests and everything that will need to be modified. However, the term *guarantor* also expresses a guarantee that all comments and suggestions that may appear regarding the new text during all the comments stages will be discussed. Finally, the last label the legal expert acquires is *finisher*. At this level it is an effort to express not only the fact that it is a work that must correspond to its surroundings (part of the *guarantor*'s work), but also that it is a work in which all formal requirements must be observed.

None of the legislative experts we asked felt they were the authors of the texts, one writing: "*Over the years I have completely abandoned what naturally challenges every author. That is, that the text is a product of my inner uniqueness and personality, and that I am its true, fully-fledged author, as if I were writing poetry. I do not perceive this in any way. I am able to free myself from this authorial relationship to the text. I think this is alright – I am not writing a novel, poetry, even a scientific article or treatise. I am writing a law. Of course, I am never the sole author of the text.*" Legislators seem to perceive themselves primarily as a tool of the system ensuring that its individual components fit together. One of the main features of these tools is that they do not speak for the system, but merely prepare documents, or directly prepare the actors empowered to speak – their superiors.

Conclusion

In order to understand the law-making process, in particular the parts associated with the drafting of legislation itself, it has proven to be important to find out how the legislative experts themselves describe their work, including their interpretation of their work and description of their roles (analyst, guard, guarantor, finisher or, generally, tool). This approach will make it possible to identify their attitude towards the writing process, especially whether it is a creative activity, a fully formalized process consisting of routine activities without any space for creativity, or a creative activity heavily regulated by rules (legal or other social rules). When analyzing the legislators' individual testimonies, there was a difference between the theoretical concepts that clearly point to the idea of law-making as an activity that includes significant creative elements, and the findings from a pilot survey (in-depth interviews). Legislative experts perceive their activities as more formal – even willing to describe themselves as tools. Even though there is some "emotional investment" (some legal experts follow the draft until the last stages, although they are no longer active players in the process), the description of the content of the work itself is closer to a creative activity in which the experts choose the steps according to the given conditions and try – within the given limits – to support the comprehensibility of the text as much as possible. In doing so, they construct the addressees' expectations, the expected interpretation, or consider the implications of the use of individual words and phrases, constantly confronted with methodological recommendations or rules for constructing normative text. The result is therefore often a compromise.

In spite of the declared formality of statutory drafting, it is also clear there is no single correct style or correct procedure. The result (normative text) and legislative work itself are influenced by external factors. Not even the drafting itself has clear and strict rules, despite the fact that there are written and unwritten rules (such as legislative conventions) known to the legislative experts.

References

Bentham J., "Nomography", *The Works of Jeremy Bentham: Volume III.* (William Tait 1843).

Boháč R., *Legislativní proces: (Teorie a praxe)* (Tiskárna Ministerstva vnitra 2011).

Bourdieu P., "The Force of Law: Toward a Sociology of Juridical Field" (1987) 38 The Hastings Law Journal 814–853.

Braibant G., "Qui fail la loi?" (1993) 64 Pouvoirs: Revue française d'études constitutionnelles et politiques 43–46.

Capitant H., "Comment on fait les lois aujourd'hui" (1917) 91 Revue Politique & Parlementaire 305–317.

Chritiansen M. R. and Eskridge Jr. W. N., "Congressional Overrides of Supreme Court Statutory Interpretation Decisions, 1967–2011" (2014) 92 Texas Law Review 1317–1541.

Cyrul W., "Lawmaking: Between Discourse and Legal Text", *Legislation in Context: Essays in Legisprudence* (Routledge 2016).

Cvrček F. and Novák F., *Legislativa: Teoretická východiska a problémy* (Vydavatelství a nakladatelství Aleš Čeněk 2017).

Filip J., "Ústavní soud a problémy legislativy v ČR", *Otázky tvorby práva v České republice, Polské republice a Slovenské republice: sborník příspěvků z mezinárodního vědeckého sympozia "Aktuální otázky tvorby práva v České republice, Polské republice a Slovenské republice", Praha, 29. -30. 11. 2004* (Vydavatelství a nakladatelství Aleš Čeněk 2005).

Hammersley M. and Atkinson P., *Ethnography: Principles in Practice* (3rd Routledge 2007).

Jellum L. D., *Mastering Statutory Interpretation* (Carolina Academic Press 2008).

Jestaz P., "Les sources du droit: Le déplacement d'un pôle à un autre" (1996) 27 Revue générale de droit 5–19.

Kaufmann J.-C., *L'entretien compréhensif: L'enquête et ses méthodes* (3e Armand Colin 2011).

Kyritsis D., *Shared Authority: Courts and Legislatures in Legal Theory* (Hart Publishing 2015).

Mańko R., *W Stronę Krytycznej Filozofii Orzekania.: Polityczność, Etyka, Legitymizacja.* (Wydawnictwo Uniwersytetu Łódzkiego 2018).

Mill J. S., *System of Logic Ratiocinative and Inductive: Being a Connected View of the Principles of Evidence and the Methods of Scientific Investigation* (JM Robson ed University of Toronto Press 1974).

Remy D., *Légistique: L'art de faire les lois* (Romillat 2004).

Robinson C. A., *The Bureaucracy and the Legislative Process: A Case Study of the Health Care Financing Administration* (University Press of America 1991).

Savigny C. F. von, *Vom Beruf unsrer Zeit für Gesetzgebung und Rechtswissenschaft* (Mohr und Zimmer 1814).

Sitte C., *Der Städtebau nach seinen künstlerischen Grundsätzen: Ein Beitrag zur Lösung Modernster Fragen der Architektur und Monumentalen Plastik unter Besonderer Beziehung auf Wien* (Carl Graeser 1889).

Sobek T., *Právní myšlení: Kritika moralismu* (Ústav státu a práva AV ČR ve spolupráci s Vydavatelstvím a nakladatelstvím Aleš Čeněk, Plzeň 2011).

Šín Z., *Tvorba práva: Pravidla, metodika, technika* (2nd C.H. Beck 2009).

Wagner R., *Das Kunstwerk der Zukunft* (Otto Wigand 1850).

Weber M., *Economy and Society: An Outline of Interpretive Sociology* (G Roth and C Wittich eds University of California Press 1978).

Wintgens L. J., "The Rational Legislator Revisited. Bounded Rationality and Legisprudence", *The rationality and justification of legislation: essays in legisprudence* (Springer 2013).

Wróblewski J., *Teoria racjonalnego tworzenia prawa* (Zakład Narodowy im. Ossolińskich 1985).

Contributors

Paweł Chmielnicki Dr hab., Full Professor at Faculty of Law and Administration Lazarski University. He is particularly interested in exploring functional relationships among various norms determining the achievement of predefined goals of human activities. The year 2009 marked what P. Chmielnicki considers to be his most important scientific achievement, namely, the discovery of the existence of clear long-term trends in the legislative process. This discovery had no precedent in any earlier similar research by other scholars, either in Poland, or in any other country. For the purpose of the above described research, P. Chmielnicki developed an original, interdisciplinary research method which comprised both elements of expert analysis (evaluation of research data), and mathematical modelling of the obtained results. The discovery itself was described in a number of publications, of which the most important ones included: "Activity Rules of Economic Man in Society as the Source of Legal Norms", Warsaw: LexisNexis, 2010; "Pochodzenie, tworzenie i efektywność prawa" (*The Origins, Making, and Effectiveness of Laws*), Warsaw: LexisNexis, 2014; "Tworzenie instytucji gospodarki a ustawodawstwo polskie" (*Making of Economy Institutions and Polish Acts*), Warsaw: Wolters Kluwer business 2015.

Rafał Chybiński, PhD student at Chair of Theory and Philosophy of Law of the University of Wroclaw. He has published many articles about philosophy of law and banking law. His current research interests are Marxism, economic philosophy and problem of insolvency of banks.

Alexandra C. Evans is a Senior Lecturer in the School of Taxation & Business Law at UNSW Business School at The University of New South Wales (UNSW) in Sydney, Australia, where she primarily teaches income tax law courses to Masters students. Prior to joining UNSW, she: practised in the Tax & Revenue Group at Ashurst in Sydney, Australia, from 2005 to 2009; taught Contracts and Remedies in the undergraduate program at Sydney Law School in Sydney, Australia, and was a research assistant to Professor Lee Burns, Associate Professor Celeste Black and Professor Richard Vann at the Parsons Centre for Corporate & Commercial Law at Sydney Law School in Sydney, Australia. Alexandra holds a Bachelor of Arts / Bachelor of Laws (Honours), a Masters in Law (specialising in Tax Law) and a PhD (in Tax Law) from The University of Sydney, Australia. Alexandra attended Harvard Law School in the United States of America (USA) on a doctoral exchange in 2013. During that time, she undertook research for her PhD thesis and audited courses in US income tax law. Alexandra's current research focuses on the Australian domestic income tax rules that apply to business vehicles (companies and trusts) but her research has also covered alternative business vehicles in the USA (LLCs, partnerships and S Corporations), domestic property law in Australia and the treatment of real property under Australia's network of bilateral Double Taxation Agreements.

Dominik Góra, PhD student at the Department of Theory and Philosophy of Law at the University of Wrocław, associate of the Center for Research on the Problems of Electronic and Computer Communication in Wroclaw. The main field of interest is the impact of new technologies on the law and its functioning in the information society. Author of several Polish and English-language scientific publications, participant and speaker at many national and international conferences and scientific symposia. Contact e-mail: dominik.gora@uni.wroc.pl.

Joanna Kuźmicka-Sulikowska Dr hab., PhD in legal science with habilitation, professor at the University of Wrocław in the Unit of Civil Law and Private International Law and Director of the Clinical Legal Education Workshop in the frame of the Institute of Civil Law at the Faculty of Law, Administration and Economics at the University of Wrocław; ORCID 0000-0002-7699-5150; legal counsel. Author of numerous publications in the field of civil law, including the monograph "Principles of tort liability in the light of new tendencies in Polish legislation" (Warsaw 2011), "Tortious liability in the law of selected foreign states" (Wrocław 2011), "The idea of limitation of claims and its realization in the Polish Civil Code" (Wrocław 2015) and commentary "Financial liability of public officials for gross violation of the law. Commentary" (Wrocław 2013) and co-author of the commentary to the Civil Code: "Civil Code. Commentary", ed. E. Gniewek, P. Machnikowski, 8th Edition (Warsaw 2017) and 9th Edition (Warsaw 2019). A member of the editorial board of the Journal of the Foundation of University Legal Clinics "Klinika". Contact e-mail: joanna.kuzmicka-sulikowska@uwr.edu.pl.

Rafał Mańko received his master's degree (*magister*) in law from the University of Warsaw (2003), his PhD in law (*graad van doctor*) at the University of Amsterdam (2014) and most recently his habilitation (*doctor habilitatus* degree also known as '*venia legendi*') in law from the University of Wrocław (2019). He is an author of two monographs, one on European private law (*Prawo prywatne w Unii Europejskiej. Perspektywy na przyszłość*) published by the University of Warsaw Postgraduate School of European Law in 2004 and another on critical theory of adjudication (*W stronę krytycznej filozofii orzekania. Polityczność,* *etyka, legitymizacja*) published by the Łódź University Press in 2018. He has published over 60 scientific articles and chapters in monographs, and co-edited a volume on *Law and Critique in Central Europe: Questioning the Past, Resisting the Present* together with Adam Sulikowski and Cosmin Cercel (published by the British critical legal publisher Counterpress in 2016). His academic interests focus on various aspects of critical legal theory, especially with regard to adjudication and the political, socio-economic transformation (the phenomenon of legal survivals), as well as the relations between law and ideology. He is also researching the legal identity of Central Europe, especially from the perspective of critical comparative legal studies, defending the idea of a Central European Legal Family. Since 2014, he has been affiliated as external fellow at the University of Amsterdam Centre for the Study of European Contract Law (since 2020 – Amsterdam Centre for Transformative Private Law).

Dobrochna Minich, Doctor of Law and Master in Political Science. Assistant professor at Faculty of Law and Administration Lazarski University. Author of numerous publications on legal theory, constitutionalism and legal philosophy. Contact e-mail: dobrochna.minich@lazarski.pl.

Sanita Osipova Dr. iur. prof. University of Latvia. In 1998 received a doctorate degree in (Dr. iur.) law from the University of Latvia. Doctoral work "Laws of Lübeckand its influence in the cities of the Hanseatic League". Since 2006 – Professor University of Latvia, Faculty of Law. Since 2011 – Judge Constitutional Court of the Republic of Latvi. Scientific interests:Legal history (history of family law, History of justice – especially history court system, judges independence and notarie), Legal sociology, State law, legal ethics. Contact e-mail: sanita.osipova@lu.lv.

Adam Sulikowski Critical constitutionalist and legal philosopher. Full professor at the University of Wroclaw and at the University of Opole. Author of 6 monographs and over 50 scientific articles on constitutional theory, postmodern and post-Marxist philosophy of law and social theory. The head of the organizing committee Critical Legal Conference 2015, President of the Association for Research on the Sources and Functions of the Law "Fontes".

Martin Škop is employed as associate professor at Department of Legal Theory, Faculty of Law, Masaryk University, Brno, Czech Republic (Ph.D. in 2004 at Masaryk University in *Theoretical Legal Sciences*). As a teacher, he participates in teaching legal philosophy, legal theory, sociology of law and media law. To his scientific interests belong critical legal studies, law and literature, and sociology of statutory drafting. He published four monographs in Czech (*Law and*

Violence; Law in Postmodern Situation; Law and Passion; ...Law, Language, Narrative) and many peer-reviewed articles. He is a chair of *Argumentation* conference organized in Brno every two years with WoS indexed proceedings. For years 2019-2023, he was appointed to the office of Dean of the Faculty of Law.

List of Figures

Lex et Res Publica
Polish Legal and Political Studies

Edited by
Anna Jaroń

Vol. 1 Anna Jaroń: Socio-Economic Constitutional Rights in Democratisation Processes. An Account of the Constitutional Dialogue Theory. 2012.

Vol. 2 Stanisław Filipowicz: Democracy – The Power of Illusion. 2013.

Vol. 3 Teresa Dukiet-Nagórska (ed.): The Postulates of Restorative Justice and the Continental Model of Criminal Law. As Illustrated by Polish Criminal Law 2014.

Vol. 4 Agnieszka Kupzok: Enforcement of Patents on Geographically Divisible Inventions. An Inquiry into the Standard of Substantive Patent Law Infringement in Cross-Border Constellations. 2015.

Vol. 5 Alicja Jagielska-Burduk / Wojciech Szafrański: Legal Issues in Cultural Heritage Management. A Polish Perspective. 2016.

Vol. 6 Maciej Mataczyński (ed.): The Takeover of Public Companies as a Mode of Exercising EU Treaty Freedoms. 2017.

Vol. 7 Maciej Barczewski (ed.): Value of Information. Intellectual Property, Privacy and Big Data. 2018.

Vol. 8 Paweł Smoleń, Marcin Burzec: Introduction to Polish Tax Law. 2018.

Vol. 9 Łukasz Pohl, Konrad Burdziak: Judicial Interpretation of the 1997 Criminal Code Provisions on Self-Defence. 2019.

Vol. 10 Adam Szot: Judicial Review of Administrative Discretion. The Influence of Court Decisions on Administrative Actions. 2019.

Vol. 11 Michał Peno / Konrad Burdziak (eds.): The Concept of Modern Law. Polish and Central European Tradition. 2019.

Vol. 12 Leszek Leszczyński / Bartosz Liżewski / Adam Szot (eds.): Potential of Precedent in the Statutory Legal Order. 2019.

Vol. 13 Łukasz Bolesta: In Search of a Model for the Legal Protection of a Whistleblower in the Workplace in Poland. A legal and comparative study. 2020.

Vol. 14 Paweł Chmielnicki / Adam Sulikowski (eds.): New Perspectives on Legislation. A Comparative Approach. 2020.

www.peterlang.com

www.ingramcontent.com/pod-product-compliance
Ingram Content Group UK Ltd.
Pitfield, Milton Keynes, MK11 3LW, UK
UKHW020835290926
15470UKWH00004B/1367

9 783631 793626